# Dependency Politics

Ryan Jablonski's *Dependency Politics* examines how democracy works in aid-dependent countries. He draws on over six years of fieldwork to investigate relationships between donors, NGOs, politicians and voters. He shows aid dependency changes politicians' behavior and voters' assessments of politicians' performance. He reveals that voters don't simply reward politicians for aid, rather they condition their votes on beliefs about how politicians influence aid delivery. This leads to a "visibility–uncertainty" paradox where aid can either enhance or erode democratic accountability. Revisiting assumptions about the effects of foreign aid on political behavior, he also explains how aid can cause citizens to vote against their interests and sometimes benefit opposition candidates over incumbents. Drawing on surveys, interviews, focus groups, and field experiments, Jablonski challenges conventional wisdom about foreign aid and offers lessons for balancing trade-offs over aid effectiveness, political capture, and capacity-building. This title is also available as Open Access on Cambridge Core.

Ryan Jablonski is Associate Professor of Political Science at the London School of Economics and Political Science. He specializes in the political economy of public service delivery in low-income democracies, with particular expertise in foreign aid, voting behavior, and elite politics. His research is published in leading political science, international relations, and economics journals including the *American Political Science Review, Journal of Development Economics, Proceedings of the National Academy of Sciences (PNAS), World Development, International Studies Quarterly, British Journal of Political Science*, and *World Politics*. His research has been supported by the British Academy, the World Bank, the UK Department for International Development, the United States Agency for International Development (USAID), and others.

# Dependency Politics

## *How Foreign Aid Shapes Electoral Behavior*

RYAN JABLONSKI

*London School of Economics and Political Science*

Shaftesbury Road, Cambridge CB2 8EA, United Kingdom

One Liberty Plaza, 20th Floor, New York, NY 10006, USA

477 Williamstown Road, Port Melbourne, VIC 3207, Australia

314–321, 3rd Floor, Plot 3, Splendor Forum, Jasola District Centre, New Delhi – 110025, India

Cambridge University Press is part of Cambridge University Press & Assessment, a department of the University of Cambridge.

We share the University's mission to contribute to society through the pursuit of education, learning and research at the highest international levels of excellence.

www.cambridge.org
Information on this title: www.cambridge.org/9781009789080
DOI: 10.1017/9781009789127



First published 2026

Cover image: Ryan Jablonski

*A catalogue record for this publication is available from the British Library*

*Library of Congress Cataloging-in-Publication Data*
NAMES: Jablonski, Ryan author
TITLE: Dependency politics : how foreign aid shapes electoral behavior / Ryan Jablonski.
DESCRIPTION: 1. | New York : Cambridge University Press, 2026. | Includes bibliographical references and index.
IDENTIFIERS: LCCN 2026000702 (print) | LCCN 2026000703 (ebook) | ISBN 9781009789134 hardback | ISBN 9781009789080 paperback | ISBN 9781009789127 ebook
SUBJECTS: LCSH: Democracy – Developing countries | Economic assistance – Political aspects – Developing countries | Elections – Developing countries | Political participation – Developing countries | Liability (Law) – Political aspects – Developing countries | Political planning – Developing countries
CLASSIFICATION: LCC KZ1318 .J33 2026 (print) | LCC KZ1318 (ebook)
LC record available at https://lccn.loc.gov/2026000702
LC ebook record available at https://lccn.loc.gov/2026000703

ISBN 978-1-009-78913-4 Hardback
ISBN 978-1-009-78908-0 Paperback

# Contents

*List of Figures* — *page* vii
*List of Tables* — ix
*Acknowledgments* — xi

1 Introduction — 1
1.1 The Argument — 4
1.2 The Scope of the Argument — 11
1.3 Evidence and Research Design — 13
1.4 The Case of Malawi — 14
1.5 Contribution to Existing Research — 17
1.6 Plan of the Book — 21

2 Understanding Relations between Politicians and Donors — 23
2.1 Why Do Politicians Interact with Donors? — 25
2.2 Why Do Donors Interact with Politicians? — 32
2.3 How Donors and Politicians Bargain Over Policy — 35
2.4 How Often Do Politicians Interact with Donors? — 39
2.5 Who Interacts with Donors? — 42
2.6 Conclusions — 44

3 A Theory of Foreign Aid and Elections — 46
3.1 Limitations of Existing Theory — 47
3.2 Outline of the Argument — 53
3.3 A Formal Model of Foreign Aid and Elections — 57
3.4 Implications — 66
3.5 Proofs — 69

4 The Electoral Politics of Aid Distribution — 73
4.1 The Distributional Politics of Foreign Aid — 76
4.2 Foreign Aid in Malawi, Kenya, and Sierra Leone — 79
4.3 Hypotheses — 81
4.4 Foreign Aid Data — 81
4.5 Voting Data — 83
4.6 Estimating the Effects of Voting on Aid — 84
4.7 Estimation Results — 85

4.8 Foreign Aid Before and After Kenya's 2002 Election 87
4.9 Conclusions 92

5 The Effects of Aid on Voter Behavior 95
5.1 What Does Existing Evidence Say About Aid and Voting? 98
5.2 Hypotheses About Aid on Voting 100
5.3 Study Context 102
5.4 Study Details 103
5.5 Examining Voter Knowledge 112
5.6 Effects of Foreign Aid 115
5.7 Conclusion 120

6 The Effects of Aid on Politician Spending Behavior 122
6.1 How Does Foreign Aid Affect Spending Policy? 123
6.2 Theorizing the Effects of Aid on Spending Policy 130
6.3 Hypotheses 133
6.4 A Study of Aid and Policymaking 133
6.5 Politician Knowledge of Donor Activities 136
6.6 Conclusions 152

7 Conclusions: Understanding Democracy in Aid-dependent Countries 155
7.1 Politics Beyond Malawi 158
7.2 Policy Implications 161

*Appendix A Survey Details* 165
*Appendix B Interview Details* 170
*Appendix C Further Details, Chapter 4* 175
*Appendix D Further Details, Chapter 5* 180
*Appendix E Further Details, Chapter 6* 182

*References* 191
*Index* 205

# Figures

| | | |
|---|---|---|
| 1.1 | Aid dependency in Malawi | *page* 16 |
| 2.1 | Donor versus nonrecurrent government spending, 2010–2022 | 28 |
| 2.2 | Donor and politician interactions | 40 |
| 2.3 | Influence of donors on politician decision-making | 41 |
| 4.1 | Foreign aid per capita in Sierra Leone, Kenya, and Malawi | 79 |
| 4.2 | Distribution of foreign aid in Sierra Leone, Kenya, and Malawi | 83 |
| 4.3 | Effects of vote share on aid spending per capita | 86 |
| 4.4 | Voting during the 2002 Kenya election | 88 |
| 4.5 | Foreign aid before and after the 2002 election | 91 |
| 5.1 | Map of surveys and groups | 107 |
| 5.2 | Citizen and teacher knowledge of donor and politician spending | 113 |
| 5.3 | Distribution of accurate knowledge of donor and council projects | 114 |
| 5.4 | Effect of aid receipt on outcome variables (95 percent CI) | 116 |
| 5.5 | Effect of not being eligible for aid on outcome variables (95 percent CI) | 118 |
| 5.6 | Effect of being selected (but not receiving) aid on outcome variables (95 percent CI) | 119 |
| 5.7 | How respondent priors condition the effects of aid (95 percent CI) | 120 |
| 6.1 | Sampled constituencies | 136 |
| 6.2 | Primary schools and foreign aid projects | 137 |
| 6.3 | Donor knowledge quiz | 138 |
| 6.4 | Example treatment map with aid information | 140 |

6.5 Example control map with no information 141
6.6 Effects of school characteristics on the school selection 146
6.7 Effects of aid information on the school selection 148
6.8 Effects of school characteristics on the school selection for politicians in the aid information treatment 149
6.9 Effects of school characteristics on the school selection for politicians in the donor report treatment 151
7.1 Citizen beliefs about donor influence 160
7.2 Citizen beliefs about donor help 161
D.1 Effect of SMS messages on outcome variables (95 percent CI) 181
E.1 Example donor oversight report 189

# Tables


| | | |
|---|---|---|
| 1.1 | Summary of the argument | *page* 12 |
| 2.1 | Frequency of politician interaction with international donors | 43 |
| 2.2 | Frequency of politician interaction with local donors | 44 |
| 4.1 | Summary variables | 84 |
| 4.2 | Estimate of KANU vote share on aid distribution | 92 |
| 5.1 | Experimental groups | 105 |
| 5.2 | Treatment groups and messages | 109 |
| 5.3 | Outcome variables | 111 |
| 6.1 | Correlates of donor knowledge | 140 |
| A.1 | Local councilor sample statistics | 167 |
| A.2 | MP sample statistics | 168 |
| B.1 | Interviews of donors and NGO officials | 171 |
| B.2 | Interviews of elected officials | 172 |
| B.3 | Interviews with ADCs | 172 |
| B.4 | Interviews of bureaucrats | 172 |
| E.1 | The effect of covariates on survey attrition | 184 |
| E.2 | Effect of treatment on attrition due to politician contesting a school location | 187 |

# Acknowledgments

In many ways, I have been working on this book for well over a decade and have incurred debts to many generous friends, family, collaborators, colleagues, and students who have participated in the research, offered critiques, read half-baked drafts, shared coffee, or provided an encouraging word or two.

First, thank you to Richard Dreesen and the Cambridge team, who supported and guided this process. Two reviewers provided extraordinarily constructive feedback. George Ofosu, Haley Swedlund, Matthew Winters, Axel Dreher, Mirko Heinzel, Adam Harris, Johan Ahlbäck, and Alex Yeandle generously devoted time to my book workshop and provided smart and honest feedback that I needed.

All the surveys, interviews, and experiments described in this book were a team effort. Especially, this book would not have been possible without the brilliant Brigitte Seim, who was a coequal conspirator on many of these field projects. Johan Ahlbäck also spent much time in Malawi making sure the resulting data and analysis made sense. Brigitte and Johan are also coauthors on articles and working papers which I draw on in Chapters 5 and 6.

I also have a number of additional people to thank for their dedicated assistance with fieldwork activities. My (then) PhD student Alex Yeandle conducted brilliant interviews with donor officials. Jimmy Mkandawire was a capable research manager and troubleshooter. Bright Chimatiro, Francis Kamungu, Frank Sulamoyo, Richard Ganiza, Frazier Mkwaila, Hector Honde, and Felix Chauluka were capable enumerators and spent much time stuck in potholes, floods, and broken cars on behalf of these projects.

I am also lucky to have had very talented students who were willing to work on this project. Luzia Kirschbaum, Tetsekela Anyiam-Osigwe,

Maheen Rasul, Pola Legowska, Diane Jung, and Lila Rota have my thanks for competently completing many data wrangling, desk research, literature review, and proofreading. Petra Matsi and Nonne Engelbrecht spent time in Malawi helping to keep our projects on track. I also owe thanks and apologies to the many clever students at the London School of Economics and Political Science (LSE) who have discussed half-baked versions of these ideas in seminars and lectures.

I have presented aspects of this research at many workshops and conferences, including the American Political Science Association (APSA), the International Political Economy Society (IPES), The Political Economy of International Organizations (PEIO), the Political Economy of Aid and International Development Society (PEADS), and various workshops and seminars at the LSE, King's College London, University College London, Duke, the University of North Carolina at Chapel Hill, Indiana University, AidData, and elsewhere. I am particularly thankful for feedback from Daniel Berliner, Sarah Brierley, Sara Hobolt, Mathias Poertner, Mark Copelovitch, Tyler Pratt, Kathleen J. Brown, Stefano Jud, Maia King, Mathias Krönke, Dan Honig, Christina Schneider, Joachim Wehner, Brad Parks, Ariel BenYishay, Ryan Powers, Helen Milner, and Michael Tierney.

I am also indebted to my PhD advisors, Stephan Haggard and J. Lawrence Broz whose advice still informs my work. During my PhD, I also benefited from many conversations that eventually informed this book, especially with Clark Gibson, Craig McIntosh, Karen Ferree, Emilie Hafner-Burton, Susan Hyde, Steven Oliver, Branislav Slantchev, Brigitte Seim, Francisco Cantu, Megumi Naoi, Erik Gartzke, and David Lake.

I am also indebted to many unnamed public officials, nongovernmental organizations, donors, and focus group participants in Malawi for honest discussions about these issues.

Finally, this work would not have been possible without the encouragement of my wife Laurie.

For financial assistance, I am thankful to the British Academy, the AidData Research Center, the LSE and The Suntory and Toyota International Centres for Economics and Related Disciplines (STICERD). I am also thankful to the LSE Open Access Books Fund for helping to facilitate open access to this book.

I

# Introduction

In 2014, Felix Mwela, a thirty-five-year-old farmer, was elected as a local councilor in Southern Malawi, largely due to his promises to deliver roads and bridges and to improve school buildings. However, in an interview two years later, he said the only thing he had successfully funded was a small classroom construction project. Even this project was funded by the council only on the condition that the community fire their own bricks. Some constituents had started to wonder if Felix was stealing money rather than funding projects.

To address his fiscal dilemma, Felix said in an interview that he had developed a "very productive relationship" with foreign nongovernmental organizations (NGOs) and donors as an alternative way to help his community. He named two NGOs specifically who had helped with restoring a road, building a bridge and borehole digging. While admitting that they often did things without consulting him, he emphasized the importance of NGOs and donors for his work:

> The main challenge I have in meeting my goals is the source of funds. Since I don't have access to the constituency funds, it is tough for me to bring development to the area or ward. My hands are tied and no one seems to come and help me.... Unless I start asking for funds from the NGOs, it is rare that I am assisted.[1]

As Felix found, it is hard to be a politician without money. Surveys in low-income democracies consistently show that voters want politicians to prioritize new and more effective public services.[2] Yet politicians in

[1] From an interview with a local councilor in Southern Malawi. His name was changed to protect anonymity. See Appendix B, Interview B5.

[2] For instance, according to Arab Barometer, Asian Barometer, and AmericasBarometer, 33 percent of citizens claim that the quality of public services is their most important

the world's poorest democracies rarely have funds to deliver things such as new schools, access to clean water, and health clinics. Instead, most oversee meagre budgets that are dominated by recurrent expenses like salaries. Especially without access to powerful friends and partisan connections, it is hard for many politicians in poor democracies to improve public services or to demonstrate that they are working hard on behalf of voters.

For many politicians, building relationships with donors and NGOs offers a solution to their fiscal challenges. Unlike governments, donors oversee budgets that are mostly focused on nonrecurrent development expenses. In the world's most aid-dependent countries, donors are often the main way in which new infrastructure is funded and delivered. Even where governments funds are used, donors frequently act as cofinancing partners. Since many donors are hesitant to channel such funds through low-capacity governments, the only way many politicians can access such funds is by building relationships with donors or their agents, NGOs. This is a book about the relationships between donors and politicians and the ways in which they shape politics in low income, aid-dependent democracies. It is not an exaggeration that donors have as much impact on politics in many democracies as most traditional electoral and legislative institutions. Yet, while many scholars have noted the political leverage of donors, we have surprisingly little social science theory or microlevel evidence on how donors shape the motivations, beliefs, and behavior of voters and politicians.

To illustrate the importance of these donor relationships, consider the challenges that many aid-dependent governments face in funding new infrastructure and services without donor support. In terms of overall expenditures, foreign aid represented about a third of all public expenditure in the world's least developed countries from 2000 to 2020.[3] However, this statistic understates the true influence of donors over social spending. Most poor governments spend the vast majority of their budget on wages and debt servicing. If we subtract this recurrent expenditure and focus instead on new spending on infrastructure like roads, schools, or clinics, donor spending mostly far exceeds that of the government. For instance, in highly aid dependent countries such as Malawi, Sierra

issue. This proportion increases to over 80 percent in most African countries (Grossman and Slough 2022).

[3] In countries classified by the United Nations as Least Developed, the median donor expenditure totaled 46 percent of government expenditure from 2000 to 2020 (World Bank 2024).

Leone, Bangladesh, and Mali, projects and loans from donors have sometimes totaled 70–90 percent of all public investments in social sectors.[4] These fiscal constraints make public sector investments all but impossible without donor support for many politicians and governments.

Donor influence is also reflected in their geographic footprint, and close networks with local governments. Today, much aid spending happens through well-defined and geographically specific development projects, most likely facilitated by one or more NGOs or private contractors. This means that donors or NGOs are present in many communities and often have close relationships with politicians and civil servants in those communities. In Kenya, there are over 8,000 NGOs with investments in every district in the country.[5] In Bangladesh, over 90 percent of villages host at least one NGO.[6] In Malawi, donors are present in almost every school, health center, and hospital. In fact, I show in Chapter 5 that citizens are more familiar with what donors have recently done in their communities than what their own local government has done.[7]

The importance of donors for politics and social services is also reflected in how politicians spend their time. While cross-national statistics are difficult to come by, politicians in aid-dependent countries often have very close relationships with donors. In surveys I conducted in Malawi, 58 percent of MPs report meeting with donors regularly, most on at least a monthly basis. In comparative terms, more than half of MPs claim to meet with donors more frequently than they attend formal legislative sessions and about a fifth claim to meet with donors more than they meet with their constituents.[8] Studies in other contexts have reached similar conclusions. For instance, a study of Japanese aid in Uganda by Baldwin and Winters (2023) shows that MPs were involved in lobbying for 40 percent of aid projects and that councilors were involved in mobilization in over 50 percent of aid projects. Brass et al. (2018) likewise show how politicians and NGOs in Kenya invest in collaborative relationships in order to deliver more effective public services.[9]

4 International Monetary Fund 2018, 2020; Bangladesh Ministry of Finance 2024.

5 Brass 2016; Jablonski 2014; Seim, Jablonski, and Ahlbäck 2020.

6 Brass et al. 2018.

7 See Chapter 5.

8 Author surveys with 100 MPs in Malawi. See Appendix A for details.

9 See also Jablonski (2014), Briggs (2012), Lewis (2004), Bräutigam and Segarra (2007), and Mercer (2003).

## 1.1 THE ARGUMENT

How do these relationships between donors and politicians matter for electoral behavior? My answer to this question starts with the observation that donors have a voice in most major spending decisions in highly aid-dependent democracies. Consider a simple policy decision like where and how to build a new school. In many democracies, this decision might be made by an elected council or a parliament, often as part of a longer-term education development plan. The final project would likely be managed by and contracted through a professional civil service.

That same decision in an aid-dependent democracy might look very different. Given the scarcity of social infrastructure budgets, most aid-dependent governments will be forced to rely partly or wholly on donors to fund the school. At the least, this control over the purse will give donors a voice in the planning of the school and veto power over the final budget. While elected officials may have substantial input, donors will often have a seat in related policy committees and will also often earmark funds or impose conditions on their use.

To illustrate, in Malawi this decision over the school funding would fall to elected politicians sitting on district councils. In making the funding decisions, councilors might choose to reach out to donors to finance or cofinance the project, or they might seek to use their council infrastructure budget, which is known as the Local Development Fund.

But, even if councils rely on their own Local Development Fund, donors would still have substantial input. While the Local Development Fund is formally part of the budget, it is almost entirely donor-funded. Donors and NGOs sit on committees that allocate and monitor this funding, and these committees often place earmarks and conditions on its use, for instance, the prioritization of some issues over others. Because of this role in prioritizing some projects over others, councils commonly have to compete with other districts to propose projects that will be attractive to donors.[10]

In addition to having a veto over funding, donors and NGOs would also most likely be involved in the planning and implementation of the school. In Malawi, NGOs and donors are generally members of the district committees that advise the council on community needs and funding

[10] For evidence on the operation and funding of LDFs in Malawi, see Chasukwa and Banik (2019) and International Monetary Fund (2018).

priorities.[11] This membership gives donors a strong voice, and sometimes veto power, over most basic infrastructure spending. This comingling of donor, NGO, and politician voices is a characteristic of development planning within many aid-dependent governments.[12]

This role of donors and NGOs in spending decisions has also increased over time. Through several means, donors have increasingly circumscribed the role that low-income governments play in infrastructure spending. One way donors do this is by channeling foreign aid through (or partly through) NGOs and multilateral organizations. At the time of writing, donors channeled about 45 percent of all foreign aid through the public sector in the world's least developed countries. The remaining 55 percent is largely channeled through NGOs or multilateral organizations.[13]

But even where donors do spend within the public sector, this spending almost always has strings attached. Less than 1 percent of donor spending in the world's least developed countries is provided in the form of budget support (compared to 3 percent globally). This means that, for all but a miniscule share of foreign aid, governments remain accountable to donors for how the funds are used and mostly have to involve donors or NGOs in the planning and implementation process.[14] Among other challenges, these restrictions mean that foreign aid cannot be included in a government's normal budget planning process.

The dominance of NGOs and other organizations in the development process means that many, if not most, development decisions result from a complex and extra-legislative collaboration between development organizations, politicians, bureaucrats, and senior ministers. A foreign aid project might start with high-level meetings between relevant ministers and donor representatives. If it is a large project, the negotiations with government officials can take many months and involve dozens of meetings with different government and development stakeholders. Once a project is funded, its implementation might involve dozens more NGOs and local government officials who were not even involved in the original negotiation, each in turn putting their stamp on the project.

[11] Area Development Committees and District Education Committees are the primary for discussing education-related issues at the district level. NGOs regularly participate in both committees.

[12] Lewis 2004; Brass 2012a; Mercer 2003; Van de Walle 2001.

[13] OECD 2024.

[14] Based on 2020 OECD statistics (OECD 2024). See also Dietrich (2013) for discussion on this point.

Together, this dominant role of donors and NGOs in the budgetary process means that, unlike in many richer democratic contexts, infrastructure spending decisions in aid-dependent democracies are rarely wholly or mainly the prerogative of legislatures. Instead, it is apt to think of much public spending in aid-dependent democracies as a kind of bargaining process. Politicians, donors, and other stakeholders like NGOs have power in this bargaining process: Politicians need donors to bring the funds or projects they require in order to develop their constituencies and placate voters. But donors also need politicians to design, deliver, and sustain many development projects. This analogy of a multilateral bargain is the one I refer to frequently in this book. I will later argue that the ultimate outcome of this bargain – such as whether politicians get development in their district – will depend on the divergence of preferences between donors and politicians, as well as the power of each actor.

As I describe further the structure of these aid bargains also powerfully shape the incentives and responsibilities of politicians and voters in ways that matter for our understanding of elections, voting, and democracy in aid-dependent countries.

### 1.1.1 How Donors Affect Politician Behavior

In aid-dependent democracies, it is an undeniable fact of political life for many politicians that they need to bargain with donors and foreign NGOs to deliver significant development to their constituents. This book investigates several ways in which this aid dependence changes politicians' behavior.

For instance, aid dependence changes politicians' prioritization of effort and time. Because of the importance of donors for political survival and policymaking, politicians invest a lot in building relationships and collaborations with donors and their representatives. One consequence of this investment is that politicians have less time for other activities, such as legislation and constituency service. While it is difficult to calculate the exact allocation of politicians' time, I offer a number of pieces of evidence to support this reprioritization effect. For instance, I show survey and interview evidence that politicians prioritize donor relationships over more traditional legislative activities. Furthermore, I show that the frequency with which politicians meet with donors compares favorably with the frequency of other official activities.

Additionally, aid dependence changes how politicians conceptualize the role of their offices. Despite having no constitutional mandates to work with donors, many politicians in Malawi describe working with donors as a core part of their job. In interviews, I asked politicians in Malawi to describe their role in government. Most stated that supporting, negotiating, or monitoring development projects (most likely from donors) is of primary importance. One councilor said his primary responsibility is, "[take] the development from the District [Council] to the ward when there is money from local development funds and other donors from different organizations." One MP when asked about his responsibilities stressed the importance of addressing hunger and health issues in his constituency, and when asked about specific actions, he mentioned – not legislative work – but "discussions" and "meetings" with donors to bring reproductive health projects and food aid to his constituency.[15]

These politician investments in donor relations are further shaped by the incentives of *voters*. When donors are a primary source of public spending, voters have incentives to value politicians that are capable of building effective relationships with members of the international development community. For instance, Malawian voters, when asked in a focus group what makes for a good politician, emphasize, not just legislative and bureaucratic effectiveness but also the capacity to work with foreign development organizations (for instance, by being fluent in English) and the ability to facilitate foreign aid.[16] In Chapter 5, I show evidence that foreign aid spending also changes how voters perceive politician effort and performance.

I show that aid dependence also changes how politicians campaign and win elections. Instead of, or in addition to, campaigning on legislative accomplishments, politicians campaign by claiming credit for projects facilitated wholly or partly by donors.[17] Indeed, when I asked politicians in Malawi in a survey, what they had done for their constituents, the majority talk about projects funded or facilitated by donors. Furthermore, I show that politicians visit donor projects frequently in order to take credit (rightly or wrongly) for their role in delivering services.[18]

Finally, aid dependence changes how politicians consider and implement policy decisions. Because of the dominance of donors in funding and facilitating infrastructure, effective policymaking requires politicians to consider the views and activities of donors when making almost any policy decision – regardless of whether that decision involves donors or

[15] Author interviews, see Appendix B for details.
[16] Author focus groups, see Appendix B.
[17] Cruz and Schneider 2017; Springman 2023; Ijaz 2025.
[18] See especially Chapter 5.

not. This influence is difficult to overstate: In a survey of 101 elected councilors in Malawi, for instance, ninety six of them stated that they very often consider what NGOs and donors do when making policy decisions about development.[19] In a policy experiment with Malawian politicians in Chapter 6, I provide causal evidence that politicians substantially adjust their spending priorities when they learn about new donor projects in their constituency.

This policy codependence means that effective policymaking requires a much higher level of knowledge and collaboration than it otherwise would. For instance, I show that politicians mostly struggle to learn about the activities of all the NGOs and donors in their area and invest a lot of effort and time in staying abreast of these activities. These high information and coordination costs also mean that many spending decisions that politicians make are overly duplicative and inefficient.

### 1.1.2 How Donors Affect Voter Behavior

The complex relationships between politicians and donors make it hard for citizens to condition their vote on the quality of public services in aid-dependent democracies. To illustrate this point more concretely, suppose, as a citizen in an aid-dependent democracy, you observe a health clinic being built in your community. How might this affect your beliefs about incumbent effort and subsequent voting behavior? On the one hand, if it seems that the government was responsible for facilitating the clinic to be built in your community, you might infer that your incumbent politician worked hard on your behalf. You might therefore choose to reward that incumbent with your vote. On the other hand, suppose that the project was wholly or partly delivered by a donor-funded NGO. In this case, you might struggle a lot with how to attribute credit. It is certainly possible that your incumbent politician lobbied for or otherwise facilitated the clinic to be delivered into your community. However, given the opaque nature of most donor spending, it will be difficult for you to confirm the scale of political involvement. Claims by politicians themselves are not necessarily trustworthy.

Depending upon your beliefs about political involvement, it is also possible that this clinic could make you *less* likely to support the incumbent. Suppose, for instance, the NGO built a clinic in a

[19] Survey with 101 elected councilors in Malawi, see Appendix A.

neighboring community rather than in your own; or suppose that the project was mismanaged. In such cases, you might be rather annoyed that your incumbent did not do more on your behalf to influence the NGO's decision.

This illustrates two important tenets of my argument about voter behavior: First, the effect of public services and foreign aid on voter behavior depends a lot on what voters *believe* about the capacity of politicians to influence the delivery of those services. When voters believe that politicians have good relations with donors, we should see a stronger relationship between aid and voter behavior than when voters do not hold such beliefs. Second, the opaque nature of much public spending in aid-dependent democracies means that voter beliefs about aid spending will often be uncertain and biased. As a consequence, I show that voters commonly make incorrect inferences about politician performance from observing development projects.

The fact that voting is conditional on beliefs means – contrary to what is often assumed – that there is not a simple relationship between foreign aid and electoral outcomes. On the one hand, foreign aid can sometimes allow incumbents to claim credit (sometimes rightly, sometimes wrongly) for quality services. On the other hand, politicians are also sometimes blamed for the actions of donors. When donors prioritize ineffectively, ignore certain communities, or deliver subpar services, politicians receive a share of the blame. Depending upon voter knowledge and the nature of aid delivery, foreign aid can either help or harm incumbents' electoral chances.

This argument implies that the effect of foreign aid on voting will be heterogenous and will depend upon what voters believe about the process of aid delivery. If voters believe that incumbents have influence over donors, and that foreign aid is delivered in a manner that transparently benefits a majority of voters, then we should expect that foreign aid will help incumbents win elections. However, if these conditions are not met, then it is unlikely that aid will benefit incumbents and may harm their electoral chances.

Among other pieces of evidence for these claims, I discuss an experiment in Chapter 5 which examines how voters respond to foreign aid after receiving different kinds of information about politicians' and donors' role in that aid delivery. I show that, depending upon what voters assume about the aid distribution process, aid can have positive, negative, or null effects on perceptions of incumbent performance and voting.

### 1.1.3 How Donors Affect Democracy

In order for democracy to work effectively, voters need to be able to hold politicians accountable for their actions.[20] That is, they need to be able to observe what politicians do and punish or reward them at the polling booth based upon those actions. I argue that aid dependence affects accountability in two main ways: First, it makes politicians' effort more *visible*. Absent donor support, most politicians in aid-dependent democracies are severely budget constrained and have little or no opportunity to help the majority of their constituents, especially with improvements in infrastructure or social services. When voters do not observe government policies, they have little opportunity to assess the quality of politician performance. This kind of low-information environment can also lead to higher levels of corruption, vote buying, and identity-based voting.[21] However, with the support of donors, politicians have the potential to deliver more services and demonstrate their performance to more of their constituents.

Second, aid dependence makes voters more *uncertain* about the relationship between public spending and politician effort. While voters might see more public services, they will struggle to distinguish between the work of donors or NGOs and those of politicians. As I emphasized in Section 1.1, many public spending decisions are made outside of a legislative context and through a multilateral bargaining process between donors, NGOs, bureaucrats, and politicians. Even a well-informed voter might be uncertain about the role of all the officials involved. This uncertainty problem is exacerbated by political incentives for politicians to deceive voters about their role in development projects and their ability to negotiate with donors.[22] This uncertainty effect can erode electoral accountability, and cause low performing and corrupt incumbents to remain in power longer than they would otherwise, often to the detriment of public welfare and democracy.

The effects of donors on accountability and democracy will depend a lot upon the scale of these uncertainty and visibility effects. When foreign aid increases the visibility of politician effort – while not substantially increasing the uncertainty or inaccuracy of voter beliefs – foreign aid can make it easier for voters to identify those politicians that work hard on their behalf. On the other hand, if a primary effect of aid is to increase

20 Przeworski, Stokes, and Manin 1999.
21 Keefer and Khemani 2005; Ferraz and Finan 2008.
22 Cruz and Schneider 2017.

voter uncertainty about what the government does, or if aid makes it more possible for poorly performing politicians to deceive voters, then donors can be quite harmful for democracy and accountability.

As an extension of this argument, I argue that some kinds of aid delivery will be better for democracy and accountability than others. I also engage with debates about the trade-offs involved in different modes of aid delivery and propose policy reforms.

Together, these arguments imply that aid dependence meaningfully transforms how democracy works. In Table 1.1 I summarize some main mechanisms of this transformation. In the left column I provide a list of ways that governance differs between aid-dependent democracies and similar, but nonaid-dependent, democracies. This is not meant to be a comprehensive list; however, I think it is fair to say that most aid-dependent democracies share these characteristics to some degree. Next, in columns 2–4, I summarize some key claims I make in this book about how these governance effects matter for politician behavior, voter behavior, and democratic accountability. I develop each of these claims as I move forward in the book.

## 1.2 THE SCOPE OF THE ARGUMENT

The objective of this book is to assess the impacts of foreign aid and foreign donors on electoral behavior within aid-dependent democracies. These are countries that fit three criteria: (1) they hold competitive or semi-competitive elections, (2) they have a high level of poverty, and (3) they depend upon foreign funding for a large proportion of social or infrastructure spending. Depending upon how strictly we define aid dependency and democracy, these criteria encompass about 45–60 countries. As the highest proportion of these countries are in sub-Saharan Africa (including my main case of Malawi), much of the evidence from this book focuses on this region.[23] As I discuss in Chapter 2, these aid-dependent countries share specific characteristics, including an inability to self-fund new public services, deep ties to foreign donors, and collaborative policymaking between foreign and domestic actors.

By foreign donors, I mean organizations or countries that are either provide foreign aid or are recipients of foreign funds. This means that

[23] There are forty five low- and middle-income countries that have multi-party, contested elections and above average levels of aid as a percent of GDP (4.8 percent of GDP) (Hyde and Marinov 2012; World Bank 2019b). These are mostly in Sub-Saharan Africa, East Asia and the Pacific Islands.

TABLE 1.1 *Summary of the argument*

| Governance in aid-dependent democracies | Consequences for . . . | | |
|---|---|---|---|
| | **Politician behavior** | **Voter behavior** | **Democracy** |
| Governments have limited ability to fund new public services without donor help. | Politicians seek to influence donor spending decisions in favor of constituents. | Voters infer politicians' influence efforts from observing foreign aid spending. | Foreign aid can help voters make better inferences about politicians' effort and preferences. |
| Legislatures often share de facto policymaking authority with donors. | Politicians prioritize donor relationships over legislative activity. | Citizens condition their votes on foreign aid rather than just legislative activity. | Legislative service is less likely to reflect politician quality. |
| Many public spending decisions depend on bargains between bureaucrats, politicians, donors and NGOs. | Politicians struggle to stay informed about donor activities and to coordinate effective policy decisions. | Voters struggle to infer which organization deserves credit for public spending. | Voters often attribute the effort or preferences of donors to politicians (and vice versa). |
| Credit for public spending is often shared and unclear. | Politicians campaign by claiming credit for foreign aid. | Voting decisions depend on how foreign aid is distributed and what voters believe about who deserves credit. | Effects of foreign aid on incumbency are uncertain and heterogenous. |

my discussion will focus on typical bilateral and multilateral donors such as the United Kingdom or the World Bank; however, my discussion will also focus a lot on NGOs that benefit from foreign funding. And, except where necessary for clarity, I often use the term donor to refer to multilateral donors, bilateral donors, and foreign-funded NGOs.

As I discuss in Chapter 2, most aid-dependent countries are characterized by a high level of delegation from donors to NGOs, and NGOs make key decisions about how and where foreign aid funds are spent. These close partnerships between donors and NGOs, combined with the intermingling of funds, mean that it is difficult to make clear distinctions between the activities of traditional donors and NGOs. Likewise, the vast majority of NGOs in low-income democracies are donor-funded, especially if involved in infrastructure.[24]

These close partnerships between donors and NGOs, combined with the large geographic footprint of NGOs, also mean that some of the most politically important donor relationships, particularly at the local level, are between NGOs and politicians, rather than between politicians and the representatives of major bilateral and multilateral donors.

## 1.3 EVIDENCE AND RESEARCH DESIGN

Research on foreign aid and its political consequences has often been approached from a macro-lens, for instance by analyzing relationships between aid spending and political or economic outcomes at the country or sector level. While such research is useful for assessing questions around donor motivations and for studying the aggregate relationship between aid and growth, cross-national data is quite a blunt tool for studying democratic processes like voting and elections. Additionally, it is often difficult to infer causation from cross-national data, since donors explicitly or implicitly condition aid on the very political outcomes we are interested in (such as the functioning of democratic institutions and electoral outcomes). These and other estimation and reliability issues with cross-national data place limits on what we can learn from much of the past data on the political effects of aid. To address this limitation, this book adopts a microlevel approach, examining the perspectives of voters, politicians, and aid workers through surveys, interviews, and field experiments, primarily in Malawi. The research design involves gathering data from multiple sources, including surveys with politicians and citizens, field experiments, and secondary data on aid distribution and government spending.

[24] Brass (2012a), for instance, estimates that over 90 percent of NGO funds in Kenya are donor funded and only about 1 percent are government funded. In Malawi, only 38 out of 1,169 NGOs report that they primarily rely on their own income (NGORA Malawi 2024).

The first set of surveys focus mostly on the relationships between politicians and donors. Between 2014 and 2018, I and fellow researchers conducted three surveys in Malawi encompassing almost all elected officials (460 politicians). These surveys ask questions about politicians' interactions with donors and NGOs. They also test politicians' knowledge of donor activities. I use these data especially in Chapters 2 and 6 to assess the relationships between politicians and donors and the extent of politicians' knowledge of donor activities.

A second set of surveys look at how citizens and teachers view donors and politicians. These surveys were conducted in 2016 and include 314 teachers and 2,019 citizens across 311 randomly selected schools throughout Malawi. In Chapter 5, I also use these data to draw inferences about what citizens know about donor activity in their community and to examine the implications of aid on election outcomes.

As a main test of the theory, I describe two field experiments (in Chapters 5 and 6). The first is an information experiment with voters to assess how a foreign NGO project changed expected voting behavior. The second field experiment tests how politicians' spending decisions change when they learn about foreign aid projects in their constituencies.

To provide more detailed information on perceptions and motivations, I supplement these data with interviews and focus groups with bureaucrats, elected politicians, community leaders, donors, NGOs, and voters. These interviews focus on how respondents view donors and politicians and how respondents make decisions about development and voting.

## 1.4 THE CASE OF MALAWI

Despite the broad scope of the argument, much of the analysis in this book focuses on the case of Malawi. This narrow focus is driven by the questions I am asking. By looking at a single case, I can contribute detailed and locally representative evidence about the ways in which politicians and voters respond to foreign aid. This kind of microlevel analysis would not be possible without such a deep dive into a single case. However, this narrowness does come at a cost. While I draw on cross-country evidence where possible, there are limits to my ability to assess cross-country heterogeneity.

Malawi is an apt case. Malawi has held mostly competitive elections since a referendum and donor pressure encouraged then-president

Hastings Banda to hold elections in 1994. At the national level, incumbents have lost elections three times (in 1994, 2014, and 2020). At the local level – where much of my evidence will come from – elections are often highly contested and turnover is often well over 50 percent.[25]

Additionally, as the seventeenth most aid-dependent country in the world in terms of GDP, Malawi is representative of the situation faced by many of the world's most aid-dependent democracies. Foreign donors are omnipresent and play a dominant role in funding social services. There are about twenty three international donors and over 1,200 registered NGOs scattered across each district in Malawi.[26] Often these donors spend close to a billion dollars on social infrastructure and services, doing things like funding schools, training teachers, provisioning health supplies and providing access to clean water.[27] Amidst this aid dependency, Malawi remains one of the most impoverished and unequal countries in the world. The United Nations Development Programme (UNDP) ranks Malawi 170 out of 188 countries in human development with over 77 percent of the population living below a poverty rate of $1.90/day.[28]

Like in many aid-dependent countries, the role of donors in the Malawian economy rivals that of the government. In most years the amount of spending funded by donors exceeds the total amount of government expenditure. From 2010 to 2020, donor spending averaged about 92 percent of the government budget. While this ratio of government to donor spending is similar to other African countries, it is higher than the aid dependency elsewhere (the average for aid recipient countries is 41 percent[29]). This dominance of donors over the budget is even more true in the social sectors.[30] These donor investments are present in almost every school, health center and hospital in Malawi.[31]

[25] For instance, out of 462 council seats contested in the 2019 election, 287 were contested by incumbents and only eighty two (18 percent) were won by incumbents.

[26] NGORA Malawi 2022; Peratsakis, Christian, Joshua Powell, Michael Findley, Justin Baker, and Catherine Weaver 2012.

[27] OECD 2024.

[28] UNDP Jan 2016.

[29] World Bank 2017.

[30] For example, in 2021 donors spent 993 million on social services and infrastructure against the government's social services budget of about 364 billion (OECD 2024; UNICEF 2023).

[31] For instance, I estimate using survey data with teachers that donors invested in 44 percent of all primary schools over a five-year period. See Chapter 5.

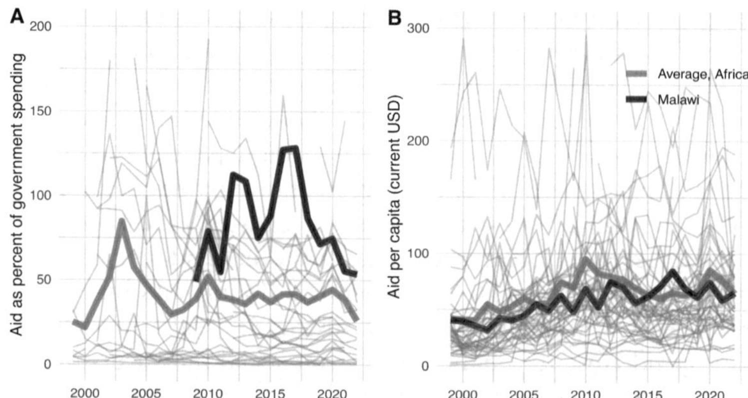


FIGURE 1.1 Aid dependency in Malawi
*Note:* This figure shows average Official Development Assistance (ODA) over time as a percent of central government expense (Panel A) and in per capita terms (Panel B). Light lines show the values for all countries in Africa. Dark lines show values for Malawi and the average for Africa. I omit data for Somalia due to its extreme values. Data is from the World Bank World Development Indicators.

This aid dependence is exacerbated by the government's budget constraints. The government's $364 million budget in 2020 for social spending was almost entirely taken up with recurrent expenditure: primarily salaries.[32] Something as basic as building a new school is impossible for all but the most well-connected of politicians. In most years, less than 2% of the government's education budget is available for capital expenditure, making new construction nearly impossible in many areas.[33]

In Figure 1.1, I plot aid dependence in Malawi relative to the rest of sub-Saharan Africa. In terms of aid per capita received, Malawi is similar to many countries in Africa (Panel B). However, due to its high rate of poverty and unstable agriculture based incomes, Malawi has a quite low tax base. This means that aid as a share of central government expenses (Panel A) is quite high.[34]

Despite Malawi's high aid dependency, most of Malawi's donor funding is not channeled through the government. Due to donor concerns over

[32] Out of Malawi's total budget, about 80% is recurrent. In sectors like education the share of recurrent spending is closer to 90 percent (Mlusu 2021).

[33] In 2021, this works out to $6.3 million across a population of 5.5 million students. In comparison, the UK spends about 10 percent of its education budget on capital expenses.

[34] In the ratio of aid to government expenses, Malawi (at 91% from 2010 to 2020) is similar to the DRC (75%), Mali (73%), Rwanda (69%), Mozambique (69%), Ethiopia (67%) and Burundi (120%).

corruption or mismanagement, donors in recent years have withdrawn most budget support and set up a number of service delivery operations that parallel those of the government. Of Malawi's $1.5 billion aid budget in 2019, only $140 million was funded by grants. This fact makes donors an independent and important provider of public services. This use of nongovernmental channels to deliver aid is increasingly the norm for donors, particularly in lower income countries. As I point out later, this lack of government ownership also challenges voters' ability to assess the links between political behavior and public welfare.

This combination of high aid dependency, electoral pressure and off-budget funding makes Malawi an apt case for my argument. Because of this economic dependency, I show that politicians have strong incentives to invest in donor relationships as a source of public spending and voters have strong incentives to value politicians with links to donors, which have meaningful consequences for voting and elections.

However, it's worth noting also that Malawi is also in some ways an unlikely case to observe a strong effect of foreign aid on political outcomes. Several influential theories have suggested that the political consequences of aid are largest in contexts where recipient governments have unconstrained access to donor funds, or where donor foreign policy interests are substantial.[35] Malawi is instead a case where donors have very few policy interests, budget support is meagre, and aid often comes with strings attached. In the Conclusion, I will discuss in further detail how some of the findings in this book might differ by context.

## 1.5 CONTRIBUTION TO EXISTING RESEARCH

A primary contribution of this book is to debates about how foreign aid affects electoral behavior in democracies. While the vast majority of foreign aid now goes to democratic or semi-democratic countries, we lack reliable theory or evidence about how foreign aid affects voting and elections. As I show, many theories we do have are more tailored to autocratic environments and modalities of aid that no longer persist. Moreover, contrary to what most theories have presumed, there does not appear to be a simple relationship between foreign aid and incumbent voting. Often empirical findings observe instead that foreign aid has very

[35] Bermeo 2016; Bueno de Mesquita and Smith 2009; Morrison 2014.

mixed effects on voting and support for incumbent politicians.[36] Some studies have even suggested that aid may have negative or null effects on support for incumbent politicians.[37] In this book I introduce a micro-founded theory about when and why foreign aid might change voter beliefs and behavior. This theory builds on insights from retrospective voting literatures and suggests alternative hypotheses about when foreign aid might help or hurt incumbents. Experimental evidence on voting in Malawi broadly supports these theories.

This book also speaks to the consequences of foreign aid for democracy and political accountability. One long-standing criticism argues that foreign aid undermines democracy by allowing poorly performing or unaccountable governments to take credit for the work of donors, or to reward supporters with opportunities for corruption.[38] Other scholars point to the ways in which foreign aid shifts control over policy. Since foreign aid is rarely channeled through legislative institutions, and donors are primarily accountable to foreign rather than domestic publics, politicians may feel that they have no ability to affect development and voters may struggle to link their welfare to politician performance.[39] These effects may be further reinforced by the effects of aid on eroding the fiscal basis of the state: because aid-dependent governments are not as dependent upon citizens for revenue, aid may erode citizens' ability or willingness to demand rights and services from the government.[40]

To the extent these critical arguments are correct, aid may not just be ineffective, it may actually be harmful. Foreign aid might reduce incentives for political liberalization, undermine voter accountability, entrench autocratic rule and foster corruption. However, these critical arguments often rely on assumptions about the behavior of voters, politicians and donors which are too rarely stated or tested explicitly. Using formal theory and data on how aid impacts voting and voter beliefs, I argue for a more mixed and conditional effect of aid dependency on democracy

36 Sexton and Zürcher 2023; Briggs 2015; Ijaz 2025; Springman 2023; Baldwin and Winters 2023; Brass 2016; Cruz and Schneider 2017.

37 Sexton and Zürcher 2023; Briggs 2019; Blattman, Emeriau, and Fiala 2016.

38 Cruz and Schneider 2017; Jablonski 2014; Djankov, Montalvo, and Reynal-Querol 2008; Ahmed 2012; Gibson, Hoffman, and Jablonski 2015; Mesquita and Smith 2009; Bräutigam and Knack 2004; Guiteras and Mobarak 2015; Brown 2001; Tangri and Mwenda 2006; Isaksson and Kotsadam 2018; Van de Walle 2001.

39 Mkandawire 2010; Lewis 2004; Lewis and Madon 2004; Brass 2016; Koch and Weingart 2016; Resnick and Van de Walle 2013.

40 Moss, Pettersson Gelander, and Van de Walle 2006; Morrison 2014; Martin 2023; de la Cuesta et al. 2022; Eubank 2012; Ahmed 2019; Albers, Jerven, and Suesse 2023.

and accountability. Despite the role of donors in development, I show that politicians are still seen by many voters as a key agent and mediator of development spending. Foreign aid can therefore help accountability by providing a mechanism to improve the visibility of politician effort and performance. Nonetheless, I also show how foreign aid changes the information environment and often leads to less informed voting and unaccountable policy.

This book also informs our understanding of retrospective voting and accountability in low-income democracies. Political scientists often note the challenges that voters in low-income settings face in assessing politician performance, even where voters have accurate and comparative information about government services.[41] I show that aid dependency is an underappreciated explanation for this gap between welfare and voting behavior: by making voters uncertain about the role of politicians (relative to donors) in service delivery, aid dependency means that voters will often be uncertain about the link between public welfare and politician (rather than donor) performance. This uncertainty implies that voters will often make inefficient voting decisions, that politicians will have incentives to manipulate the beliefs of voters in their favor, and that politicians may substitute more easily attributable clientelistic and personalistic forms of service delivery.

Additionally, this book helps explain how politicians prioritize their time and effort. An often noted fact is that politicians and voters in poorer democracies (relative to the Global North) often seem to place less value on legislative activities relative to more direct forms of constituency service.[42] Political scientists have pointed to the role of clientelism, accountability and education as explanations for this deprioritization of nonlegislative service.[43] I argue that a complementary explanation is the importance of donors in mediating service delivery: where legislatures are fiscally constrained, or where politicians lack legislative influence, investments in donors can substitute for traditional forms of legislative

41 Dunning et al. 2019; Cruz, Keefer, and Labonne 2021; Humphreys and Weinstein 2012; Grossman and Slough 2022; Slough 2024; Cruz, Keefer, and Labonne 2021; Martin and Raffler 2021; Jablonski et al. 2022; Keefer and Vlaicu 2008; Berliner and Wehner 2022; Ashworth, Mesquita, and Friedenberg 2018; Buntaine et al. 2018.

42 Humphreys and Weinstein 2012; Mattes and Mozaffar 2016; Barkan et al. 2010; Ofosu 2024; Lindberg 2010.

43 Keefer and Khemani 2009; Stokes et al. 2013; Ofosu 2019; Weitz-Shapiro 2014; Keefer and Vlaicu 2008.

service delivery and provide a supplementary source of credit claiming opportunities.

Also this book contributes new experimental and survey data on how politicians learn about their constituencies, and the links between information and policymaking.[44] While a growing number of experimental studies emphasize the role of information in distorting policy, this book is one of the few attempts to look at how politicians learn about donors, or how gaps in donor knowledge might shape public policy. As such, this book also informs long-standing debates about how donor fragmentation and choices around aid ownership can alter the policymaking environments in low-income settings.[45]

While this book is about the politics of aid dependence, some of the theories offer insight into how politics work in democracies with similarly complex forms of fiscal governance. Claims I make about the opacity of public spending, and the difficulties of identifying the source of funding, mirror arguments about the ways in which petroleum or mineral wealth might change voting behavior and democratic accountability. As political scientists like Michael Ross and Laura Paler have noted, voters in resource dependent economies face similar struggles in identifying the size of infrastructure budgets and the source of funding.[46] It is likely that the visibility and uncertainty effects I discuss in Chapters 3 and 5 can also help us understand voting these contexts. Additionally, some of the ways in which politicians and donors bargain over spending in aid dependent democracies mirror similar kinds of bargaining relationships between government authorities, and especially the bargains between central and local governments in decentralized democracies.[47] Like in aid dependent democracies, it is likely that these bargaining relationships, and the distribution of bargaining power, alters accountability and incumbency in ways that are similar to those I identify here.

44 Jablonski and Seim 2023; Liaqat 2020; Pereira 2020; Gulzar, Hai, and Paudel 2021; Rogger and Somani 2023; Auerback, Singh, and Thachil 2024; Grossman, Platas, and Rodden 2018; Buntaine, Hunnicutt, and Komakech 2021; Broockman and Skovron 2018.

45 Knack and Rahman 2007; Acharya, De Lima, and Moore 2006; Gehring et al. 2017; Qian 2015; Wright and Winters 2010; Gibson, Ostrom, and Shivakumar 2005.

46 Ross 2012; Paler 2013; de la Cuesta et al. 2019; Paler et al. 2023.

47 Brollo et al. 2013; Brollo and Nannicini 2012; Grossman and Lewis 2014; Grossman, Pierskalla, and Boswell Dean 2017.

## 1.6 PLAN OF THE BOOK

To set the stage for the argument, Chapter 2 discusses how and why politicians interact with donors and foreign NGOs. Drawing on interviews and surveys with politicians, bureaucrats and donors in Malawi, I explain some of the fiscal and political challenges faced by politicians in Malawi and in aid-dependent countries generally, and how these challenges motivate politicians to bargain with donors as a way to deliver services to constituents and take credit for improvements in constituent welfare. I then discuss some empirical findings from Malawi about the frequency with which politicians say they interact with donors and the challenges that some politicians face in building donor relationships.

Building on this foundation, Chapter 3 provides a microfounded theory of how politicians lobby donors and how these aid bargains shape voting behavior and electoral accountability. Extending insights from formal models of retrospective voting and distributional politics, I argue that foreign aid often serves as a signal of politicians' performance and preferences in what are otherwise information-poor environments. However, I show that foreign aid can also increase voter uncertainty and misinformation about the link between welfare and incumbent performance. I derive implications for voting, democratic accountability, and politician behavior.

Chapter 4 examines theoretical claims about how politicians lobby and bargain with donors to achieve electoral advantages. First, I look at the correspondence between electoral geography and aid distribution over time in Malawi, Kenya and Sierra Leone. The analysis shows how ruling parties have biased aid in favor of ruling party coalitions. Additionally, I discuss the case of the 2002 transition in Kenya from then President Moi's KANU party to Mwai Kibaki's NARC party and illustrate some of the ways in which politicians in the new government were able to bargain for a shift in donor resources toward NARC areas.

Chapter 5 examines what voters in Malawi know about donor activities in their communities, and how foreign aid changes voter behavior and beliefs about incumbent performance. I show using original survey data that aid recipients often struggle to distinguish between the role of governments and donors in development funding. Next, I use experimental and panel data to test hypotheses about how foreign aid (and beliefs about foreign aid bargains) change voter behavior and perceptions of incumbent performance. The results are broadly consistent with the theoretical predictions in Chapter 3.

Chapter 6 examines what politicians know about donor activities in their constituencies and how donors affect their policy behavior. Extending the theory in Chapter 3, I show how foreign aid can distort policymaking when donors fail to adequately consult with or inform politicians about their activities. I then discuss an experiment with Malawian politicians involving their choices over the allocation of school resources. Consistent with the theory, I show that these allocation decisions were influenced by donor activities in their constituencies and politicians' knowledge of those activities.

Finally, Chapter 7 expands on what these findings imply for the functioning of democratic institutions. I also discuss in more detail the scope conditions of the argument and consider reforms to international development policy.

# 2

# Understanding Relations between Politicians and Donors

> I have a close relationship with [Donor Name]. Using my influence, they have constructed 18 school blocks in my constituency.
>
> – Member of Parliament, Malawi[1]

> [Our projects] are an advantage for [politicians] because most of the time government budgets have no room for infrastructure projects. The biggest chunk of the government education budget goes into salaries. So there is very little room for other projects . . . When reporting on joint sector review, [politicians] refer to projects we've funded as their achievements in the year.
>
> – Portfolio coordinator for a bilateral donor in Malawi[2]

As the above extracts illustrate, politicians in aid-dependent democracies often rely on donors to deliver services to their constituents. The purpose of this chapter is to set the stage for the rest of the book by explaining how and why many politicians have become so reliant on donors for the delivery of social services and, by extension, why politicians have become reliant on donors for pleasing constituents and winning elections.

I will begin the argument by explaining the gap between the demand and supply of social services in aid-dependent democracies. I will show that politicians often face a similar problem to that faced by Felix in Chapter 1: they represent constituents that desperately need and demand investments in core social services and infrastructure, but they have little or no budget to meet these demands. I will then provide evidence that this economic dependency has led to a *political* dependency: in order

[1] Interview B4, see Appendix B.

[2] Interview A3, see Appendix B.

to cater to voters, politicians in aid-dependent democracies seek out relationships with donors, attempt to shape donor decisions, and claim credit for donor investments. Likewise, voters often prefer to elect politicians who have close relationships with donors.

In the second part of the chapter, I will turn to the question of when, why, and how donors choose to build relationships with elected officials. Like politicians, donors have a choice in how to deliver social services. They can invest on their own or they can involve governments in their decisions. I show that donors often characterize this delegation choice as a trade-off between effectiveness and sustainability: excluding governing officials from development decisions can lead to more effective spending (or at least what donors believe to be more effective spending). However, limiting delegation can also lead to less sustainable investments and lower state capacity. In practice, donors' attempts to balance these trade-offs lead to complex and multilateral bargains between foreign donors, nongovernmental organizations (NGOs), and governing authorities over the delegation, prioritization, and allocation of development funds.

In the final part of the chapter, I provide evidence on how politicians interact and bargain with foreign donors. Using surveys with Malawian politicians, I assess how these interactions vary across donor type and political office. Consistent with my broader argument about the costs and benefits of delegation, I show that politicians are especially likely to invest in donor relationships when they face higher budget constraints, greater electoral risk, or have higher levels of education.

This chapter especially relies on two original sources of data. The first is a set of thirty-eight interviews I and fellow researchers conducted in Malawi with donors, MPs, local councilors, bureaucrats and local development committees.[3] These interviews focus on the nature of politician and donor relationships and how each respondent views their roles and responsibilities in development spending. The second sources of data is a survey I and collaborators conducted in 2017 with nearly all elected councilors and MPs in Malawi (460 politicians; 72 percent of all elected officials).This survey asked several questions about donor interactions which I will use to make inferences about the frequency and causes

[3] Most of these interviews and surveys were conducted in collaboration with Brigitte Seim, Johan Ahlbäck or Alex Yeandle with the assistance of Jimmy Mkandawire, Bright Chimatiro, Francis Kamungu, Frank Sulamoyo, Richard Ganiza, Frazier Mkwaila, Hector Honde, and Felix Chauluka in Malawi.

of donor–politician interactions. Further details on these interviews and surveys are in the Appendix.[4]

## 2.1 WHY DO POLITICIANS INTERACT WITH DONORS?

### 2.1.1 The Gap Between Citizen Demands and Fiscal Reality

If an incumbent wants to remain in office in a poor democracy, they are well advised to prioritize efforts to improve the quality and availability of public services, jobs and infrastructure.[5] This point is well illustrated by surveys in low-income countries. Afrobarometer surveys in thirty-four African countries, for instance, suggest that about 80 percent of Africans rate public services – and especially water, health, and education – as among "the most important problems facing this country that government should address."[6]

Further, many voters would prefer their elected representatives prioritize service delivery over other official duties, even when service delivery is not their primary responsibility. For instance, 31 percent of respondents across Africa say that the "most important" responsibility of their Member of Parliament is to "deliver jobs or development" compared to only 16 percent who said that the most important responsibility is to "make laws for the good of the country."[7]

This demand for local development is also reflected in how politicians themselves define their roles. For instance, I asked Malawian politicians to describe their "primary responsibility" as a Member of Parliament (MP) or councilor. Fifty-eight percent of councilors and 43 percent of MPs mentioned bringing development or services to their area as their primary responsibility. The next most frequent response had to do with representing their area or making laws.[8]

4 See Appendix B.

5 Jablonski et al. 2022; Grossman and Slough 2022; Banerjee et al. 2011; Gottlieb 2016; Cruz, Keefer, and Labonne 2021.

6 Of Afrobarometer respondents those that mention public services, 78 percent say that improving health, education or water should be the government's priority(Afrobarometer Round 8 Data from 34 countries).

7 Afrobarometer Round 4 Data from 34 countries. The other options were "listen to constituents and represent their needs." (45 percent), "monitor the president and his government" (5 percent), or "none of these" (1 percent). See also Mattes and Mozaffar (2016) and Ofosu (2024) for further discussion on this evidence.

8 This was an open ended question. I coded each response based on whether the politician mentioned development or services in their constituency. See Appendix A for survey details.

However, voter demand for local service delivery creates a dilemma for politicians in aid-dependent countries. Countries are often aid dependent precisely *because* they are severely fiscally constrained in their ability to deliver new and effective public services. Politicians – especially if they are not well connected – often have little or no means to deliver new public services to their constituents without the assistance of donors.

This gap between constituent demands and fiscal supply comes across strongly in interviews and surveys. I asked interviewed politicians the biggest challenge they faced in their job. The most common answer by far was the challenge they faced in gaining access to funds and delivering on the development projects demanded by citizens. This is particularly true of politicians who were in minority areas or not well connected.[9] As one councilor put it:

> The lack of political affiliations is the biggest barrier to fulfilling my goals: if you don't have connections in the government or in political parties, you cannot achieve your goals. Since for you to get projects, we vote at the council, so if you don't have friends then there is nothing for you.[10]

Several officials also emphasized the large gap between citizen expectations or needs and fiscal reality, especially when it comes to infrastructure development:

> The resources that we are given at the council for development are not enough. I made a lot promises to the people during campaign period. But most of these are not being fulfilled. And as such I feel I have to not stand in 2019 because people feel I cheated.[11]

> The resources, usually demand by far surpasses supply. The supply side is a complete failure on our part. The resource envelope is very small. Most projects we require in this district are infrastructural e.g. health centers and schools. Infrastructural projects require a lot of resources.[12]

The fiscal challenges facing by politicians in Malawi are also apparent from an examination of the government budget. Budgets for social sectors like education and health are often over 90 percent recurrent,[13]

9 The link between partisanship and local budgets have been noted in several contexts. See for instance Dunning and Nilekani (2013) and Bussell (2019).

10 Interview B5, Appendix B.

11 Quoted from survey with a local councilor. See Appendix A.

12 District Commissioner. Interview D3, Appendix B.

13 In the education sector, the overall level of recurrent spending is about 90 percent. About 70 percent of this recurrent budget is taken up by wages and another 24 percent in basic operating expenses (World Bank 2010b).

meaning that less than 10 percent is available to the government to deliver on new services, capital projects, and development initiatives.[14] If we look at budgets for new capital expenditures (e.g., new schools, clinics, or water points), the fiscal challenges for politicians are even more dire. In the education sector, for instance, less than 2 percent of Malawi's government budget is often available for new capital expenditure. In comparison, countries like the United Kingdom often spend more than 10 percent on capital expenses in the education sector, or about 2,000 times what the government of Malawi is able to spend per student.[15] While Malawi is more aid-dependent than many low- and middle-income countries, it is far from alone in its dependence on donors for the development of social services. In Sierra Leone, for instance, less than 2 percent of primary and secondary education funds are spent on capital expenses, a number which is dwarfed by donor capital expenses in this sector.[16]

As a solution to their fiscal dilemma, many politicians seek the assistance of donors or NGOs. To see why this might be attractive to a fiscally constrained politician, consider how the budgets of governments and donors differ. By definition, official development assistance (or foreign aid) must have the goal of promoting and targeting the economic development and welfare of recipient countries. In practice, this means that donors often spend the majority of their budgets on exactly the things that constituents demand the most: new and high-impact public service projects like schools, roads, infrastructure, and health clinics. For example, if we look at 2023 budgets, official donors spent $31.6 billion in the world's least developed economies. Of this, the largest share by far went to fund social or economic development (41 percent and 13 percent, respectively). Less than 2 percent was budget support to the government.[17]

[14] World Bank 2010b; Mlusu 2021.

[15] Mlusu 2021

[16] In 2019, Sierra Leone had a budget for primary education of $33.9 million. Only 0.5 million of this was spent on capital expenditures against donor expenditures of $21 million. (World Bank 2021).

[17] OECD (2024). Donors do sometimes earmark funds for recurrent expenditure (e.g., maintenance funds on development projects); however, a persistent cause of project failure is that recurrent expenses most often have to be picked up by governments. For example, Hood, Husband, and Yu (2002) estimates that the ratio of recurrent expenditure to investment expenditure of World Bank projects ranges from 0.003 to 0.074.

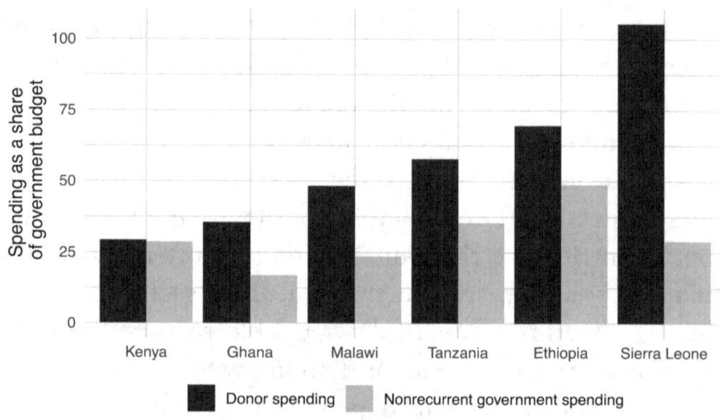


FIGURE 2.1 Donor versus nonrecurrent government spending, 2010–2022
*Note:* This graph averages nonrecurrent (capital) expenses and donor spending as a share of government budgets from 2010 to 2022 (excluding missing data). Data on donor spending are from World Bank (2024). Data on recurrent expenses are compiled primarily from government statistics offices and yearly budget reports.

To illustrate the importance of donors for funding nonrecurrent expenses more generally, in Figure 2.1, I compare government nonrecurrent expenses with donor budgets across six aid-dependent countries: Ghana, Kenya, Malawi, Ethiopia, Tanzania, and Sierra Leone. In each case, donor spending exceeds what donors spend on capital expenses, most often by a considerable degree. In Ghana, Malawi and Sierra Leone, aid represents more than twice the government budget for nonrecurrent expenses.[18]

The contrast between what donors and governments spend on social infrastructure is often especially stark. In Malawi donors spent $993 million in 2022 on social services and infrastructure against the government's social services budget of about $364 million. Additionally, since the government's budget goes almost entirely into funding salaries, donor spending on the development of social services is often several times what the government spends on nonrecurrent expenses.[19]

18 This likely understates governments' economic dependency since governments also include some donor funds as part of their budget calculations for capital expenditures. Also note that not all donor spending would necessarily be considered nonrecurrent (e.g., administrative expenses).

19 It is difficult to calculate these figures exactly, but, assuming a level of recurrent spending of 75 percent (based on the 2023/24 budget numbers), donor spending in 2022 was about twelve times government spending on nonrecurrent social spending (OECD 2024; UNICEF 2023; Malawi Ministry of Finance 2024).

Poor countries have long been economically dependent on donors. However, what has changed in recent decades is that donors have, in several important ways, increased their leverage relative to governments in how foreign aid is prioritized and distributed in low-income states. This increasing leverage has made it important for politicians to build relationships with donors and to be able bargain over the delivery of aid to their constituents. As a consequence, governments and politicians are not just dependent on donor funding, they are dependent on donor relationships and goodwill.

One manifestation of this shift in donor relations is the sharp drop in donor willingness to provide budget support to low-income countries. Budget support is money that goes directly into the government budget to be spent through official government channels. As of 2020, only about 3 percent of global aid from Organisation for Economic Co-operation and Development (OECD) countries went to budget support; whereas about 52 percent was allocated to specific donor-funded projects.[20] Further the amount of budget support has been decreasing substantially over time. In 2002, donors distributed about $98.6 billion in budget support. In 2023 donors distributed less than $6 billion, only about 11 percent of which went to the world's least developed countries.[21]

Of the aid that does not go to budget support, most is delivered through and by NGOs or multilateral organizations, or channeled through government ministries with specific programmatic aims. The OECD estimates that about 45 percent of foreign aid from major donors is channeled through nongovernmental channels in low income countries;[22] however, this proportion increases substantially for states with low levels of government capacity. At the lowest decile of governance, Dietrich (2013) estimates about 90 percent of aid will bypass the government. Moreover, this dependence on external actors has been increasing. Between 2005 and 2017, the share of bilateral aid bypassing recipient government coffers in Sub-Saharan Africa and being channeled directly through NGOs increased from about 5 percent to more than 29%.[23]

20 OECD 2020.

21 OECD 2024; Tierney et al. 2011.

22 2020 numbers from (OECD 2024).

23 Dietrich 2021.

### 2.1.2 From Economic to Political Dependency

The fact that politicians are economically dependent on donors also means that they are politically dependent on donors. In order to meet voter demands, politicians in aid-dependent countries have incentives to invest time and resources in attracting donors to their community and finding ways to earn a share of credit for what donors have done.

The importance that politicians place in building and maintaining relationships with donors and foreign NGOs in Malawi likewise comes across clearly in interviews and surveys. Some councilors even justified their plans to run for MP office as a way to strengthen their relationships with donors and gain better access to donor funding. One stated "an MP has a better chance to meet donors." Another stated that he wants to be an MP "because it's easy to access international organisations."[24]

It was also clear from interviews that a reason for building these relationships was to claim credit for bringing new services to their constituents. For instance, we asked all interviewees to describe projects they recently delivered to their constituents. They mentioned eighteen separate projects, most of which were funded and delivered by donors. Only three were clearly funded and delivered through legislative appropriation. As one MP bragged: "I also have a close relationship with [donor name]. Using my influence, they have constructed 18 school blocks in my constituency."[25]. Another councilor stated, "I interact with donors on a monthly basis and they consult when they want to come up with a project."[26]

Studies outside Malawi have come to similar conclusions about the frequency of donor–politician interactions and credit claiming. Baldwin and Winters (2023) analyze political involvement in eighteen water, education and health projects funded by Japan's Grant Assistance for Grassroots Human Security Projects Program in Uganda. Even though these projects formally bypassed government bureaucracies, interviews with project staff confirmed that politicians were nonetheless involved in various aspects of the grants. In 40 percent of funded programs, MPs helped to lobby for funding, and councilors helped to mobilize the community in 50 percent of cases. Politicians also often provided bureaucratic assistance or helped to oversee aspects of the implementation process.

24 Author survey with 460 politicians. Responses are from an open ended query asking politicians why they plan to leave office. See Appendix A.

25 Interview B4, see Appendix B.

26 Appendix B.

Likewise, Cruz and Schneider (2017) provide an account of how mayors in the Philippines claimed credit for a World Bank community development program called KALAHI. Despite the fact that the program was distributed based on transparent, programmatic criteria, mayors would nonetheless try to fraudulently claim credit for the spending. Often, they would participate in groundbreaking ceremonies; or even post billboards of themselves with KALAHI projects, or name KALAHI projects after themselves. As evidence for credit claiming, Cruz and Schneider (2017) look at how mayors' visits changed in response to KALAHI. If mayors are claiming credit for aid, we would expect that mayors would be more likely to campaign in KALAHI villages. And this is exactly what Cruz and Schneider (2017) show: In villages with a KALAHI project, mayors are 55 percent more likely to visit compared to villages without a project.

One reason why it is so important to take credit for donor projects is that this credit claiming shapes voter perceptions. One piece of evidence for this point is the extent to which voters attribute aid spending to the actions of politicians. I will examine this attribution effect in Chapter 5. I will document that indeed citizens in Malawi often misattribute donor spending to politicians (and vice versa). I will also show that beliefs about attribution change voting preferences and perceptions of politician performance.

Citizens often struggle to correctly attribute public spending in aid-dependent democracies. In Uganda, for instance, Springman (2023) examines the impact of a randomized health NGO health intervention. He documents that the intervention was largely attributed to the actions of the President's office, and that the program increased satisfaction with the President's performance in health service provision, despite the rather minimal role of the government in delivering the program, and the fact that allocation decisions were largely random and programmatic.[27]

Voters' perceptions that politicians can influence donors and NGOs often also leads to an electoral preference for well-connected incumbents who can influence spending in constituents' favor. Ijaz (2025) provides evidence on this from Pakistan. She conducted an experiment in which she had 1,000 undergraduate students choose between voting for hypothetical candidates with experience at the World Bank or comparable experience elsewhere. Even though candidates working for the World

[27] Springman notes that 60–70 percent of citizens believe that the President has "a lot" of power over NGO project locations.

Bank are no more likely to be rated as qualified, students are significantly more likely to prefer voting for them, presumably because of their greater ability to influence World Bank funding.[28] Voters in Malawi also express a preference for politicians who can build effective relationships with donors. In 2016, I conducted a focus group with thirty voters across four wards. When asked about what makes an effective politician, some emphasized the importance of donor relationship building. One group argued that "a good representative should be educated so that he can able communicate with the foreign organisation in English when the organization is bringing development."[29]

## 2.2 WHY DO DONORS INTERACT WITH POLITICIANS?

Why do donors involve recipient governments and politicians in their decisions? After all, politicians often do not share the interests of donors. As I will show in Chapters 4 and 6, politicians frequently advise donors to spend on politically important communities and family members rather than the most needy communities. Additionally, governments in aid-dependent states often suffer from poor accounting, high levels of corruption and non-transparent procurement. Given this, why don't donors simply provide all of their funds to contractors and NGOs and exclude the government entirely?

In fact, many aid officials agree that money would be more effectively spent by donors and NGOs than politicians. As one interviewed official at an international charity in Malawi put it: "A politician is not a development practitioner. It has no strong monitoring system. The money would be better with an NGO."[30] Several other donor representatives expressed similar sentiments.

Interviewees sometimes described specific ways in which politicians put personal motivations over the interests of the community. One donor talked about the problem of delivering aid after a recent cyclone (Cyclone Freddy) in the following terms:

> [T]o get into district [the NGO] needed approval from district government. To get approval they had to invite stakeholders from community to do a workshop, have to book a venue, have to have lunch allowances, fuel must be paid for.... This took several days: they were just standing there waiting to help with

28 See also Guiteras and Mobarak (2015) for similar evidence.

29 See Appendix B for focus group details.

30 Interview A6 Appendix B.

humanitarian assistance with people who had lost everything and faced people from local government who stopped it for their own personal benefit.[31]

However, there are a couple of challenges donors face in going alone. A major problem is information and capacity. Consider the problem that you might face in managing even a relatively simple foreign aid project like building a primary school in a remote and high poverty area. Unless your organization is well integrated into the community, it's unlikely that you could amass the resources and community support to build this project without help, or to maintain it over time. Additionally, it's unlikely that you have enough information about local community needs and related government initiatives to find the most effective location and resourcing for this project. The best solution to this problem is often to involve local government officials. The government is most often best placed to know community needs, and align the investment with efforts by other government offices and development agencies.[32]

There are also potential long-term consequences for government capacity in going alone. If donors are responsible for delivering social services, governments might underinvest in the capacity for local service delivery. For instance, governments might struggle to budget for the maintenance of donor funded infrastructure, or might fail to develop the kind of procurement capacity needed to deliver future infrastructure. As a consequence, donors by going it alone can create a long-term dependency on further donor support and investment. In interviews, donors are often explicit about this trade off between development effectiveness and capacity building. As a representative of one major bilateral donor in the Malawian education sector explained:

> It would be easier for us if we did everything with [implementation partner] and just went and did it...Something as simple as building a school is a lot easier for an NGO than going through official government systems. But you don't want aid to go on forever, the government has to be able to do things on their own. If the government has to follow up on NGOs doing things, that will become their expertise (rather than building the schools). There is a risk that we set ourselves up for permanent cycle of development.[33]

31 Interview A2 Appendix B.

32 For further discussion and evidence on the logic of donors delegating to governments, see Hawkins et al. (2006), Gibson, Ostrom, and Shivakumar (2005), and Swedlund (2017b).

33 Interview with programme office at major bilateral donor organization in Malawi; See Appendix B; Interview A2.

Citizens can also pay costs when NGOs fail to sufficiently consult communities and coordinate with governments, or when they lack sufficient information about community needs. When interviewing government officials in Malawi about this subject, lack of coordination was a frequent complaint about the efforts of donors. Many officials complain that donors fail to consult local development plans, or take into account community needs and budgets. One Malawian high-level district bureaucrat (a District Commissioner) put it this way:

> Our relationship with donors is not productive. They come to fund their own projects not projects that the (district) council wants. What we would have loved is for them to come and look at the council's district development plan. From the plan, look at the needs and priorities. The problem with NGOs is that they are accountable to their donors not the partners they work with. I feel donors are not addressing the problems we are facing. The major problem is low literacy levels and if this is not addressed the people will remain poor.[34]

Other studies have likewise noted the value that donors place in engaging host governments. In one particularly enlightening study, the political scientist Ryan Briggs surveyed 115 World Bank officials (Task Team Leaders) about the kinds of World Bank projects that they felt were most likely to be approved and favored by host governments. One of the best predictors of both was whether the location of a project was in an area that favored the incumbent or the opposition party. He also found that projects in a president's hometown were seen as being easier to implement, suggesting that World Bank officials recognize the importance of obtaining government buy-in for project success, even if it comes at the cost of more efficient distributional decisions.[35]

So, in theory, donors and private contractors might be capable of delivering aid effectively; however in practice it is difficult to replicate the knowledge and capacity of local government officials. As a result, most donors have committed to giving governments at least some discretion over foreign aid wherever possible. For instance, this method of operation is enshrined in the 2005 Paris Declaration on Aid Effectiveness, which committed over 100 signatories from multilateral agencies and governments to rely on local government institutions for the provision of development services when possible.[36] The World Bank's policy,

[34] Interview with District Commissioner in Malawi; Appendix B; Interview 1B.

[35] Briggs 2021.

[36] The Paris Declaration committed donors to use "a country's own institutions and systems, where these provide assurance that aid will be used for agreed purposes." OECD (2005).

for example, is to rely on government systems for financial management and oversight unless the government has demonstrated its inability to manage these tasks.[37]

## 2.3 HOW DONORS AND POLITICIANS BARGAIN OVER POLICY

As this demonstrates, politicians, and donors are often in a mutually dependent relationship and, as a consequence, much public service delivery requires bargaining and compromise. A lot of interactions and bargaining occurs especially during the design and conceptualization of aid projects. Many major aid projects begin with a request from a host government to support local development initiatives. Subsequent discussions around priorities will often involve stakeholders throughout many levels of government. These layers of authority can be highly complex. Consider for instance the World Bank's Agriculture Productivity Project (KAPP) in Kenya.[38] This project was initiated in 2004 as an attempt by the government to increase investment in agriculture productivity and technology. The initial design of the project was largely overseen by the government and the World Bank, though many details were managed by a steering committee consisting of nominees from 11 separate ministries and departments, farmer associations, NGOs, civil society groups, and community-based organizations. Final decisions over the allocation and procurement of funds were also complex and decentralized, with many funding decisions involving a mix of local authorities, NGOs, community organizations, universities, farmer cooperatives, and other stakeholders. World Bank task team leaders also retained considerable oversight throughout the project, and cancelled or delayed funds at points due to concerns about mismanagement.[39] While this was a particularly complex project, this kind of multilateral decision-making process is not unusual.

Because donors are involved in many aspects of development, aid workers often have regular and institutionalized meetings with high level bureaucrats and politicians to make decisions about development priorities and funding. In interviews with donor representatives, all claim to meet with public officials, often on a weekly basis. The most frequently mentioned meetings were with civil servants in relevant government ministries (especially principal secretaries). Donors also discussed meeting

37 World Bank 2010a.

38 It later became the Kenya Agricultural Productivity and Agribusiness Project (KAPP).

39 World Bank 2019a.

with MPs or sitting in on parliamentary meetings, particularly when negotiating budgets and development plans.

It is worth noting, however, that major donors primarily engage with national representatives, most often members of the ruling party or of the (often politically appointed) civil service. Especially noteworthy is the exclusion of local officials. Despite the fact that districts are nominally in charge of the allocation of primary education funding in Malawi, only one donor representative working on education could recall a meeting with a district authority. This does not mean that local governments are excluded from decisions about development aid, but it does mean that their input into decisions often happens later in the spending process, often after donors have finalized priorities and channeled funds to contractors, NGOs or bureaucrats. The level of politician input into programme design also varies a lot across projects and donors. On one hand, most donors have explicit requirements to engage with the government, and often emphasize the extent of delegation to public officials. For example, one donor representative described their decision-making process as follows:

> Unlike us going to a district ourselves and just doing it, we know who to approach, where they need support most, which districts have got the most problems.... We go to government and say we have X money, which districts should we go to? It has always been like that.[40]

But, on the other hand, this delegation and consultation is incomplete and varies a lot across donor and development programme. In interviews, donors often emphasize that their decisions rely on objective criteria first and politician priorities second. For instance, one donor explained how they handle what they see as poor government decisions:

> [Politicians] want the schools to go to a district just because they come from there, they want to show the government is doing something in that area so they prioritise that area at the expense of others who have more need...To manage risk we make the process as transparent as possible. We develop a criteria with them with objective indicators.[41]

This incomplete delegation comes across especially in interviews with politicians. When asked about their relationships with donors, politicians – almost universally – complain about an insufficient level of

[40] Interview A5, see Appendix B.

[41] Interview with donor, Malawi; Appendix B; Interview A3.

consultation about donor activities in their constituencies. To quote a local councilor:

> [With donors] it's a top down approach, for instance, if a donor just says we want to come to village A or B and maintain teacher houses. The question would be to see if it falls under the District strategic plan.... The challenge now comes that we can't deny a project from a donor because it's not number one on our list.... So if UNICEF say want to construct a toilet, we wouldn't say don't come because you will disturb our development plan. We would still let them come, say this was number 4 on the priority list then we knock it off the list and still seek to address 1, 2 and 3.[42]

Further, when politicians do describe working with donors and NGOs, they frequently describe a process, not of delegation, but of *persuasion.* As one MP described:

> I interact with NGOs and donors on a weekly basis. For instance just last week, I was with [NGO Name]. I was putting up a proposal to them to install piped water for us at [Hospital Name]. Their response was very positive. I feel a bore hole is not appropriate for a hospital set up. They promised to help; I will be meeting them again this week.[43]

Politicians do not only influence the design of donor projects, they also shape the implementation and procurement. Often politicians will be institutionally involved in implementation, for instance, if funding is allocated through a government ministry or committee. However, even if funds are allocated through an NGO or private contractor, there is almost always a process of engagement with politicians and bureaucrats, many of whom serve as critical gatekeepers.

In Malawi, for instance, a key government gatekeeper is the District Commissioner (DC). These are senior, nonelected bureaucrat responsible for coordinating district development activities and budgets. Among other things, a District Commissioner is responsible for making sure that donors engage with appropriate stakeholders and align their work with district development plans. Oftentimes District Commissioners will involve key local stakeholders in this process, including elected councilors, traditional authorities, Area Development Committees, and Village Development Committees. Here is how one official described this process:

[42] Appendix B, Interview D3.
[43] Appendix B, Interview B2.

All the projects that the NGOs do in this area consult our office and we make decisions together. Sometimes NGOs come to the traditional office or get invited to the District Commissioners office for the meetings. This meeting includes the councilors and the traditional authorities and even the Member of Parliament if he is not in the parliament.[44]

Local development committees (called Area Development Committees, or ADCs) especially play an important role in foreign aid spending in Malawi. These are councils of village leaders, along with elected councilors, MPs, and traditional authorities that help advise the government about the development needs of communities in their area. The same commissioner emphasized in this point:

Each time when the NGOs has a project they involve the ADC, they ask them ideas like the good place for the project to take place and to organise people to be in the committee to monitor the project. They also entrust the Area Development Committee with the supervising the materials and everything happening at the project. Only that the other decisions like the type of project to bring is already decided by the NGO themselves they only come and ask the small issues only.

This engagement with local stakeholders can influence donor spending in important ways. For instance, in one district, a District Commissioner explained how ADCs and traditional authorities can override NGO aid delivery decisions that they might not agree upon:

When an NGO comes to do its projects, it goes to the DC and the DC sends it to the traditional authority and the traditional authority takes it to the ADC. The ADC is made up of chairman and his vice from village development committees so the NGO would come and explain their project to the ADC and the ADC decides which area should benefit from the project. In those meetings there are the councilors, the group village heads, the MP and even the traditional authority and we all agrees the areas to benefit from the development projects, no one can change that, and that's how its done.

The fact that politicians and donors have to bargain with one another at various stages of aid design and distribution process means that *both* have considerable influence over what happens to foreign aid. As a test of this claim, in Chapter 4, I empirically evaluate whether the political interests of ruling parties affects where aid projects go. I show across three countries (Kenya, Malawi, and Sierra Leone) that there is a systemic spatial bias in aid spending in favor of supporters of incumbent parties.

44 Appendix B, Interview B1.

These findings are consistent with other academic studies documenting patterns of political biases in aid distribution.[45]

It is also not hard to find anecdotal accounts where politician interests won out over donor interests. In an infamous case, Human Rights Watch documented a systemic effort by the Ethiopian government to deny foreign food aid and microfinance to families that supported opposition parties prior to the 2010 election.[46] Citizens who requested food aid before the 2005 election in Zimbabwe were likewise routinely turned away if they could not document their support for the ruling party.[47] In Pakistan, foreign emergency relief for the 2010 flooding was allegedly withheld from key opposition strongholds.[48] In The Philippines, political connections appear to play a role in who benefited from storm relief efforts.[49] A study in Kiamba County, Kenya showed that HIV/AIDS patients from tribes affiliated with opposition parties were discriminated against in access to drugs provided by foreign donors.[50]

## 2.4 HOW OFTEN DO POLITICIANS INTERACT WITH DONORS?

Despite the fact that donors are such an important source of funding for politicians, few studies have attempted to gather systemic data about how frequently politicians interact with foreign donors; or about why different kinds of politicians and donors might engage in more frequent interactions. My collaborators and I attempted to address this gap in the case of Malawi. We asked nearly all elected politicians in Malawi (72 percent) to describe their relationships with donors and NGOs.[51] The results provide further evidence that politicians invest in donor relationships, and do so for financial and electoral reasons.

We asked politicians several related questions. We asked each to describe how frequently they meet with international donors, local donors (typically NGOs), and citizens about development issues. Additionally, to assess the importance of these interactions for policy decisions, we conducted a follow-up survey with 110 randomly selected

45 Hicken, Atkinson, and Ravanilla 2019; Dreher et al. 2019; Brass 2016; Bommer, Dreher, and Perez-Alvarez 2022; DiLorenzo 2023; Min et al. 2023; Masaki 2018; Briggs 2014.

46 Human Rights Watch 2010.

47 McGreal 2008; Tweedie 2005.

48 Rashid 2010.

49 Hicken, Atkinson, and Ravanilla 2019.

50 Kagotho, Bunger, and Wagner 2016.

51 See Appendix A for statistics on the sample versus the population.

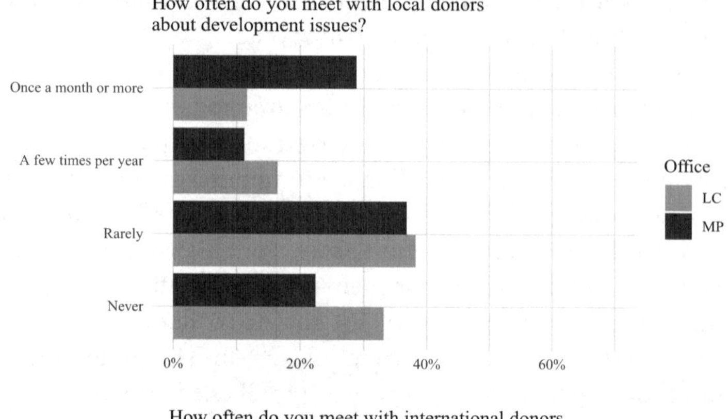


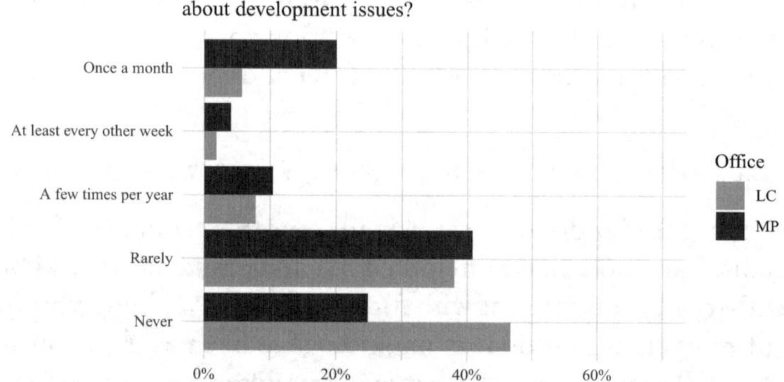


FIGURE 2.2 Donor and politician interactions
*Note:* Data from a 2016 survey in Malawi with 187 MPs and 353 local councilors. See Appendix A for further details.

councilors asked more specific questions about how donors consult politicians about development decisions.[52]

First, consider the frequency of interaction. In Figure 2.2, I plot the frequency of politician interactions with donors. On average, 58 percent of MPs and 52 percent of local councilors claim to meet with donors. Thirty-three percent of MPs and 8 percent of local councilors meet with donors on at least a monthly basis. To validate that these were substantive meetings, we asked politicians to describe their most recent interaction with donors. Eighty percent described a specific interaction with a donor or NGO. Most also named a specific project that was being delivered to

[52] See Appendix A Section A.1 for details.

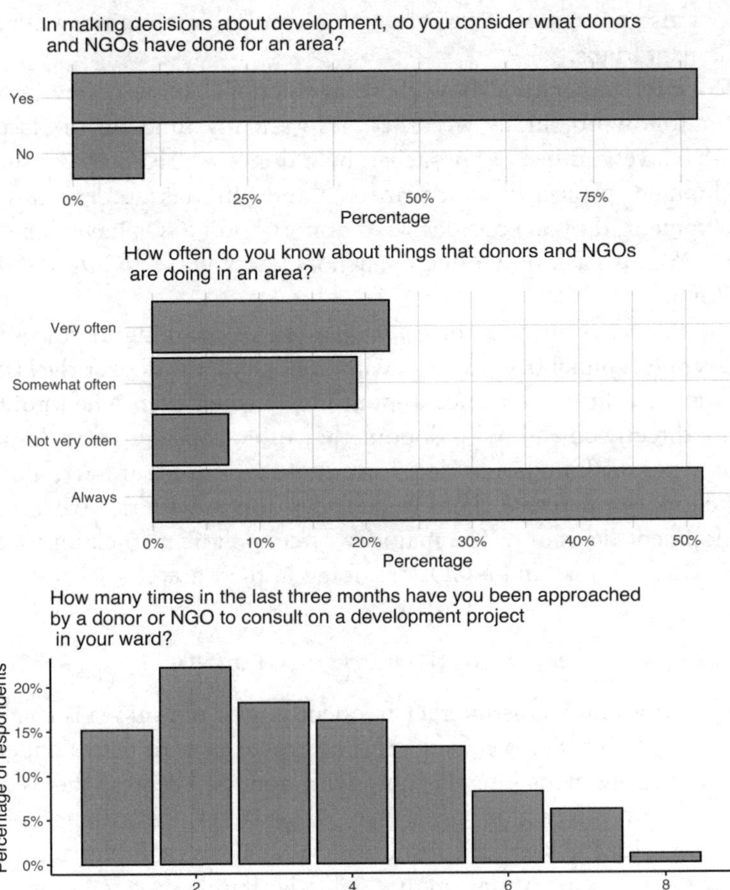


FIGURE 2.3 Influence of donors on politician decision-making
*Note:* Data from a survey in Malawi with 101 incumbent local councilors. See Appendix A for further details.

their constituency. Consistent with the statements of aid officials, councilors are about 10 percent less likely to meet with international donors, and are about 20 percent percentage points more likely to have worked with local donors.

To put these relationships in context, about 65 percent of politicians claim to meet with citizens on at least a monthly basis. About 20 percent of MPs and about 5 percent of councilors meet with local or international donors more than they meet with constituents. As the Malawi Parliament meets for two months out of the year, the frequency of interactions with donors also compares favorably with politician interactions with fellow parliamentarians.

To better understand how these interactions shape policy decisions, in our follow-up survey we asked "How many times in the last three months have you been approached by a donor or NGO to consult on a development project in your ward?"[53] and "In making decisions about development, do you consider what donors and NGOs have done for an area?" We also ask how often councilors know what NGOs and donors are doing.

The results confirm a consistent pattern of meaningful consultation. On average, councilors have met with donors 3.4 times over the last three months, or a little over once a month.[54] Further, even when politicians do not directly consult with donors, they often consider what donors are doing when making policy decisions. As shown in Figure 2.3, almost all councilors (90 percent) claim to consider donor activities when making development decisions. The majority of councilors also claim to always know what donors and NGOs are doing in their area.[55]

## 2.5 WHO INTERACTS WITH DONORS?

While many politicians interact frequently with donors, it is clear from this survey that there is considerable heterogeneity. To better understand why some politicians interact more with donors, I regress the frequency of politician interaction on a set of variables describing politician characteristics.[56] I show the results of this analysis in Tables 2.1 and 2.2.

The data appear to confirm that politicians are motivated to meet with donors due to fiscal constraints. Politicians who are not connected to the ruling party (the DPP) are substantially more likely to interact with both local and international donors. The frequency of interaction, on an ordinal scale, is 24–32 percent higher for opposition candidates. This effect seems particularly strong for local councilors. Since MPs are less

53 To make sure these data are not just measuring NGO participation in council activities, enumerators were also required to clarify that "I am asking about the times you, individually, have been approached, not about the times the council has been approached."

54 The frequency appears a bit higher than in Figure 2.2, possibly due to the fact that we asked about NGOs rather than just local donors.

55 See further discussion and evidence on what politicians know about donors in Chapter 6.

56 Frequency of interaction is coded ordinally: Never = 0; Rarely = 1; A few times per year = 2; Once a month = 3; Once a month or more = 4; Once every other week = 5; Once a week = 6; Daily = 7.

TABLE 2.1 *Frequency of politician interaction with international donors*

| Variable Name | All Politicians (1) | MPs (2) | Councilors (3) |
|---|---|---|---|
| Ruling Party | −0.281** | −0.362 | −0.294** |
| | (0.118) | (0.317) | (0.123) |
| Male | 0.006 | −0.339 | 0.124 |
| | (0.169) | (0.360) | (0.190) |
| Age | −0.0004 | 0.025* | −0.008 |
| | (0.006) | (0.014) | (0.006) |
| Level of Education | 0.218*** | 0.196** | 0.230*** |
| | (0.048) | (0.086) | (0.061) |
| Length of Residence | −0.184** | −0.243 | −0.150 |
| | (0.093) | (0.191) | (0.106) |
| MP | 0.258* | – | – |
| | (0.144) | – | – |
| Member of Cabinet | −0.055 | −0.076 | – |
| | (0.192) | (0.559) | – |
| Percent Votes | 0.179 | 0.203 | 0.082 |
| | (0.248) | (0.527) | (0.281) |
| Constant | 0.927* | 0.577 | 1.032* |
| | (0.486) | (1.108) | (0.546) |
| Observations | 453 | 123 | 330 |
| $R^2$ | 0.112 | 0.108 | 0.065 |

*Note:* *p<0.1; **p<0.05; ***p<0.01
This table shows coefficients from regressions of politician characteristics on the frequency of interaction with international donors (on an ordinal scale). Based on surveys with 125 in-office MPs and 335 local councilors in Malawi. Effective sample is slightly smaller due to missing data and nonresponse.

involved in service delivery and are not bound by council-level budget constraints, this weaker relationship is perhaps not surprising.

That data also support my claim that politicians are partly motivated to meet with donors due to concerns about election outcomes and voter persuasion. Councilors who won elections by a tighter margin are also more likely to meet with donors. A 10 percent lower vote share is associated with about 9.5 percent more interactions with local donors (on an ordinal scale). Again, this electoral effect appears not to hold for MPs.

Only one other politician characteristic appears strongly predictive: Better educated politicians at all levels are more likely to interact with donors. Part of the reason for this may have to do with language barriers.

TABLE 2.2 *Frequency of politician interaction with local donors*

| Variable Name | All Politicians (1) | MPs (2) | Councilors (3) |
|---|---|---|---|
| Ruling Party | −0.243* | −0.180 | −0.323** |
| | (0.141) | (0.414) | (0.137) |
| Male | 0.006 | −0.632 | 0.288 |
| | (0.201) | (0.470) | (0.213) |
| Age | −0.004 | 0.012 | −0.010 |
| | (0.007) | (0.018) | (0.007) |
| Level of Education | 0.208*** | 0.170 | 0.231*** |
| | (0.058) | (0.112) | (0.068) |
| Length of Residence | 0.017 | −0.193 | 0.137 |
| | (0.111) | (0.249) | (0.119) |
| MP | 0.197 | – | – |
| | (0.172) | – | – |
| Member of Cabinet | −0.221 | −0.331 | – |
| | (0.229) | (0.730) | – |
| Percent Votes | −0.495* | 0.370 | −0.951*** |
| | (0.294) | (0.687) | (0.314) |
| Constant | 1.055* | 1.597 | 0.770 |
| | (0.578) | (1.446) | (0.612) |
| Observations | 454 | 123 | 331 |
| $R^2$ | 0.074 | 0.053 | 0.079 |

*Note:* *p<0.1; **p<0.05; ***p<0.01
This table shows coefficients from regressions of politician characteristics on the frequency of interaction with local donors (on an ordinal scale). Based on surveys with 125 in-office MPs and 335 local councilors in Malawi. Effective sample is slightly smaller due to missing data and nonresponse.

Politicians who are less fluent in English will struggle more to interact with most donors. It is also likely that some donor officials seek out more highly educated politicians.

## 2.6 CONCLUSIONS

In this chapter, I show how politicians in aid-dependent contexts are economically and politically dependent on donors. Because of the fiscal constraints in aid-dependent contexts, politicians lack the means to deliver on voter demands for development and public services without donor assistance. Further, in order to build a reputation for effective service delivery, politicians often seek to influence donor activities and claim credit for donor-led development. Likewise, I show how donors are dependent upon the support of politicians and other government officials in order to deliver effective and sustainable development.

Politicians' economic and political dependence on donors motivates them to build relationships with donors, often in order to bargain with donors over the allocation and prioritization of development funds. Using survey and interview data from Malawi, I establish that most politicians meet with donors, many on a regular basis. These interactions are particularly common among politicians who lack connections to the national government, who were elected in more competitive constituencies, and who are better educated. Further, even among politicians who do not regularly engage with donors, almost every politician claims that donors influence their decisions.

Building on this foundation, in Chapter 3, I introduce some theory explaining how donor relationships shape election outcomes and the behavior of voters and politicians.

# 3

# A Theory of Foreign Aid and Elections

> I invite a number of NGOs to my area, for example [omitted]. I lobby for projects when there is a chance to do so.
>
> – Member of Parliament, Malawi[1]

Political scientists often argue that foreign aid benefits incumbents and harms democratic accountability. In this chapter, I develop a micro-founded theory to examine both effects. I will show that the likely effect of aid on political outcomes is more heterogeneous and complex than usually assumed. This chapter forms the main theoretical argument of the book. The following chapters will empirically investigate the theory.

Certainly we have reason to be concerned about the negative effects of foreign aid on elections and democracy. Famously corrupt dictators like Mobutu Sese Seko in Zaire, Ferdinand Marcos in the Philippines, and Daniel arap Moi in Kenya benefited substantially from the largess of western aid. This aid very likely helped such leaders deliver a much higher level of public services to their citizens and supporters than otherwise would have been possible. It is likely such spending helped to dampen opposition to their regimes from citizens and civil society.[2] More recently, semi-authoritarian regimes in Pakistan, Uganda, Rwanda, and Tanzania have used foreign aid to consolidate power and funnel jobs, contracts, or other resources to political supporters.[3]

If it is true that foreign aid prolongs the tenure of unaccountable or authoritarian leaders, then foreign aid has the potential to considerably

[1] Interview B19, see Appendix B.

[2] Brown 2001; Heckelman and Knack 2008; Bechtolsheimer 2012.

[3] Tangri and Mwenda 2006; Brown 2005; Tripp 2012; Ali 2009.

harm democracy. Many scholars publishing on this question have made exactly this claim.[4] However, there are a couple of reasons we might be skeptical of a universal claim that aid helps incumbents and harms democracy. For one, international donors, particularly in the post-Cold War era, are less willing to turn a blind eye to abuses of political power or the misuse of foreign aid.[5] Indeed, donors have often leveraged the promise of foreign aid to persuade political leaders to undertake costly political reforms or to hold elections.[6]

Additionally, the argument that foreign aid helps incumbents makes some questionable assumptions. Perhaps most importantly, it assumes that citizens credit, and reward *politicians* rather than donors for the benefits they receive from foreign aid. If we look at the kind of aid that leaders like Mobutu and Moi received early in their terms, this is probably a reasonable assumption. Much aid was given unconditionally and budget support was high. From a citizen's perspective, then there was often little or no difference between public services or jobs that were funded by the government and donors. As shown in Chapter 2, this is an unreasonable characterization of aid distribution today. A vanishingly small amount of aid is given in the form of budget support. The allocation and prioritization of aid today is better conceptualized as a bargaining process between politicians and donors. Further, most foreign aid today is given to democratic or semi-democratic countries and is given in the form of discrete projects, and where the role of donors in delivery is more transparent.

I will begin with a brief discussion of existing theories of foreign aid and elections, and explain why these explanations are inadequate for understanding the contemporary effects of aid on elections. Then, building on the formal political science literature on retrospective voting, I will provide an alternative set of predictions.

## 3.1 LIMITATIONS OF EXISTING THEORY

Many scholars have proposed a relationship between foreign aid and incumbent tenure or elections. These existing theories are important for understanding the history of aid and governance; however, I argue they are insufficient to explain patterns of political behavior in multicandidate

4 Ahmed 2019; Bräutigam and Knack 2004; Eubank 2012; Brown 2001; Morrison 2014.

5 Bermeo 2016.

6 Dietrich and Wright 2015; Resnick and Van de Walle 2013.

electoral settings, particularly in the post-Cold War era of international development.

### 3.1.1 Theories of Aid, Taxation and Voting

One influential body of theory points to the fact that foreign aid does not depend on taxing citizens, building on insights by influential scholars like Douglas North and Margaret Levi about the role of taxation in explaining state formation. While there are various versions of this argument, most point to the fact that foreign aid allows governments to raise revenue without raising taxes. Because taxation requires the extractive redistribution of income, governments that are funded by taxation require some level of compliance by taxpayers. In exchange for such compliance with taxation demands, the payers of tax might demand more political power and demand that political leaders use budgetary revenue more responsibly. For this reason, many political historians have pointed to taxation as one of the drivers of democracy and modern state formation.

Such arguments have been particularly influential in explaining the resilience of aid-dependent authoritarian regimes. If authoritarian regimes can maintain a low tax rate, this may reduce citizens' incentives to engage in politics or protest an underperforming regime. If so, aid-dependent authoritarian governments might have an easier time remaining in power and feel less need to provide reform or development to their citizens.[7] Because of this purported link between citizens' demands for political rights and taxation, some influential scholars have argued that aid is therefore a "curse" for politics and democracy.[8]

These aid curse arguments might also have relevance for voting behavior in democracies. If voters care more about what happens to tax revenue than other forms of revenue, this logic suggests that citizens will be more willing to invest in political accountability and transparency when taxes are high.[9] Since foreign aid can allow governments to spend money without raising taxes, foreign aid may therefore lower accountability relative to the counterfactual case where governments are forced to raise tax revenue. This may, in turn, lead to lower levels of

[7] Morrison 2014; Bräutigam and Knack 2004.

[8] Djankov, Montalvo, and Reynal-Querol 2008; Moyo 2009; Morrison 2007.

[9] North and Weingast 1989; Dynes and Martin 2021; Brautigam, Fjeldstad, and Moore 2008; Martin 2023; Ross 2012.

political mobilization against a poor performing regime.[10] We may therefore observe higher levels of corruption and lower levels of political responsiveness in aid-dependent regimes.

These arguments accurately describe several features of politics in aid-dependent contexts. Governments that rely on tax revenue seem to spend more effectively and engage in less corruption.[11] Additionally, citizens who pay taxes are more engaged in politics and appear more willing to monitor public spending.[12] Yet there are reasons to question whether theories of aid and taxation are a complete explanation of how foreign aid affects voter behavior. For one, the extent to which foreign aid (particularly when it is not part of the government's budget) undermines taxation remains contested. Some empirical studies have shown a small negative correlation between taxation and foreign aid dependence,[13] while other work has raised credible questions about whether these effects are causal or generalizable across aid dependent countries.[14]

However, a more substantial critique is that such arguments may make unreasonable assumptions about how voters think about foreign aid. This class of argument often requires us to assume that citizens care less about responsible governance when funds come from donors rather than from taxation. But is this true? If, as an engaged and responsible citizen, you learn that the government is misusing or stealing the money that should have gone to your community, why should you care whether that money came from taxation or from donors? Both scenarios will equally harm your community. And indeed, if we look at the evidence, there is substantial evidence that voters do care about the responsible use of foreign aid, and often engage in effective actions against the misuse of such funds.[15]

In one of the more thorough tests of the links between aid and accountability, de la Cuesta et al. (2019) provide citizens in Uganda and Ghana with experimentally assigned information about development projects funded by taxation and foreign aid. Contrary to what is often assumed,

[10] Bräutigam and Knack 2004.
[11] Brollo et al. 2013; Gadenne 2017.
[12] Martin 2023; Weigel 2020; Paler 2013.
[13] Eubank 2012; Thornton 2014; Albers, Jerven, and Suesse 2023.
[14] Prichard 2016; Morrissey 2015.
[15] Reinikka and Svensson (2005), for instance, describes a highly successful newspaper campaign against corruption in (mostly) aid-funded education grants in Uganda. In Malawi, likewise, protests against donor-funded medicine theft have been widespread in recent years. See also Ross (2012) for a version of this argument in the context of oil revenue.

they show that changing the sources of funding has no impact on citizens' willingness to support or petition for greater accountability. In a related study, de la Cuesta et al. (2022) find that in a lab-like setting, citizens are more likely to punish leaders who misuse funds in a treatment meant to mimic taxation. However, once citizens are reminded of their ownership over foreign aid, there is no identifiable difference in citizens' willingness to sanction leaders who misuse tax versus nontax budgets. Consistent with my argument later, findings such as these suggest that citizen beliefs and knowledge about the budget *process* matter a lot more for accountability than the *composition* of the budget.

If government spending really engenders greater accountability than donor spending, we would also expect that politicians would prefer donor to government spending. However, it is difficult to find evidence that this is the case. In a survey experiment, Findley et al. (2017) manipulate Ugandan MPs' information about cofinanced development projects and show that politicians supported projects more when they believed the projects were government funded rather than donor funded. The authors provide some evidence that these results are driven by politicians' perceptions that governments have less control over donor versus government projects, and their beliefs that there were more opportunities for corruption and patronage in government projects compared to donor projects. At the least, results such as these should make us question whether politicians value foreign aid as much as aid curse theories would have us assume.

These aid curse theories are also inadequate to explain political decision making in multi candidate settings like during democratic or semi-democratic elections. Suppose that citizens in an aid-dependent country are choosing whether to support an incumbent or a challenger. The aid-curse logic earlier suggests that these citizens might invest less in political participation or protest as a consequence of foreign aid or lower taxation; however, it seems unlikely that citizens' preferences for one politician or another will often depend on the composition of revenue or level of taxation, particularly if revenue is mostly fixed across election cycles.[16]

This existing class of theory also does not take into account the substantial challenge voters face in distinguishing between donor and

[16] In order for citizen preferences to depend upon the budget, it would have to be the case that a politician could commit to providing more foreign aid than a challenger. While we could point to some rare cases where donors have conditioned aid on election outcomes, for example, see Faye and Niehaus (2012), this is the exception rather than the rule.

government spending. Even in the most transparent political systems, untangling the fiscal composition of government spending is not an easy task, even for politicians and bureaucrats. Substantial evidence suggests that citizens are frequently confused about whether spending is funded by donors or tax dollars, and often attribute more spending to the government or donors than is in fact the case.[17] Consistent with this claim, in Chapter 5, I show that Malawian citizens often misattribute government spending to donors and vice versa.

### 3.1.2 Theories of Elite Capture

An alternative version of the aid curse argument claims that what drives the perverse effects of aid on politics is not so much the composition, but rather the *size* of the budget.[18] In perhaps the most influential version of this argument, political scientists Bruce Bueno de Mesquita and Alastair Smith argue that larger budgets help incumbents by making it more costly for the beneficiaries of regime largess to switch allegiances.[19] Because a challenger is unlikely to share resources in an equivalent manner to the incumbent, regime change is risky for the incumbent's winning coalition. As the share of revenue controlled by the government increases, we might therefore observe that political elites become more loyal and less willing to defect to challengers.

This logic is useful for explaining elite defection in autocratic settings; however, its relevance is less obvious in democratic contexts, where spending is more focused on public goods and winning coalitions are too large to be easily coopted with private transfers. Models such as Bueno de Mesquita and Smith (2009) also point out that aid can be more costly for leaders in democratic settings due to the costs for democratic leaders in granting policy concessions to donors.

But even if we accept that these elite capture theories are accurate, we have to grapple with some substantial empirical challenges. It is not true that foreign aid always helps incumbents remain in power. Particularly for democratic countries or for aid after the post-Cold War era, the relationship between incumbent tenure and foreign aid appears quite

[17] Cruz and Schneider 2017; Dietrich, Mahmud, and Winters 2018; Baldwin and Winters 2023.

[18] Brollo et al. 2013; Bueno de Mesquita and Smith 2009; Svensson 2000.

[19] Bueno de Mesquita and Smith 2009.

weak.[20] Further, attempts to estimate the effect of foreign aid on election outcomes have been inconclusive. In some cases, foreign aid appears to help incumbents win elections, and in other cases foreign aid appears to hurt incumbents.[21] I will elaborate further on this evidence for a link between aid and voting in Chapter 5. We might also question the fiscal assumptions of elite capture theory. Much of this theory assumes that foreign aid expands the government's discretionary budget. That is, the government can effectively spend the money where and how they wish. However, I have argued that this is not a fully satisfactory way to look at foreign aid. While governments often have influence over foreign aid, very little aid is given in the form of direct budget support. Even when aid is channeled through the government, officials often have severe limitations in how they spend the money. Likewise, fiscally constrained governments often have little flexibility to reallocate existing expenditure in response to foreign aid.[22]

### 3.1.3 Theories of State Legitimacy

A final branch of argument has been influential: some have argued that foreign aid is a mixed blessing for governments because aid erodes trust and state legitimacy. The claim is that if citizens start to see donors, rather than the government, as being the main source of public services, then citizens might no longer seek to hold the government to account for poor services. If so, citizens might start to disengage from politics; or, alternatively, they might seek to punish a government that they see as abrogating their responsibility to citizens.[23]

There are important concerns. However, a challenge with this critique is that it assumes that voters can easily distinguish between donor- and government-funded spending. As I have argued, voters often struggle to make this distinction. Further, given the extent to which social spending in aid-dependent contexts is co-produced by public officials and donors, this distinction is not a meaningful one in many contexts. Given this, I will argue that what matters more for voters than the composition of revenue is what public officials actually do with that revenue.

20 Bermeo 2016; Licht 2010; Yuichi Kono and Montinola 2009.

21 Briggs 2019; Knutsen and Kotsadam 2020; Cruz and Schneider 2017.

22 McGillivray and Morrissey 2000; Seim, Jablonski, and Ahlbäck 2020. See also Chapter 2.

23 Djankov, Montalvo, and Reynal-Querol 2008; Moyo 2009; Bräutigam and Knack 2004; Mkandawire 2010.

Indeed, if we look at the empirical evidence, it does not seem to be the case that voters condition their views of the government on whether spending is donor or tax funded. Several wellpowered experimental studies have examined whether informing citizens about aid, or being exposed to aid, causes disengagement, lower trust, or less tax compliance.[24] Almost all suggest that informing citizens about foreign aid has little to no effect on these outcomes.[25]

## 3.2 OUTLINE OF THE ARGUMENT

How does foreign aid matter for politics in an environment where aid is coproduced with donors and where politicians compete in elections? As a starting point for this analysis, I draw on models of retrospective accountability,[26] one of the main "workhorse" models of how government performance and spending affect voting. Retrospective voting models assume that citizens do not respond to spending because of the material benefits *per se*, but rather because the provision of material benefits gives citizens information about the preferences and performance of incumbents. This information, in turn, will affect citizens' beliefs about the future performance of the incumbent.

How does foreign aid provide information about incumbent performance and preferences? To illustrate, suppose the World Bank helped to fund a school in your community. If the project is successful and you believe that your incumbent politician lobbied hard to get funding for the project, or if you knew that the government cofunded or managed the project, you might become more positively inclined to the incumbent. The fact that you benefited from the project more than others could signal that the politician cares about your interests. The fact that the government was involved in the project suggests that your incumbent politician is working hard to improve education. After observing this project, you might reasonably expect that the incumbent will continue to work hard

[24] Blair and Roessler 2021; de la Cuesta et al. 2019; Sacks 2012.

[25] See Blair and Winters (2020), O'Brien-Udry (2021), Dietrich and Winters (2021), and Martin (2023) for discussions of these debates.

[26] For example, Ashworth (2012) and Fearon (1999). The logic of the model is especially similar to that of scholars who consider retrospective voting or agency problems with multiple inputs to the policy process, for example, Ashworth, Mesquita, and Friedenberg (2018) and Slough (2024). Structurally, the model also has a lot in common with models of special interest politics like Persson and Tabellini (2002), Grossman (2001), and Dixit and Londregan (1996). A key difference here is that it is the government that is doing the lobbying rather than special interests.

to deliver public services that benefit you and your community if they win the election.

But foreign aid can also provide you with a *negative* signal of incumbent performance and preferences. Suppose instead you learn that you failed to benefit from a new World Bank education project. If you believe that the government played a role in the negotiations with the World Bank, you might be annoyed that the government did not do more to make sure that funds went to your community. Such inequities in service provision might even be reinforced by opposition politicians who could use the project to argue that the government does not care about you, or doesn't have a good enough relationship with the World Bank to make sure that funds are distributed equitably.

Likewise, if the project was not particularly effective or if you felt like the funds were misused, then you might doubt the government's ability to manage funds effectively. The consequence of this project might be that you are less inclined to believe that the incumbent works hard and cares about your interests.

But these are only the most straightforward of cases. A distinctive and unfortunate characteristic of foreign aid is that citizens usually have incomplete information about the role of different stakeholders in shaping aid distribution. Unlike what would be the case with legislative appropriations, for example, it is difficult – if not impossible – for most citizens to untangle the relative role of donors and politicians in prioritizing and allocating foreign aid. This problem is exacerbated by the incentives that public officials have to mislead citizens about the role of the government in foreign aid.

Often this information problem exists because data on donor spending simply does not exist in a way that can be consumed by voters. To illustrate, it was estimated that less than 5 percent of official NGOs in Malawi provide legally mandated reports to the government about the allocation of their spending (encompassing over 90 percent of NGO spending). Similar gaps in reporting exist in many countries. So, even if governing officials or voters wanted more information, it's not clear where or how they would get it.[27] As I will show later, it is an empirical fact that voters

[27] Based on a 2016 investigation by the NGO Board of Malawi. In response, The Council for Non-Governmental Organizations in Malawi (CONGOMA) agreed that there was a gap in accountability between aid recipients and NGOs, but argued that NGOs nonetheless had "upward accountability" due to their compliance with *donor* reporting requirements. See "90% of aid to NGOs can't be traced" (2016) and CONGOMA (2016) for discussion.

often do not have accurate information about the role of the government in development projects.[28]

This uncertainty has important consequences for citizens' ability to infer politician performance and preferences from observing public spending in aid dependent countries. First, this uncertainty means that foreign aid will usually be a noisy signal of incumbent performance. Voters who lack information about the role of politicians in foreign aid delivery are not going to be able to make accurate inferences about how hard politicians worked on their behalf.

Additionally, aid spending can provide an *incorrect* signal of politician performance. Suppose a citizen believes an incumbent is influential with donors. Such a citizen is likely to have high expectations of the incumbent, and will be particularly likely to credit an incumbent for an effective aid project, or to blame an incumbent for an ineffective or poorly allocated project. If the citizen's beliefs are incorrect, this can lead to incumbents being blamed (or praised) for what are in fact the decisions of donors.

Conversely, a citizen who believes an incumbent is not influential will be inclined to attribute effective spending to the actions of donors rather than of the incumbent. This under-crediting of the incumbent, will mean that high performance incumbents can be disadvantaged by aid dependence. It may also lead to incumbents underinvesting in effective service delivery.

One implication of this argument is that the effects of foreign aid on political outcomes will be heterogeneous and dependent upon what citizens *believe* about the process of foreign aid delivery. If voters believe that (1) incumbents are influential and (2) that foreign aid is effectively delivered in a way that benefits the majority of voters, then we should expect that incumbents will benefit electorally from aid. However, if either of these two conditions is not met, then it is unlikely that aid will benefit incumbents, and may in fact do them electoral harm. I will discuss in some detail evidence on this point in Chapter 5.

This argument also matters for our understanding of the effects of foreign aid on electoral accountability and democracy generally. Political scientists often define accountability as the extent to which voters are able to identify and reward politicians who have characteristics that

[28] See also Springman (2023), Cruz and Schneider (2017), Baldwin and Winters (2023), and De Juan, Hofman, and Koos (2023) on this point.

voters prefer.[29] From this perspective, foreign aid (and aid dependence generally) can either be good or bad for electoral accountability. The net effect of aid on electoral accountability will depend on what I call the *visibility* and *uncertainty* effects of foreign aid.

The visibility effect refers to the fact that aid can provide voters with novel and useful information about incumbent performance and effort. As I discussed in Chapter 2, one of the central challenges politicians face in contexts of small budgets and weak state capacity is how to demonstrate credibly to voters that they have in fact worked hard on their behalf. Absent foreign aid, most politicians would have little means to affect the welfare of the vast majority of potential voters. However, foreign aid gives that information constrained incumbent the means to also influence the behavior of donors and NGOs and to thereby claim credit for a wider scope of public service delivery. This visibility effect implies that voters will often be more capable of distinguishing those politicians who are working hard on their behalf from those that are not.

However, pushing against the visibility effects is the uncertainty effect. The uncertainty effect refers to the fact that aid dependence makes voters more uncertain about the role of the incumbent in shaping public spending decisions. Because of the ubiquitous role of donors and NGOs in almost all public spending in many aid-dependent democracies, it is far from trivial to make accurate inferences about politician performance from spending outcomes. This means that while the actions of incumbents are more visible with foreign aid than without, voters are able to glean far less useful information from observing those actions.

This argument implies that foreign aid can be either a curse *or* a blessing for democracy. Where voters are able to make correct inferences about the manner in which foreign aid is delivered and the role of donors versus governments, the visibility effects will prevail and foreign aid can provide useful information to voters about the preferences, capacity, and effort of incumbent politicians. In such circumstances, foreign aid can improve electoral accountability and encourage higher government performance. Conversely, when voters are poorly informed, foreign aid can harm accountability and can help keep poorly performing leaders in power.

A key assumption of my argument is that voters consider carefully the process by which public services are delivered to their community and

[29] For example, Fearon (1999), Ashworth (2012), and Przeworski, Stokes, and Manin (1999).

condition their vote accordingly. It is of course possible that some voters do not have the ability or inclination to engage in this kind of sophisticated retrospective reasoning. An alternative assumption, for instance, would be that citizens simply condition their vote on their own personal or national welfare, independent of the process by which that welfare came about, or of whether that welfare is due to the actions of donors or politicians.

This assumption – at least as a generalization about political behavior in low income democracies – is wrong. As I noted in Chapter 2, an almost universal characteristic of aid dependent, low-income democracies, is the extent to which citizens care about, and condition their voting upon, the quality of local public services. Unsurprisingly, citizens therefore invest a lot of time and effort in learning about how services are delivered. A growing body of evidence confirms that voters in low income democracies consider carefully things like the relative role of elected versus nonelected officials in delivering services, the level of efficiency or corruption in spending, and the relative role of national versus local officials.[30]

There is less evidence about how foreign aid spending affects voter behavior; however, in Chapter 5, I will examine in some depth what voters know about foreign aid in their communities and how this information shapes their votes. Consistent with the arguments in this chapter, I will show that citizens indeed know a lot about foreign aid in their community and condition their vote – and their beliefs about politician performance – on foreign aid spending in a way that is both accurate and sophisticated.

To more completely and clearly specify the assumptions of this argument and the conditions under which we might observe positive and negative effects of aid on elections and accountability, I turn to a formal exposition of this theory. Next, I return to a discussion of some of the broader implications of the argument for democracy and development policy.

## 3.3 A FORMAL MODEL OF FOREIGN AID AND ELECTIONS

Consider a problem of the following sort: A donor announces a foreign aid project which will benefit $N > 2$ equally sized communities. The

30 Martin 2023; Buntaine et al. 2018; Baldwin 2013; Slough 2024; Grossman and Slough 2022.

donor announces that each community $i$ will receive an investment of value $x_i$ out of the budget $x$. In this model, the size of the aid budget is irrelevant, so it will be helpful to hold $x$ constant and assume $x = 1$.

As a starting point for the analysis, I assume that the donor simply chooses to allocate aid equally, so $x_i = x/N = 1/N$. As long as voters are well-informed, this assumption does not matter substantially for what follows.[31] Later, I will also consider how the results of the model would change if the donor has heterogeneous preferences across communities.

In response to this donor announcement, an incumbent politician can lobby the donor to consider a different allocation of funding. Specifically, the incumbent can propose that the donor redistribute a fraction of the budget $a$ toward $n < N$ communities that the incumbent prefers (e.g., for partisan, electoral, or ethnic reasons).[32]

The donor can reject this proposal, accept it in whole, or accept it in part. If the donor rejects the proposal, each community $i$ just gets $x_i$. If the donor accepts the proposal, then $a < x$ is distributed equally to the incumbent's preferred communities. Aid in the remaining communities is reduced by $a$. If the donor accepts the proposal in part, then $\lambda a < x$ is distributed equally to the incumbent's preferred communities. Note that since the aid budget is fixed, the incumbent can never make a proposal to redistribute more than $a = \frac{N-n}{N}$.

As $\lambda$ determines the extent of redistribution, $\lambda$ is also a measure of how effective the incumbent is at bargaining for her preferred set of voters. $\lambda$ also gives us a way to conceptualize different modalities of aid. If $\lambda = 1$ then the incumbent has full control over the allocation of aid. This is equivalent, for instance, to assuming that aid is delivered as budget support. If $\lambda = 0$ then the incumbent has no control, as if aid were wholly channeled through an NGO with no government involvement. If $0 < \lambda < 1$, then the incumbent shares control with the donor as with most project or programmatic aid.

31 As long as communities know the budget, the donor's division of $x$ does not change inferences about incumbent type. One could also justify this allocation rule by assuming that communities have flat priors about what they should receive from the donor, and therefore make inferences *as if* the donor intended aid to be distributed equally regardless of whether that is true in fact.

32 I assume here that the incumbent's coalition size, $n$ is fixed, for example, by partisanship or ethnicity. While I think this assumption to be realistic and parsimonious, it is not essential. We could instead allow the incumbent to choose their own coalition size. Since incumbents only care about reelection, they would always maximize $n$ at $n = N-1$. This oversize coalition would highly advantage the incumbents over challengers, but would not otherwise change much of what follows.

Each aid-eligible community observes the donor's announcement and their own welfare. For now, I also assume that communities know $\lambda$ (I will later relax this assumption). However, communities do not know for sure whether the incumbent has recommended them to the donor, or the final allocation of aid funds. Incumbents, of course, might prefer to tell communities about their lobbying efforts, but such claims would not usually be credible as all politicians have incentives to make such claims regardless of whether they have actually lobbied on a community's behalf.

To operationalize communities' uncertainty over incumbent behavior, we can think of politicians as coming in two types. Politicians of type $\theta_i = 1$ are those that prefer to lobby for community $i$. Politicians of type $\theta_i = 0$ are those that would prefer funds to go communities other than $i$. Politicians know their own types, but those preferences are unknown to communities. However, each community has a prior about whether a politician is of their preferred type: $p(\theta_i) = Pr(\theta_i = 1)$. Incumbents will only lobby the donor on behalf of their own type.

Equivalently, it will be helpful in what follows to think of communities as having a type. Any community has type $\theta_i = 1$ if it is preferred by the incumbent and type $\theta_i = 0$ if it is not preferred by the incumbent.

Communities expect that their welfare will increase in proportion to the aid which they receive. So, if the incumbent does not lobby, then each community $i$ expects welfare in proportion to what the donor originally allocated:

$$u(x_i) = x_i + \epsilon \tag{3.1}$$

So if the incumbent lobbies for community $i$, then communities receive the following utilities:

$$u(x_i, a|\theta_i) \begin{cases} = x_i + \frac{\lambda a}{n} + \epsilon, & \text{if } \theta_i = 1 \\ = x_i - \frac{\lambda a}{N-n} + \epsilon, & \text{if } \theta_i = 0 \end{cases} \tag{3.2}$$

In these utility functions, I assume that $\epsilon$ is symmetric and unimodal with mean equal to zero and variance equal to $v(\epsilon)$. This means that welfare outcomes are uncertain; however, each community expects welfare in proportion to the aid allocation they receive.

The game proceeds as follows: After observing welfare $u(x_i, a)$, each community independently decides whether to support the incumbent or a challenger in an election. Unlike in the models of aid politics discussed earlier, the effects of aid on this decision do not depend directly on the amount of aid delivered or the budget composition, but rather what foreign aid reveals about the incumbent's type, $\theta_i$.

Why might communities prefer to elect their own type? The idea behind this decision rule is that voters are trying to maximize the future benefits they receive from the government. If a community learns that an incumbent is more likely than the challenger to prefer their community to another, then that community might reasonably infer that the incumbent will continue to deliver services to their community after the election, and to lobby for their preferences in future policy deals.

Note that we do not have to make any assumptions about the donor or the size of the aid budget in order for voters to prefer politicians of their own type. An incumbent that shares a community's preferences in negotiations over aid is also likely to share its preferences in negotiations with fellow legislators or other actors. This also means that even small aid projects can potentially have substantial electoral consequences when they reveal new and credible information about politician preferences.

If the incumbent loses the election, then a challenger will enter into office. Challengers and incumbents come from a common pool of candidates; so, if a challenger enters office, then with probability $p(\theta_i)$ the new incumbent will be of type $\theta_i = 1$ and with probability $1 - p(\theta_i)$ she will be of type $\theta_i = 0$.

To summarize, the sequence of the game is as follows:

1. A donor proposes to allocate an aid budget, $x$, across a set of $N$ communities. The proposal includes an allocation of aid $x_i = x/N$ to each community $i$. For now, I assume the proposal is known to the incumbent and to communities.
2. Incumbents can make a counter-proposal to the donor to divert a share of the budget, $a < x$ to $n < N$ communities that share their type ($\theta_i = 1$).
3. The donor decides how much of this diversion ($\lambda$) to allow. The donor will then redistribute $\lambda a_i$ to communities of type $\theta_i = 1$ and away from communities of type $\theta_i = 0$.
4. Communities observe their welfare but do not know the actual share of aid that they have received. (Their utilities are defined by Equations 3.1 and 3.2.)
5. After observing their welfare, communities update their prior $p(\theta_i)$ over whether they believe they share the incumbent's type.
6. Communities independently decide whether to vote for the incumbent politician or a challenger. Their voting decision is based on whether they expect to receive more welfare from the challenger or the incumbent in the second period.

7. If the incumbent politician loses, the challenger comes to power. With probability $p(\theta_i)$ the new incumbent will prefer community $i$.
8. In the second period, the incumbent and donor again decide how to allocate a new aid budget across the communities.

How do communities decide between voting for the incumbent and the challenger? To solve this problem, each community calculates the probability that an incumbent is of their own type conditional on having observed their welfare in period one. A community can calculate the odds that a politician is of type $\theta_i = 1$ using Bayes' Rule (in odds form):

$$\frac{Pr(\theta_i = 1|u(x_i, a))}{Pr(\theta_i = 0|u(x_i, a))} = \frac{p(\theta_i)}{1 - p(\theta_i)} \frac{f(x_i + \frac{\lambda a}{n})}{f(x_i - \frac{\lambda a}{N-n})} \tag{3.3}$$

Since we've assumed $p(\theta_i)$ is constant across elections, each community will prefer the incumbent on instrumental grounds whenever their observed utility is more consistent with the incumbent lobbying on their behalf than not. They will vote for the incumbent whenever

$$\frac{f(x_i + \frac{\lambda a}{n})}{f(x_i - \frac{\lambda a}{N-n})} > 0 \tag{3.4}$$

From this equation, we can define the decision rule that each community will use in their voting decision: community $i$ will vote to reelect the incumbent whenever they observe $u(x_i, a) > u(x_i, a)*$. If they observe $u(x_i, a) < u(x_i, a)*$, they will vote for the challenger. In the case that a community is indifferent ($u(x_i, a) = u(x_i, a)*$), I assume that the election is a coin toss with the incumbent winning with probability $\frac{1}{2}$.

Simplifying from Equation 3.4, it follows that communities will use the following value for $u(x_i, a)*$:

$$u(x_i, a)* = \frac{1}{N} + \frac{\lambda a(N - 2n)}{2n(N - n)} \tag{3.5}$$

Given this voting strategy, how is the politician likely to respond? The incumbent in this model is only interested in reelection. From Equation 3.4, it follows that each community prefers an incumbent who lobbies to one who does not. An incumbent likewise always benefits from lobbying for redistribution as long as they have a winning coalition of voters who share their type ($n > \frac{N}{2}$). Further, the probability of voting for the incumbent is strictly increasing in $a$. It follows therefore that the incumbent will always propose to the donor to redistribute the maximum amount allowed by the budget $a = \frac{N-n}{N}$.

The following propositions define the equilibrium of this game (see proofs in Section 3.5).

**Proposition 1.** *The incumbent will lobby the donor whenever* $n > \frac{N}{2}$. *The incumbent will always propose to redistribute the maximum amount of aid allowed by the budget* ($a = \frac{N-n}{N}$). *This strategy will maximize the incumbent's chances of reelection.*

By substituting the incumbent's dominant strategy into Equation 3.5 and simplifying, it follows that each community will use the following decision rule:

**Proposition 2.** *Each community will vote for the incumbent if they observe* $u(x_i, a) > u(x_i, a)* = \frac{1-\lambda}{N} + \frac{\lambda}{2n}$. *They will vote for the challenger otherwise.*

From this framework, I am now going to consider the effects of aid on voter behavior. I will start by discussing the main effects. Next I will then discuss the implications of relaxing voter knowledge. Finally I will discuss the role of competing interests.

### 3.3.1 Electoral Effects of Foreign Aid

How will foreign aid change voter beliefs and behavior? Two conclusions follow directly from this model. First, foreign aid will benefit incumbents electorally in proportion to the incumbent's lobbying influence ($\lambda$). Second, despite aggregate benefits, the effects of aid on voting will be heterogeneous. Aid will increase incumbent votes in some communities (those of type $\theta_i = 1$) and decrease votes in other communities ($\theta_i = 0$). These backlash effects will increase as $\lambda$ increases.

Note that here I assume that communities know the size of $\lambda$, though they are uncertain about whether or not they benefit from this redistribution. Later I will consider how these conclusions differ if communities have biased or uncertain beliefs about $\lambda$ as well.

To illustrate these conclusions, consider first the simple case where voters know that $\lambda = 0$. In this case, since communities know that the incumbent has no influence, they will learn nothing about the incumbent's type from observing their own welfare ($Pr(\theta_i = 1|u(x)) = Pr(\theta_i = 0|u(x))$). Aid will have no effect on elections.[33]

[33] Of course voters might not know that $\lambda = 0$. As I show later, when we relax the assumption that voters know $\lambda$, these conclusions change substantially.

Now consider the consequences of donors delegating full authority to the incumbent: $\lambda = 1$. In this scenario, incumbents have a dominant strategy to redistribute the maximum amount of aid allowed by the budget ($a = \frac{N-n}{N}$). Communities of type $\theta_i = 1$ will share equally in the aid. Communities of type $\theta_i = 0$ will receive nothing. This follows from Proposition 1.

Since voters know what each type should receive, the voters' inference problem is straightforward. Voters of type $\theta_i = 0$ will almost certainly vote for the challenger. Voters of type $\theta_i = 1$ will almost certainly vote for the incumbent. As long as incumbents are able to lobby for a winning coalition of voters ($n > \frac{N}{2}$), the votes gained will outweigh the votes lost and the incumbent will gain electorally from foreign aid.

When we see more incomplete delegation ($\lambda > 0$ or $< 1$), the electoral effects will sit between these two extremes. Incumbents will still benefit from foreign aid; however, the scale of the electoral effects will depend on the incumbent's bargaining power $\lambda$. As $\lambda$ increases, the difference in the welfare between communities that share the incumbent's type ($\theta_i = 1$) and those that don't ($\theta_i = 0$) will also increase. As a result, communities will be better able to identify whether the incumbent shares their type as $\lambda$ increases. The following propositions follow:

**Proposition 3.** *When $\lambda = 0$, foreign aid will have no effect on voting.*

**Proposition 4.** *When $\lambda > 0$,*

*(A) incumbents will win votes in communities of type $\theta_i = 1$ and lose votes in communities of type $\theta_i = 0$;*
*(B) incumbents will benefit electorally in proportion to lobbying influence $\lambda$.*

### 3.3.2 Electoral Effects with Uncertain Voters

A key way in which foreign aid differs from other forms of spending is that voters are often uncertain about the terms of an aid project. Realistically, a voter may have only a vague idea about whether their community should receive \$10,000 or \$1,000. They may also be uncertain about how much incumbents of their type can lobby the donor. How will this change voter beliefs and behavior?

One way to operationalize uncertainty over the budget or allocation of aid is to assume that this uncertainty increases the variance in communities' prior beliefs about the welfare they should receive from any given aid project: that is, it increases $v(\epsilon)$.

As $v(\epsilon)$ increases, the welfare expected by communities of type $\theta_i = 0$ overlaps more with the welfare expected by communities of type $\theta_i = 1$. Thus higher $v(\epsilon)$ will translate into smaller positive and negative effects of aid on voting and a smaller incumbency advantage overall.

This conclusion also implies an interaction between lobbying effort, $\lambda$, and uncertainty, $v(\epsilon)$. When voters are more uncertain about aid budgets, $\lambda$ will have to be higher in order for incumbents to obtain the same electoral benefit they would get from more certain voters. One implication is that in lower-information environments, politicians will have incentives to lobby donors for more extreme levels of political favoritism in the distribution of foreign aid.

**Proposition 5.** *As $v(\epsilon)$ increases, communities will be less able to identify their type ($\theta_i$); and lobbying ($\lambda$) will have a weaker effect on voting.*

Voters are often not *just* uncertain in their beliefs about the terms of an aid project, they also often hold biased beliefs. For instance, a voter might believe that an incumbent lobbies hard on their behalf with donor (has a high $\lambda$) when in fact the incumbent does little (has a low $\lambda$). One reason for this kind of bias is credit claiming. Politicians might lie and claim credit even if it is not deserved.[34] Voters might also underestimate the role that politicians play in development (e.g., see evidence on this point in Chapter 5).

To operationalize this bias, let $\hat{\lambda}$ represent communities' belief about $\lambda$. If this belief is positively biased ($\hat{\lambda} > \lambda$), it is possible for incumbents to benefit from foreign aid even if in fact they have no influence over the terms of aid.

For instance, consider the case that $\hat{\lambda} > \lambda = 0$. Here the incumbent has no influence ($\lambda = 0$), but communities believe that the incumbent does ($\hat{\lambda} > 0$).[35] In this case, the incumbent can receive an electoral boost from aid despite doing nothing (in contrast to the perfect information case discussed earlier). To give some intuition for these results, suppose that, as a resident of some community $i$, you hear about a project that is likely to bring health supplies worth \$1,500 to three communities in your district. If you believe that the incumbent is not influential in the donor's decision process, this allocation of aid will have no effect on your voting

[34] Cruz and Schneider 2017.

[35] This assumes that incumbents can credibly lie about their influence over donors. When and why voters might form firmly inaccurate beliefs about aid is an important area for future research. See Cruz, Keefer, and Labonne (2021) and Baldwin and Winters (2023) for discussion.

decision and you should expect to receive welfare equivalent to \$500 in expenditure.

However, suppose instead you believe that the incumbent is influential ($\hat{\lambda} = 1$). Now how will this \$500 change your views of the incumbent? On one hand, you might reason that if you are of the incumbent's type you should receive more than this (about \$750). On the other hand, you know that if you are not of the incumbent's type you are likely to receive nothing since all the money would have been distributed to others. Given that \$500 in welfare is more consistent with lobbying than not, you will infer that the incumbent is of your type.

It is worth emphasizing that credit claiming is still not the ideal strategy for incumbents. Incumbents will be better off if they actually lobby rather than mislead voters (i.e., if $\hat{\lambda} = \lambda$); however, when voters are misinformed, it is possible that incumbents will benefit beyond their lobbying influence.

What if voters underestimate incumbent lobbying effort? This will be the opposite of the overestimation case: voters are going to demand *more* aid in exchange for their votes. Aid will still generally help incumbents win votes but to a lesser extent than would be the case if voters were fully informed.

**Proposition 6.** *(A) When voters overestimate incumbent lobbying effort, $\hat{\lambda} > \lambda$, incumbents will gain votes compared to a scenario where voters are informed ($\hat{\lambda} = \lambda$). (B) When voters underestimate incumbent lobbying effort, $\hat{\lambda} < \lambda$, incumbents will lose votes compared to a scenario where voters are informed ($\hat{\lambda} = \lambda$).*

### 3.3.3 Electoral Effects with Competing Interests

Up until now, I have assumed that donors always prefer to distribute aid equally across the communities. In reality, donors also have their own interests to consider. They also often have to consider the interests of bureaucrats, NGOs, multilateral organizations, and civil society. How will these additional interests change the conclusions?

Suppose instead of assuming $x_i = x/N$, we assume that the donor sets $x_i$ in according to some fixed and exogenous preference over each community $i$. If communities are fully informed about the donor's preferences, then voters will update their priors about how much each community will receive absent lobbying effort. The effects of aid on electoral outcomes will not differ substantially from the analysis earlier.

However, more realistically, we might expect that communities are uncertain about the donor's preferences. This uncertainty can potentially be quite problematic for both voters' ability to select high performance incumbents and for the incumbent's chance of winning the election.

To see this, suppose the donor rejects the government proposal and decides to distribute a substantially greater share of aid to communities of type $\theta_i = 0$, perhaps because they exhibit greater levels of need (as they often do). If $\hat{\lambda} > 0$, then communities of type $\theta_i = 0$ will mostly infer incorrectly from their greater welfare that the incumbent shares their interests: that they are actually $\theta_i = 1$ communities. Communities of type $\theta_i = 1$ will mostly infer incorrectly from their lower welfare that the incumbent *does not* share their interests: that they are $\theta_i = 0$ communities. Since communities of type $\theta_i = 0$, by definition, do not represent a winning coalition of votes, this scenario will often cost the incumbent more votes than it gains.

## 3.4 IMPLICATIONS

Most scholars of foreign aid have argued or assumed that foreign aid helps incumbents and harms accountability. In this chapter, I propose an alternative (and I believe more realistic) way to think about these effects in democratic contexts, focusing on way in which foreign aid can provide information to voters about incumbent performance and preferences.

### 3.4.1 Voter Behavior

The theory implies some new insights into the ways in which foreign aid shapes votes. First, foreign aid will rarely be apolitical. Voting effects depend, not just on how foreign aid is distributed, but on what voters *believe* about the role of the incumbent in shaping that distribution. As long as voters believe that incumbents have some influence with donors (regardless of whether that is in fact the case), then foreign aid will alter voter beliefs about incumbent performance and preferences.

Contrary to what is often assumed, this means that efforts by donors to avoid the politicization of aid by, for instance, channeling aid through NGOs, will not isolate aid from political consequences. In fact, channeling aid away from the government may create a particularly toxic political scenario in which politicians can get credit from voters despite doing little for their constituents.

Second, these propositions imply that foreign aid is both an electoral blessing and curse for incumbents. On one hand, if incumbents have control over aid, then it can help them win elections. On the other hand, foreign aid can also cost incumbents votes. Voters who fail to benefit from aid as much as expected can punish incumbents for their failure to work on their behalf. This backlash effect can be particularly costly for incumbents when voters have incorrect beliefs about the role of the government and donors in shaping aid allocation. Finally, this argument implies that electoral effects of aid will depend on the form of aid delivery. When incumbents have more control over aid distribution (and voters know this to be the case), then voters will be more capable of selecting incumbents who share their preferences. This often translates into a greater electoral advantage for the incumbent.

### 3.4.2 Democratic Accountability

The theory also provides some nuance to arguments about the aid curse and democratic accountability. Here I mean by democratic accountability the ability of citizens to identify and reelect those politicians who share the characteristics that those citizens value. In the context of this theory, foreign aid improves accountability whenever foreign aid increases voters' ability to identify politicians who share their type.

When politicians influence aid spending and voters have accurate information about that influence ($\hat{\lambda} = \lambda$), then it follows that foreign aid is beneficial for accountability since aid will help voters to better identify those politicians that share their preferences.[36] These beneficial effects will be increasing in the extent of politicians' influence over aid allocation ($\lambda$) and voter certainty ($v(\epsilon)$).[37]

I refer to this effect of increasing the visibility of politician preferences as the *visibility effect* of foreign aid. This visibility effect is potentially meaningful for voters. As I show in Chapter 2, politicians in aid-dependent (and therefore budget constrained) contexts often struggle to find ways to affect the welfare of the majority of citizens in their constituencies. For many voters, foreign aid is the main or only way that they can make inferences about their incumbent. I will discuss some further evidence on this point in Chapter 5. However, critics of aid are not all wrong. Because of the opacity of aid spending, voters will often struggle in aid-dependent countries to make accurate inferences about

[36] From Equation 3.3, informed voters will always positively update their priors whenever $\lambda > 0$ and $a > 0$.

[37] As politicians have more say, the differences in the welfare between voters of type $\theta = 1$ and $\theta = 0$ will be greater, as will those voters' ability to distinguish the type of the incumbent.

the relationship between politicians' effort and their own welfare. Additionally, voter uncertainty creates an opening for politicians to mislead voters. When voters often have incorrect beliefs about politicians' influence ($\hat{\lambda} \neq \lambda$), and lack credible ways to determine the extent of that influence, foreign aid can cause voters to incorrectly update about the probability that the incumbent shares their type. I refer to this increased likelihood of adverse updating as the *uncertainty effect* of foreign aid.

The net effects of foreign aid on electoral accountability will depend on the scale of these visibility and uncertainty effects. Uncertainty effects will be greater the more voters are uncertain about the terms of an aid project. For instance, if voters overestimate $\lambda$, for instance, due to undeserved credit claiming by politicians, then voters will be more likely to reward incumbent for aid even though – if fact – the incumbent may have done little to deserve it. At the extreme, foreign aid can cause voters to reelect incumbents that neither have influence with donors nor share the preferences of the majority of citizens.

Contrary to what is usually assumed, this theory implies that channeling aid away from the government can be the worst outcome for accountability because it *decreases* the visibility of politicians' effort, while *increasing* uncertainty about the role of the government in spending. Paradoxically, this logic suggests that donors, by trying to limit corruption and maximize transparency by limiting government influence over development, might do particular harm to incumbent governments and democratic accountability. In the short term, donors might rationalize circumventing the government as a way to create more equitable development outcomes and avoid political bias. In the long run, however, donor aid may reinforce inequality by making it possible for politicians to remain in power while working on behalf of a narrow group of supporters.

It is important to note however that these aid curse effects are not inherent to aid in this model. These curse effects occur – not because aid is fungible or untaxed, as often argued – but rather because governments and donors fail to inform sufficiently voters about development decisions, and because of the fragmentation and complexity of development decisions in aid-dependent contexts.

### 3.4.3 Politician Behavior

Finally, this theory has some implications for politician behavior. First, it suggests that politicians should seek to lobby donors in favor of those communities that are both electorally pivotal and likely to attribute foreign aid to government action. These incentives to lobby should be particularly strong when voters are more uncertain about the politician's effort or the relationship between public welfare and politician behavior ($\lambda$ or $\epsilon$). Intuitively, when spending is not a reliable signal of politician performance, politicians have to work harder to signal to voters their preferences and effort. I will argue and show evidence in Chapter 4 that this logic implies a bias in foreign aid distribution in favor of copartisan communities.

Additionally, the model helps explain when and why politicians might seek to shift voter beliefs about the role of the government ($\lambda$), for instance by claiming credit for donor activities. As with traditional forms of spending, politicians will tend to benefit electorally from accurate credit claiming. However, this model also implies a partial substitution between real and pretend effort: when voters are uncertain (about $\lambda$ or $\epsilon$), politicians can, to some extent, avoid lobbying effort by misleading voters into thinking that they have more bargaining power than they do ($\hat{\lambda} > \lambda$). This will cause voters to overestimate the likelihood that they share the incumbent's type.

I will examine these prediction especially in Chapter 4. Using data on the allocation of foreign aid in Malawi, Kenya and Sierra Leone over time, I will show that patterns of foreign aid change over time in ways that tend to benefit supporters of incumbent parties. I will also show in Chapter 5 that politicians often attempt to take credit for the activities of donors. In Chapter 6, I will also extend this argument to consider how foreign aid can affect other forms of public spending decisions.

## 3.5 PROOFS

**Proposition 1.** *The incumbent will lobby the donor whenever* $n > \frac{N}{2}$. *The incumbent will always propose to redistribute the maximum amount of aid allowed by the budget* ($a = \frac{N-n}{N}$). *This strategy will maximize the incumbent's chances of reelection.*

*Proof:*

Consider first communities that share the incumbent's type. From Equation 3.3, it follows that the odds that any such a community votes for the incumbent is strictly increasing in $a$ (since a higher $a$ makes the community more confident that the politician is of type $\theta = 1$). Note also that the maximum amount of aid that the incumbent can propose without exhausting the budget is $a = \frac{a}{N-n}$. It follows that $a = \frac{a}{N-n}$ will be the strategy likely to maximize votes for this group.

Consider now communities that do not share the incumbent's type. As $a$ increases, they become more certain that the incumbent is of type $\theta = 0$ and become *less* likely to vote for the incumbent.

Since both types of communities have common beliefs about $\lambda$, these effects are symmetric: a marginal increase in votes for communities of the incumbent's type will cost an identical share of votes in communities that do not share the incumbent's type. Thus if $n < \frac{N}{2}$, the incumbent will always prefer not to lobby and will prefer the victory probability of $\frac{1}{2}$ they get from doing nothing. However, if $n > \frac{N}{2}$, then the gains from the politicians' preferred communities will always exceed the losses from other communities. To maximize these gains, the incumbent will set the budget to $a = \frac{a}{N-n}$.

**Proposition 2.** *Each community will vote for the incumbent if they observe $u(x_i, a) > u(x_i, a)* = \frac{1-\lambda}{N} + \frac{\lambda}{2n}$. They will vote for the challenger otherwise.*

*Proof:*

From Equation 3.3 and substituting in the equilibrium values for $a$, it follows that communities positively update their prior $(p(\theta_i))$ whenever $f(\frac{n(1-\lambda)+\lambda N}{Nn}) > f(\frac{1-\lambda}{N})$ and are indifferent between electing and not whenever $f(\frac{n(1-\lambda)+\lambda N}{Nn}) = f(\frac{1-\lambda}{N})$ where $f(.)$ is the pdf of $\epsilon$.

By assumption, $f(\frac{n(1-\lambda)+\lambda N}{Nn})$ and $f(\frac{1-\lambda}{N})$ are symmetric and unimodal with unique maxima at $\frac{n(1-\lambda)+\lambda N}{Nn}$ and $\frac{1-\lambda}{N}$. From this, it follows that there is a unique solution which satisfies this equality at $u(x_i, a)* = \frac{1}{2}[\frac{n(1-\lambda)+\lambda N}{Nn} + \frac{1-\lambda}{N}]$. After simplifying, it follows that $u(x_i, a)* = \frac{1-\lambda}{N} + \frac{\lambda}{2n}$.

**Proposition 3.** *When $\lambda = 0$, foreign aid will have no effect on voting.*

*Proof:*

This follows trivially from Proposition 1. When $\lambda = 0$ the incumbent will win the election with probability $\frac{1}{2}$. In the proof for Proposition 1, I show that incumbents can always do better than this when $\lambda > 0$ and $n > \frac{N}{2}$.

**Proposition 4.** *When $\lambda > 0$,*

*(A) incumbents will win votes in communities of type $\theta_i = 1$ and lose votes in communities of type $\theta_i = 0$;*

*(B) incumbents will benefit electorally in proportion to lobbying influence $\lambda$.*

*Proof:*

First consider communities of type $\theta_i = 1$. To prove part A, it is sufficient to show that an increase in $\lambda$ increases community welfare, $u(x_i, a|\theta_i = 1)$, more than it increases the reserve price that communities demand in order to vote for the incumbent: $u(x_i, a)*$.

$\theta_i = 1$ communities will receive, in expectation, $\frac{n(1-\lambda)+\lambda N}{Nn}$ from the donor. Taking the derivative of this equation with respect to $\lambda$ it follows that an increase in $\lambda$ will increase the amount that each of these communities receives by

$$\frac{d}{d\lambda}u(x_i, a|\theta_i = 1) = \frac{d}{d\lambda}\frac{n(1-\lambda)+\lambda N}{Nn} = \frac{1}{n} - \frac{1}{N} \tag{3.6}$$

From Proposition 2, we know that communities' reservation price is $u(x_i, a)* = \frac{1-\lambda}{N} + \frac{\lambda}{2n}$. Taking the derivative of this equation with respect to $\lambda$, we get

$$\frac{d}{d\lambda}u(x_i, a)* = \frac{d}{d\lambda}\frac{1-\lambda}{N} + \frac{\lambda}{2n} = \frac{1}{2n} - \frac{1}{N} \tag{3.7}$$

Note that, from our assumptions about $n$, $\frac{d}{d\lambda}u(x_i, a|\theta_i = 1)$ is therefore always positive and $\frac{d}{d\lambda}u(x_i, a)*$ is always negative. It follows that any increase in $\lambda$ will increase votes for the incumbent among communities of type $\theta_i = 1$.

Since both types of communities in this game have common beliefs, it follows also that an increase in votes among communities of type $\theta_i = 1$ must result in a proportional *decrease* in votes in communities of type $\theta_i = 0$.

Part B follows directly. Since there are more voters of type $\theta_i = 1$ (otherwise from Proposition 1, we know the incumbent will not lobby), the increase in among $\theta_i = 1$ voters will be greater than the decrease in votes among $\theta_i = 0$ voters.

**Proposition 5.** *As $v(\epsilon)$ increases, communities will be less able to identify their type ($\theta_i$); and lobbying ($\lambda$) will have a weaker effect on voting.*

Let $f(u(x_i|\theta_i = 1))$ be the pdf of the welfare expected by $\theta_i = 1$ communities where $f(.)$ is the pdf of $\epsilon$.

In order for any such community change their prior in the incumbent's favor, it must be the case that their draw from $f(u(x_i|\theta_i = 1))$ exceeds their reservation price, $u(x_i|\theta_i = 1)*$. As $v(\epsilon)$ increases, it becomes more likely that any draw falls below the reservation price. Thus we will see more updating against type as $v(\epsilon)$ increases.

An identical logic holds for $\theta_i = 0$ communities.

**Proposition 6.** *(A) When voters overestimate incumbent lobbying effort, $\hat{\lambda} > \lambda$, incumbents will gain votes compared to a scenario where voters are informed ($\hat{\lambda} = \lambda$). (B) When voters underestimate incumbent lobbying effort, $\hat{\lambda} < \lambda$, incumbents will lose votes compared to a scenario where voters are informed ($\hat{\lambda} = \lambda$).*

From Proposition 2, we know that communities' reservation price is $u(x_i, a)* = \frac{1-\lambda}{N} + \frac{\lambda}{2n}$. Taking the derivative of this equation with respect to $\lambda$ we get

$$\frac{d}{d\lambda}u(x_i, a)* = \frac{d}{d\lambda}\frac{1-\lambda}{N} + \frac{\lambda}{2n} = \frac{1}{2n} - \frac{1}{N} \tag{3.8}$$

From our assumptions about $n$, it follows that $\frac{d}{d\lambda}u(x_i, a)*$ is always negative.

It follows that if communities overestimate lobbying, $\hat{\lambda} > \lambda$, then communities' actual reservation price will decrease. They will therefore require less aid in order to update their prior in the incumbent's favor.

Likewise if communities underestimate lobbying, $\hat{\lambda} < \lambda$, then communities' actual reservation price will increase. They will therefore require more aid in order to update their prior in the incumbent's favor.

# 4

# The Electoral Politics of Aid Distribution

The other barrier we also have is that [district name] does not have hot NGOs like World Vision, EU and UNICEF. NGO presence in a district is influenced by the Government of the day and this is heavily politicized.

– Member of Parliament, Malawi[1]

For many years I have been a victim when it comes to the allocation of schools. I don't have enough secondary schools in my area, I need one.

– Malawian Member of Parliament, complaining in Blantyre council about the allocation of USAID funding.[2]

In Chapter 3, I argued that politicians have strong incentives to lobby donors in order to increase the share of foreign aid going to electorally pivotal voters. Further, I argued that this lobbying shapes voter behavior and often (but not always) helps incumbents win elections. My goal in this chapter is to test the first part of this argument: is it the case that politicians influence donor spending? And, if so, does this influence favor electorally pivotal voters?

These are not uncontentious claims. On one hand, a number of studies offer evidence that foreign aid projects are sometimes biased in favor of areas connected to incumbent parties and presidents.[3] Yet, other analyses have found mixed or inconclusive evidence that politicians influence the

[1] Interview B4, see Appendix B.

[2] Mogha-Mana 2019.

[3] Briggs 2014, 2012; Jablonski 2014; Francken, Minten, and Swinnen 2012; Dipendra 2020; Bommer, Dreher, and Perez-Alvarez 2022; Min et al. 2023; Lio Rosvold 2020; Seim, Jablonski, and Ahlbäck 2020; Kagotho, Bunger, and Wagner 2016; Dreher et al. 2019; Bomprezzi et al. 2024; Brass 2016; Briggs 2021.

distribution of aid for political ends.[4] To reconcile such findings, some scholars have suggested that while political capture may have been a problem in the past, the oversight and accountability mechanisms that major donors now have in place strongly constrain the ability of politicians to use foreign aid for political ends. Indeed, several well-executed studies provide evidence that political capture is mainly a problem for non-traditional donors or for donors in the pre-Cold War era.[5]

Aid workers themselves also have mixed views on this subject. In Malawi, most (but not all) donors I interviewed accepted that politicians were interested in influencing foreign aid for political reasons; however, most also emphasized their high level of oversight and use of objective needs-based criteria. Many claimed that these checks are sufficient to prevent any undue political influence. Here are some examples of responses that donor program officers gave when asked about the potential for political bias:

> We select schools, we get endorsement from national and district level.... At the district level there's a council meeting that happens, where you find members of parliament, traditional authorities... Everybody would want to take the programme to their area. But when we do the objective analysis of the data, we defeat their decision.[6]

> [Politicians] want the schools to go to a district just because they come from there, they want to show the government is doing something in that area so they prioritise that area at the expense of others who have more need... To manage risk we make the process as transparent as possible. We develop a criteria with them with objective indicators.[7]

> I don't think [government officials prioritize political or personal interest].... Our systems are very transparent, no space at all for corruption or influencing from other partners.[8]

Other donors, however, were more willing to admit that there is a lot which they cannot control:

[4] Nunnenkamp, Öhler, and Sosa Andrés 2017; Anaxagorou, Efthyvoulou, and Sarantides 2020; Masaki 2018; DiLorenzo 2023; Findley et al. 2017; Dreher et al. 2022; Brass 2012b.

[5] Bermeo 2016; Dreher et al. 2019, 2022; Anaxagorou, Efthyvoulou, and Sarantides 2020.

[6] Interview portfolio coordinator an international NGO, Malawi; Appendix B; Interview A6.

[7] Interview with portfolio coordinator for bilateral donor, Malawi; Appendix B; Interview A3.

[8] Interview with official at an international donor organization, Malawi; Appendix B; Interview A4.

> We agreed with civil servants where to build [schools]. Then politicians didn't agree, said "bring those schools to this district" even though that wasn't what we agreed.... It's difficult, we can't do anything otherwise we start being political. Us, development partners, we just go by what they decide. We just give to the government. If they use it in that way, that's their responsibility.[9]

It is possible that part of the reason for these mixed expectations and findings is that this is a difficult and sensitive topic to study. Donors rarely, if ever, want to be associated with supporting politically connected citizens or helping a poorly performing politician hold on to power. Indeed, it has been my experience that donors are reticent to entertain or discuss the role of political bias in their aid portfolios. Donor likely also face information disadvantages relative to government officials: Politicians often know more about local needs and politics and may seek to mask political goals under the guise of development or at least find ways to combine both political and developmental goals.

As researchers, we also face the problem that electorally motivated bias is not easy to identify. If we observe a correlation between voting and voter characteristics, it does not necessarily imply that this relationship is causal or that there is an electoral bias in aid distribution. For instance, constituencies which strongly support the incumbent party might also be locations that are historically disadvantaged, or where, for whatever reason, many citizens are in need of support from donor communities.[10] We may also observe bias because politicians simply know more about the needs of communities inside their social and political network.[11]

A related problem is that most data we have on foreign aid spending is spatially and temporally imprecise. Major donors often track the locations that benefit from foreign aid; however, they rarely track at a sufficient level of precision to identify the exact community or even constituency that benefited from foreign aid. Often the reason for this is logistical: A donor will often select certain districts, but leave it up to an implementing partner (a government agency or NGO) to select the precise individuals or communities that will benefit. This is potentially problematic since this implementation stage is often where politicians are able to assert the most influence.

9 Interview with portfolio manager at a bilateral donor, Malawi; Appendix B; Interview A5.

10 Simson and Green 2020; Kramon and Posner 2013; Harris and Posner 2019.

11 Jablonski and Seim 2023; Jöst and Lust 2022; Duarte et al. 2019.

I address these challenges using several strategies. First, I conduct a cross-national analysis examining how aid responds to changes in patterns of electoral support for incumbent governments. For this analysis, I select three democratic countries – Sierra Leone, Malawi, and Kenya – for which we have comprehensive and relatively spatially precise data. In Malawi and Sierra Leone, this precision is due to a requirement on the part of the government that all donors report spending data to an aid management platform, which tracks the location of aid beneficiaries to a relatively high degree of precision. In Kenya, I rely on the hand coding of project completion reports published by the World Bank and the African Development Bank. These completion reports often provide extensive detail on where projects end up being distributed.[12]

These three cases are also apt in that they have a history of highly competitive elections. Because of the competitiveness of elections in these countries, politicians have strong incentives to use development spending to influence voting. In each country, these elections have resulted in substantial changes in the partisanship of ruling coalitions. These changes in governance will allow me to test whether the distribution of foreign aid changes when new governments come to power. The cross-national data also provides leverage to assess how these effects vary across countries and donors.

To help identify whether these effects are indeed driven by electoral motivations, I will examine in more depth how a major government transition in Kenya in 2002 affected the distribution of multilateral donor spending over time. By looking at how changes in the governing coalition affected aid distribution, I make a case for a causal link between the government's electoral motivations and the distribution of aid.

Finally, in Chapter 6, I take a somewhat different approach to testing for electoral bias. Rather than relying on donor data with all its problems, I ask politicians in Malawi directly to advise on the distribution of a foreign aid project. The more geographically precise data from this survey mirror and reinforce what I find in this chapter.

## 4.1 THE DISTRIBUTIONAL POLITICS OF FOREIGN AID

To test whether politicians are using aid to win votes, I start by asking what aid distribution would look like if this were happening. I then test whether the pattern of aid distribution is consistent with this expectation.

[12] These data were originally coded as part of my PhD thesis. See Jablonski (2014, 2013) for details.

To understand how a reelection-minded politician might prefer to target foreign aid, it is helpful to first think about the effects of aid from the standpoint of potential aid recipients. As I argued in Chapter 3, one of the main ways in which foreign aid influences voting is by persuading citizens to change their beliefs about the effort and preferences of an incumbent. If citizens believe an incumbent lobbied on their behalf, they might infer that the incumbent will continue to lobby for their interests. If, however, citizens observe that they did not benefit, they might infer that the incumbent failed to work on their behalf.

It follows that a primary factor that an incumbent has to consider in targeting her spending decision is how persuadable a citizen might be. For instance, if a citizen strongly supports a challenger, then it might be hard to persuade that citizen to change their mind. Incumbents will also consider how likely it is that citizens can be persuaded to engage in the costly action of voting. Citizens who are already partisan with an incumbent are more likely to pay those costs and may therefore be easier to mobilize than nonpartisans.

There is a substantial body of political science theory considering how incumbents weigh these concerns about persuasion and mobilization in their spending decisions. One possibility is that politicians will target communities with many "swing voters," which are those voters who are close to indifferent between the policy preferences of two or more candidates. The logic of this prediction is that voters who are indifferent will be more persuadable than those whose preferences are far away from those of the incumbent. While intuitive, in practice, this is often not a dominant strategy since the costs of mobilizing co-partisans are often much lower than the costs of both persuading and mobilizing nonpartisans.[13] Some have argued that these persuasion costs are particularly high among voters in low-income democracies. Campaigns in such contexts are often personal: focused on interpersonal interaction between candidates and voters, or between party brokers and voters. Where this is the case, it might be difficult to persuade those voters that are not well connected to political networks.[14] Politicians also often struggle to learn about the preferences and needs of voters outside of their core areas.[15]

Instead, what we most often observe is that politicians prefer to spend public funds in such a way as to increase the welfare of so-called core voters, who are those groups of citizens who are already well embedded into a politician's political network; often by virtue of their ethnic or kin

[13] Nichter 2008; Cox 2010.

[14] Stokes et al. 2013.

[15] Jablonski and Seim 2023; Dixit and Londregan 1996.

connections to a politician. It is often much easier for an incumbent to mobilize voters from those who are already positively disposed to her; and persuading such core voters to turn out and vote is oftentimes much easier to trying to change the opinion of a voter who is not well disposed to the incumbent. Additionally, politicians can take advantage of patronage networks among core voters. Within many societies, voters rely on local patrons – such as chiefs, village leaders, or well-connected officials – to help them make informed decisions about how to vote. Since such patrons can exchange the support of groups of voters for development spending, this can lead to transactional voting in which even a politician's closest core supporters can be up for grabs if another politician is able to commit to providing more public resources to a community.[16]

There are also some characteristics of an incumbent's distributional problem that are specific to foreign aid. As I show in Chapter 3, incumbents that want to gain electorally from foreign aid also have to consider citizen *beliefs* about the role of the government in lobbying for that aid. If a group of citizens are uncertain about the government's role in development spending, or if they do not believe that the government had influence, then there is little electoral reason to lobby donors on behalf of these citizens. These beliefs about the government's role in development spending are not equally distributed across citizens. A citizen of a more politically marginalized area, for instance, might be more sceptical of an incumbent's attempts to claim credit for aid since they know the incumbent has little history of favoring their community. Likewise, incumbents might find it easier to claim credit for aid (e.g., through participating in groundbreaking ceremonies) where they have dense social and political networks.

If incumbents target those citizens already inclined to believe in government influence and favoritism, this means that aid will be particularly likely to target those communities that are well aligned with the incumbent. Consistent with this argument, the empirical evidence on foreign aid seems to suggest that foreign aid is biased especially in favor of places like an incumbents birth area, their home area, and places with close family networks.[17]

[16] Keefer and Vlaicu (2008), for instance, consider a model in which politicians are better able to make promises of development when such promises are made to political brokers. They show that this leads to an equilibrium in which politicians make few spending commitments outside of clientelistic networks. See also Stokes et al. (2013) for further discussion and evidence.

[17] Seim, Jablonski, and Ahlbäck 2020; Dreher et al. 2019; Bomprezzi et al. 2024.

## 4.2 FOREIGN AID IN MALAWI, KENYA, AND SIERRA LEONE

To assess my argument, I examine the history of aid distribution in Kenya, Malawi, and Sierra Leone. As noted earlier, these cases are largely selected for reasons of data availability. However, they are also cases in which politicians likely have strong incentives to use foreign aid for political ends. As shown in Figure 4.1, each is a country in which citizens are highly dependent upon donors. Each country also is quite constrained in its ability to raise revenue without donor assistance.[18]

Each country also has a history of biased spending in favor of incumbent co-partisans. In Kenya, for instance, Burgess et al. (2015) studied the distribution of paved road investment over time in Kenya (from 1961 to 2002) and showed that such investment consistently favored coethnics and residents in the home districts of government officials. Other studies have shown similar biases.[19] In Malawi, several studies have noted a bias toward co-partisans of supporters of the ruling party in the distribution of goods.[20] In Sierra Leone, ruling parties are frequently accused

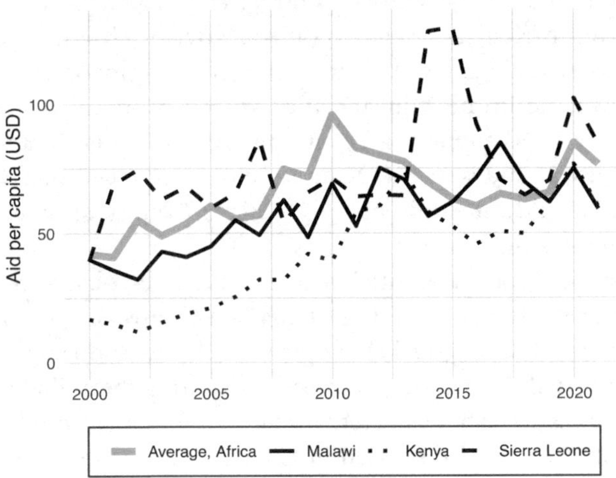


FIGURE 4.1 Foreign aid per capita in Sierra Leone, Kenya, and Malawi
Source: World Bank World Development Indicators

[18] See Chapter 2.

[19] Kramon and Posner 2013; Jablonski 2014; Briggs 2014; Alwy and Schech 2004.

[20] Jablonski and Seim 2023; Brazys, Heaney, and Walsh 2015; Chinsinga 2011; Ejdemyr, Kramon, and Robinson 2018; Kita 2017.

of diverting foreign aid and other forms of funding to co-partisan and co-ethnic voters.[21]

In Malawi, voters and political officials often note a tendency for development spending to follow partisanship. In focus groups, when asked about the role of politics in public spending, one respondent said "most politicians choose development to where they get more votes, in order to punish those who didn't vote for him." Another said, "[politicians] always think of where they come from first." A third said "In Malawi it's a syndrome. [Elected officials] always bring development to where they stay." A District Commissioner (a high level bureaucrat) likewise told us that "Whenever [we] conduct a meeting with the elected officials to identify the area where the development should go, most of them choose the area where he got more votes." In interviews, politicians also sometimes admit to political bias in favor of core voters. When asked how he made a spending decision, one politicians said "I was taking into consideration on how people voted for me so I wanted to please my people."[22]

Consistent with my argument, we also see some anecdotal accounts of politicians pressuring donors to target core voters or ethnic groups. For instance, in Kenya, a senior political advisor (Miguna Miguna) to Prime Minister Odinga tells the story in his biography of a French donor who came to the Prime Minister after with a proposal to improve the infrastructure of Kisumu, a large city on Lake Victoria. Despite the fact that Kisumu was and is in significant need of infrastructure development, but Odinga would "steer discussions to Siaya County, specifically Bondo town where he hailed from."[23]

Likewise, in Malawi, politicians are sometimes observed pressuring donors to bring funds to certain areas.[24] Perhaps, most substantially, the Democratic Progressive Party that was in power during most of the period of my analysis was often accused of limiting the ability of northern opposition constituencies to access foreign development funds, especially from the Chinese.[25] As discussed in Chapter 2, my interviews also confirm that politicians often pressure donors in ways that appear motivated by electoral concerns.

[21] Reno 1995; Robinson 2008.
[22] Voter focus groups and politician surveys, see Appendix B.
[23] Miguna 2012, pp. 176ff.
[24] Mogha-Mana 2019.
[25] Khamula 2015; Nyasa Times Reporter 2019.

## 4.3 HYPOTHESES

This argument implies testable hypotheses about aid distribution in these three countries. If incumbents are successful at capturing foreign aid for political ends, we should first observe that strong supporters of opposition parties will rarely benefit from the distribution of aid. Such groups, were it even possible to change their votes, would require a significant investment by candidates. As a result, in all but the most implausible cases, candidates will find it cheaper to purchase the votes of less ideologically opposed groups.

H1 Core supporters of the opposition party are less likely to receive foreign aid than core supporters of the incumbent party.

Depending upon the assumptions one makes, candidates will specifically target either swing or core voters. As discussed earlier, there are both theoretical and empirical reasons to believe that in these contexts electoral commitments to core voters are more credible and valuable than such commitments to swing voters and, therefore, that these voters will receive a larger share of goods.

H2 Core supporters of the incumbent party will receive more foreign aid than voters who have less support for the incumbent party (opposition and swing voters).

## 4.4 FOREIGN AID DATA

In order to identify the location of aid projects in Kenya, I rely on project completion reports published by the World Bank and the African Development Bank. These project reports usually identify where the final funds from an aid project were allocated. By reviewing these data, I am able to code the geographic coordinates of all World Bank and African Development Bank projects from 1992 to 2010.[26] It is not feasible to code data after this date due to changes in constituencies and spending rules.[27]

[26] For details on the coding of these data see Appendix C and Jablonski (2014).

[27] Kenya's first real multiparty election was in 1992, making this a reasonable place to start the analysis. In 2010, Kenya formed a new constitution which, among other things, reformulated constituency boundaries and devolved considerable spending authority to county governments. This makes it challenging to compare spending patterns before and after 2010.

I use two sources of data to code patterns of aid spending in Malawi. First, I rely on data from Malawi's Aid Management Platform. This was a platform set up by the government to provide citizens and stakeholders with public access to the details of international development projects, including the location of various components of the project. It includes reporting from 30 donor agencies on 548 projects affecting 2,119 locations. It represents approximately 80 percent of all development financing reported to the government from 2000 to 2012.[28,29]

Like Malawi, the Sierra Leone government set up a Development Assistance Database to track the activities of donors and publicly share information on the location and amounts of their spending. This database tracks donor commitments across 856 projects affecting 2,314 locations from 1992 to 2014.[30] Because of Sierra Leone's tumultuous history, I am able to include data on donor activities in Sierra Leone from 2002 onward.[31]

Using data from these sources, I code for each country the amount of funding per person committed to each electoral constituency in each year (aid per capita).[32] Since donors do not release the amount of funds going to each location, this requires making some assumptions about how aid is distributed across different project components and regions. I describe these assumptions in Appendix C. I also provide additional robustness checks and coding details.

It's important to note that these data do not include foreign budget support. Partly this is because it is nearly impossible to get visibility into the allocation of budget support. Additionally, none of these countries received large amounts of budget support during this period.[33] Since donors retain a substantial amount of control over these projects, the use of these data make for a particularly hard test of political influence.

[28] Peratsakis, Christian, Joshua Powell, Michael Findley, Justin Baker, and Catherine Weaver 2012

[29] It is difficult to match foreign aid to specific constituencies prior to 2000 as Malawi significantly redrew its political boundaries prior to the 1999 election.

[30] AidData 2017.

[31] Sierra Leone held its first elections in 1996 under a new constitution; however these were quickly followed by a coup and contested rule. In 2002 was the first election in which an incumbent (Ahmed Tejan of the SLPP) had largely uncontested control over the government.

[32] I use the project approval date as the year of each project. Donors and governments often decide on the amount and the location of aid disbursements during the planning stage of a project, so this is the most reasonable point at which to date each project.

[33] Donors cut off budget support to Kenya, in part, due to human rights abuses by President Moi. Donors have historically been reluctant to give Malawi and Sierra Leone budget support due to concerns about capacity and corruption.

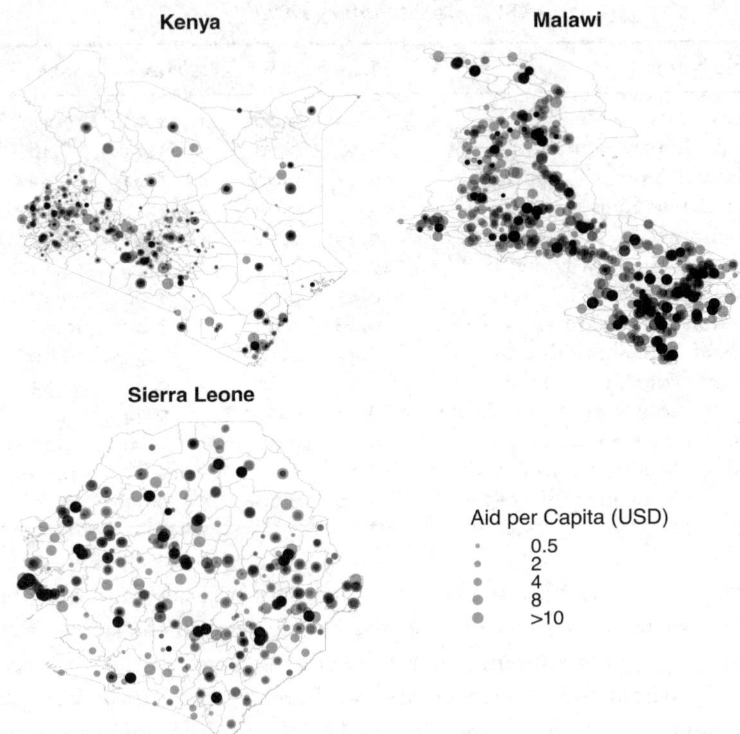


FIGURE 4.2 Distribution of foreign aid in Sierra Leone, Kenya, and Malawi
*Note:* This figure shows the geographic coordinates of each aid project in Malawi, Kenya, and Sierra Leone. The size of each dot indicates the amount of aid as a share of the constituency population.

In Figure 4.2 I plot the distribution of projects across the constituencies in each of the three countries.

## 4.5 VOTING DATA

In order to identify the political characteristics of aid recipients, I collected data on parliamentary elections for each of the constituencies in Malawi (1999–2014), Sierra Leone (1998–2014), and Kenya (1992–2010).[34]

34 I use parliamentary data for coding political characteristics since disaggregated data on presidential and other elections are not widely available for these countries. In each of these countries, partisanship largely predicts voting patterns, making this distinction mostly inconsequential. Data on voting come from the Constituency level Election

TABLE 4.1 *Summary variables*

| Variable Name | Mean | Min | Max | SD |
|---|---|---|---|---|
| Aid per Capita | 10.05 | 0.00 | 1391.22 | 39.37 |
| Bilateral Aid per Capita | 6.94 | 0.00 | 965.11 | 26.48 |
| Multilateral Aid per Capita | 7.31 | 0.00 | 1391.22 | 33.69 |
| Aid per Capita Kenya | 7.83 | 0.00 | 1391.22 | 40.60 |
| Aid per Capita Malawi | 7.99 | 0.00 | 1065.66 | 34.92 |
| Aid per Capita Sierra Leone | 20.15 | 0.00 | 476.24 | 41.17 |
| Incumbent Vote Share | 0.41 | 0.00 | 1.00 | 0.27 |
| Opposition Vote Share | 0.26 | 0.00 | 1.00 | 0.26 |
| Incumbent Vote Share Kenya | 0.43 | 0.00 | 1.00 | 0.30 |
| Incumbent Vote Share Malawi | 0.37 | 0.00 | 0.94 | 0.23 |
| Incumbent Vote Share Sierra Leone | 0.44 | 0.008 | 0.94 | 0.27 |
| Opposition Vote Share Kenya | 0.21 | 0.00 | 1.00 | 0.25 |
| Opposition Vote Share Malawi | 0.23 | 0.00 | 0.91 | 0.26 |
| Opposition Vote Share Sierra Leone | 0.40 | 0.008 | 0.93 | 0.27 |

I use several variables to measure support for incumbent parties. First, I create a variable *Incumbent Vote Share* which equals the share of votes received in each constituency by the incumbent party in the most recent previous parliamentary election. Second, I create *Opposition Vote Share* which equals the share of votes received by the leading opposition party.

I summarize all the voting and foreign aid variables in Table 4.1.

## 4.6 ESTIMATING THE EFFECTS OF VOTING ON AID

To analyze the effects of political support on foreign aid distribution, I start by regressing foreign aid per capita (In year 2000 U.S. Dollars) in each constituency on *Incumbent Vote Share* and *Opposition Vote Share*. I include both year and constituency fixed-effects.

The idea behind this linear two-way fixed effects estimation approach is to isolate how changes in aid spending responds to changes in a government's distribution of political support during elections. If the aid capture thesis is correct, then we should expect that when a new government comes to power, members of the new government should lobby for their own group of pivotal voters rather than pivotal voters of a prior government.

Archive supplemented with data from national electoral commissions (Kollman, Ken, Allen Hicken, Daniele Caramani, David Backer, and David Lublin 2020).

Formally, I estimate the following equation:

$$Log(Aid\ per\ Capita + 1)_{ijt} = \beta_1 Vote\ Share + \theta_t + \gamma_{ij} \qquad (4.1)$$

Where $Log(Aid\ per\ Capita + 1)_{ijt}$ equals the log aid per capital in country $i$, constituency $j$ and year $t$. $\theta_t$ and $\gamma_{ij}$ are fixed effects for year and constituency. Standard errors are clustered on constituency. I am interested in the coefficient $\beta_1$ which represents the effect of within-constituency changes in *Vote Share* on *Log(Aid per Capita + 1)*.

This estimation approach addresses some of the main concerns about alternative explanations. For instance, one challenge with identifying a partisan bias is that partisanship is often correlated with the needs of a community. As a result, a distributional decision that is purely motivated by need might be confused with a decision that is motivated by partisanship. However, by looking at within-constituency changes in partisanship and ethnicity, we can rule out this possibility.

That said, it is still possible that the coefficients from this model could reflect more complex, but still need-based, concerns. For instance, it could be the case that some politicians are not motivated by political concerns themselves, but are instead motivated to redress the political biases of others, which might have harmed public welfare.

I cannot rule out this possibility entirely; however, it is worth noting that this alternative account is still largely consistent with the theory of the book. If we see a partisan bias in aid, it is almost certainly the case that politicians played a key role in influencing the distribution of that aid and that some politicians (even if not all politicians) had partisan motivations for influencing that distribution.

## 4.7 ESTIMATION RESULTS

The results of this estimation in Figure 4.3 indeed suggest a consistent pattern of partisan bias. On average, the estimates suggest that a 10 percentage point increase in votes for the incumbent party would increase the amount of aid each resident in a constituency received each year by about 3 percent.

On a year-to-year basis, these effects of political capture might not seem large. However elections can result in large transformations in the political map. As I illustrate in the case of Kenya later, large shifts in power can substantially shift the allocation of foreign aid.

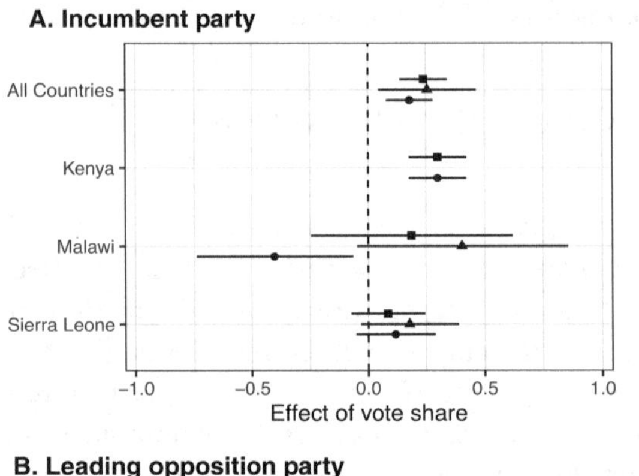


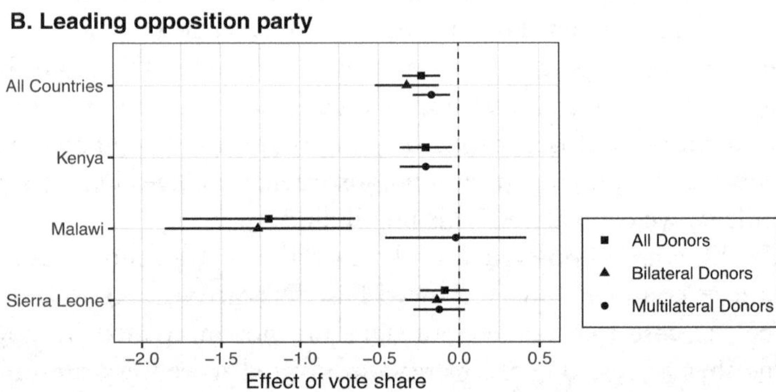


FIGURE 4.3 Effects of vote share on aid spending per capita
This figure shows the coefficients from a two-way fixed-effect regression of log aid spending per capita on the vote share of incumbent parties (Panel A) and the leading opposition party (Panel B) in each constituency, country, and year. Standard errors are clustered on constituency.

While the effects of vote share are mostly consistent across country, there is some variation. The effect sizes are largest in Kenya, which could be do to Kenya's history of ethnically biased public spending. However, as discussed later, this larger effect could also be due to Kenya's tumultuous political history. The large shifts in political coalitions during this era – and particularly after the fall of President Moi – created particularly strong incentives for the political leaders to shift the allocation of spending.

We see the most uncertain estimates in Malawi, and the effects for multilateral donors are sometimes the opposite of what I predicted. In some ways, this is puzzling: As the quotes earlier illustrate, politics plays an important role in how politicians engage with donors. Further, I will show in Chapter 6 that politicians are quite strategic in how they advise donors about spending decisions.

Despite this fact, it is possible that politicians' bargaining power in Malawi is weaker than in Kenya or Sierra Leone. And this might be particularly true with respect to politicians' relations with large multilateral donors. As one of the poorest countries in Africa, with few natural resources, Malawian politicians have few outside options if donors choose to withdraw support. And donors have a long history in Malawi of forcing reluctant politicians to do their bidding.[35]

The Malawian government's lack of bargaining power, combined with the fact that an extraordinarily high level of foreign aid in Malawi is channeled through NGOs rather than governments, may limit the ability of national governments to successfully influence the distribution of aid to the extent we see in some other countries.

## 4.8 FOREIGN AID BEFORE AND AFTER KENYA'S 2002 ELECTION

To further assess the political capture of aid, I will now go into more depth on one particularly illustrative election: the 2002 Kenya general election. Prior to this election, the Kenyan government was controlled by President Daniel arap Moi. Moi was effectively a dictator. While he held elections in 1992 and 1997, these elections were characterized by fraud and the suppression of opposition candidates.[36]

However, under pressure from donors and foreign allies, Moi agreed not to contest the 2002 election. Instead Moi endorsed his Minister for Local Government, Uhuru Kenyatta, to succeed him and to lead the governing Kenya African National Union party. But, to the surprise of many, Kenyatta did not win the election. Instead, an opposition MP named Mwai Kibaki won the presidency with 62 percent of the vote. This was the first time in Kenya's history that an incumbent party had lost an election.

One reason that this is an illustrative case for our purposes is that the 2002 election resulted in a massive shift in the geographic distribution of support for the ruling party. This point is illustrated by Figure 4.4 which shows the distribution of votes for Kenyatta and Kibaki. The core Moi

[35] Most famously, donors played an important role in forcing the autocratic President Hastings Banda to resign in 1994 (Resnick and Van de Walle 2013).

[36] Throup and Hornsby 1998.

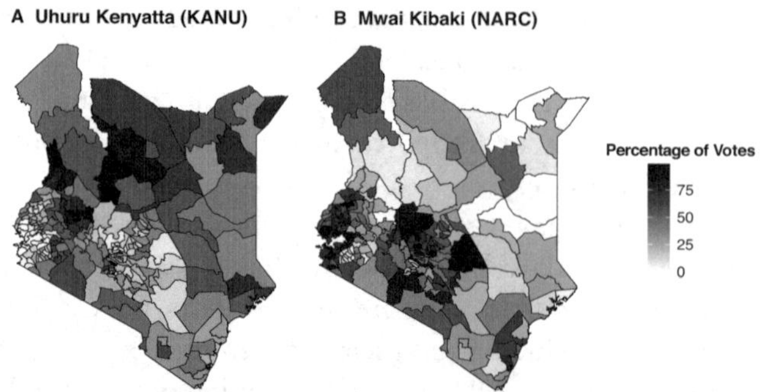


FIGURE 4.4 Voting during the 2002 Kenya election
*Note:* This figure shows the geographic patterns of voting for Uhuru Kenyatta (Panel A) and Mwai Kibaki (Panel B) during the 2002 Kenyan election.

voters in Kenya's Rift Valley and North Eastern Provinces, in particular, went from being part of the governments core support base to being part of the opposition. Many of these were members of Moi's Kalenjin ethnic group. Instead, members of the Luo and Kikuyu ethnic groups in places like Central Province and Nyanza Province were the new winning coalition under Mwai Kibaki's National Rainbow Coalition (NARC). If my argument is correct, the new government under Mwai Kibaki would have faced a lot of pressure to spend more among these new voters, and less among Moi's historical base of support.

Another reason this is a particularly illustrative case is that the Kenyan government during this period was highly dependent upon international donors. Indeed, donors were often accused of helping to prop up Moi's rule.[37] However, donor relations changed rapidly following the Cold War. Increasingly, donors took a critical view of Moi's authoritarian tendencies and severely limited government discretion over foreign aid. Most donors, for instance, suspended budget aid and started giving almost all aid in the form of project aid disbursed directly to project coordinators.[38]

Yet, despite this greater donor oversight, there is good evidence that the Moi government continued to use foreign aid and other public resources to reward political supporters and President Moi's ethnic group, the Kalenjin.[39] For instance, one of the main investments by the World Bank during this time was in Kenyan roads and health centers

37 Brown 2001.
38 Briggs 2014.
39 Branch 2011.

which were heavily concentrated in Kalenjin areas.[40] Several audits of World Bank and other donor projects during Moi's tenure also uncovered patterns of corruption, including padded contracts, suspicious financial flows, and offshore accounts in the names of powerful politicians.[41] It is likely that this diversion of resources helped to shore up Moi's electoral support during a time of declining budgets and spending.

After Kenyatta lost the 2002 election, donors restored much of the budget assistance to Kenya, and agreed to support several key initiatives of the new government. Yet the new government engaged in a similar strategy of diverting development resources. One illustrative example was the World Bank's HIV/AIDS Disaster Response Project (KHADREP) in Kenya. This 56 million-dollar project began in 2000, but expanded during Kibaki's presidency. The project funded a parastatal bureaucracy called the National AIDS Control Council (NACC) which was responsible for coordinating the HIV/AIDS response in Kenya. About $22 million went to fund NACC and ministry activities directly with the remainder going to fund initiatives from the research community, civil society, and private sector.[42]

The Kibaki government appears to have used the NACC as a tool to funnel foreign aid to political supporters. One way this happened is through favoring political supporters with preferential contracts. A World Bank integrity review conducted in the course of the project found indicators of corruption and fraud in 72 percent of grant activities reviewed, including undocumented expenses, contract collusion, inflated bids, bribery, and payments to fictitious entities.[43]

Additionally, the NACC was used as a way to funnel projects to politically important areas. The way the project worked is that regional organizations would submit proposals for NACC funding through local committees called Constituency AIDS Control Committees (CACCs). While elected officials were not formally part of these CACCs, MPs were able to control the appointment process and sometimes packed CACCs with loyal supporters.

40 Burgess et al. 2015; Briggs 2014.

41 Ensminger and Leder-Luis 2025; Rice 2007; Andersen, Johannesen, and Rijkers 2022.

42 World Bank n.d.

43 The World Bank's DIR team reviewed fifty-three grant activities and found indicators of irregularities in thirty-eight of them. While this only represents a small sample of the activities conducted under the project, it suggests a broader pattern of corruption across all grant activities.

Indirectly, elected officials were also able to manipulate procurement rules in such a way that certain grant writers were favored or mandated. This also allowed politicians to maintain a strong measure of control over how grant recipients distributed funds. Subsequent audit investigations suggest that politically affiliated grant applicants were considerably more successful at obtaining funds.[44]

If my argument is correct, we should also observe a more general quantitative shift in all foreign aid distribution right after 2002. Moi's base of support should be systematically advantaged by donor spending prior to the 2002 election, but then be systematically disadvantaged following the election.

### 4.8.1 Distribution of Foreign Aid Before and After the 2002 Election

To assess whether we observe such a shift in aid, I first show in Figure 4.5 how patterns of foreign aid changed over time from 1997 to 2006. The y-axis in these plots shows the amount of aid received by each of Kenya's 210 constituencies in each year. I standardize these data (with z-scores) so that values greater than zero indicate that a constituency received more aid than average in a given year and values less than zero indicate that a province received less than average in a given year.

Panels A and C illustrate that constituencies that voted for Moi and KANU in 1997 (at greater than 50 percent) or that are predominately made up of President Moi's Kalenjin ethnic group were systematically favored prior to 2002, but not after.[45] When Moi was in power (1997–2006), KANU constituencies received 37 percent more aid than the average constituency. Kalenjin constituencies received 87 percent more aid. After Moi left power (2003–2006), KANU constituencies received only 0.4 percent more than the average constituency, and Kalenjin constituencies received 37 percent *less* than the average constituency. Opposition parties and ethnic groups are likewise disadvantaged prior to 2002, but not after.

In order to formally test whether aid spending differed between the KANU and NARC governments, I estimate a difference-in-differences model. The idea behind this model is that we can identify the "treatment"

[44] This information comes from a 2007 World Bank Department of Institutional Integrity report investigated by the *Wall Street Journal*. "Kenya and the World Bank." *The Wall Street Journal*. March 6, 2008. See also Dionne (2017, 50ff).

[45] Kenya does not release constituency data on ethnic make-up. Ethnic groups are estimated using survey data as described in Jablonski (2014).

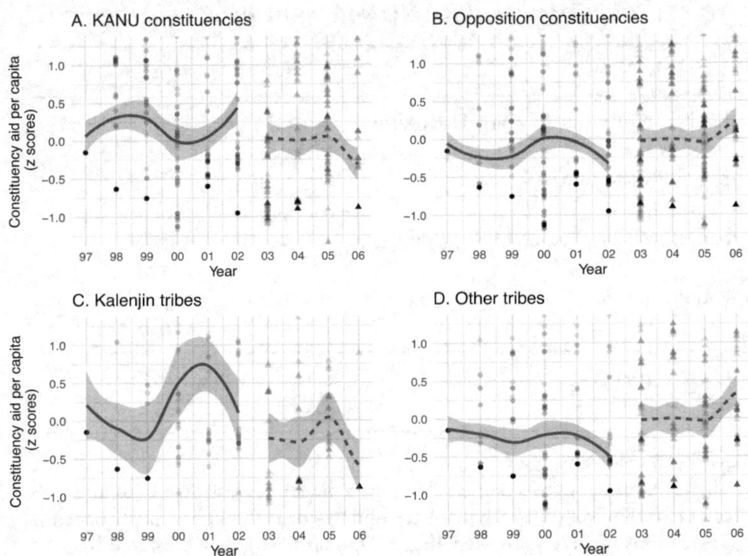


FIGURE 4.5 Foreign aid before and after the 2002 election
This figure shows patterns of aid distribution (log aid per capita) over time (in z-scores) for constituencies with more than 50 percent of votes for KANU in the 1997 election (Panel A), for constituencies with less than 50 percent of votes for KANU (Panel B), for constituencies with a majority of Kalenjin voters (Panel C), and for constituencies with a majority of other ethnic groups (Panel D). Note the y-axis is truncated to +/− 1$\sigma$ for clarity.

effect of KANU and NARC partisanship by comparing how supporters of KANU and NARC fared while KANU and NARC were in power relative to periods in Kenya's history when KANU and NARC were not in power. Specifically, I estimate the following equation:

$$Log(Aid\ per\ Capita + 1)_{it} = \beta_1 KANU\ Vote\ Share_i * KANU\ in\ power_t + \beta_2 KANU\ Vote\ Share_i + \theta_t \quad (4.2)$$

Where *KANU Vote Share*$_i$ equals the share of votes received by KANU in the 1997 election. $\theta_t$ are year fixed effects and standard errors are clustered by constituency.

The coefficient $\beta_1$ provides the effect of *KANU Vote Share*$_i$ when KANU is in power, subtracting the effect of *KANU Vote Share*$_i$ when the regime is not in power. As a result, $\beta_1$ provides a reasonable estimate of the extent to which KANU and NARC changed Kenya's aid portfolio

TABLE 4.2 *Estimate of KANU vote share on aid distribution*

| Variable Name | (1) | (2) |
|---|---|---|
| KANU Vote Share*KANU Regime | 0.993*** | |
| | (0.170) | |
| KANU Vote Share | −0.231* | |
| | (0.131) | |
| Kalenjin Tribe*KANU Regime | | 0.556*** |
| | | (0.152) |
| Kalenjin Tribe | | −0.307*** |
| | | (0.100) |
| Observations | 2,100 | 2,100 |
| $R^2$ | 0.317 | 0.306 |

*Note:* *p<0.1; **p<0.05; ***p<0.01
This table shows the coefficients from a linear regression of log aid per capita on KANU's 1997 vote share and majority Kalenjin constituencies. Regressions include year fixed effects. Standard errors are clustered by constituency.

among their constituents. I include in the analysis all years between the 1997 election and the 2007 election.[46]

The estimates in Table 4.2 confirm that KANU constituencies received significantly more foreign aid when KANU was in power and were systematically disadvantaged after KANU exited power in 2002. These estimates suggest that constituencies in which half of the votes went to KANU received about 50 percent more aid when President Moi was in power than when he was out of power. Moi's co-ethnics, the Kalenjin, were similarly advantaged: Constituencies that are majority Kalenjin received about 56 percent more aid when Moi was in power than when he was out of power.

## 4.9 CONCLUSIONS

In this chapter, I test the claim that politicians influence the distribution of foreign aid spending to benefit politically pivotal communities.

[46] The 1997 election was won handily by Moi. The 2002 election was contested by former members of the 2002 NARC coalition, Mwai Kibaki and Raila Odinga. The 2007 results were contested and resulted in a power-sharing agreement. Estimates including the full sample of observations are similar.

As evidence for this claim, I demonstrate that foreign aid changes over time in response to changes in the distribution of political support for incumbent governments. This pattern of political influence appears systematic, biasing spending for all three countries in this study and for bilateral donors and multilateral donors.

That said, politics is far from the only – or even the primary – determinant of aid distribution. It is most certainly true that community needs, poverty, and underdevelopment also matter substantially (a topic we will return to in Chapter 5). These political capture effects are nonetheless important for democracy. These results confirm that foreign aid plays an important role in electioneering in many countries and likely shapes who wins elections and stays in power.

Based on the evidence in this chapter, it is perhaps tempting to join the bandwagon of aid critics. In an ideal world, we might like to see foreign aid being spent in a purely technocratic and altruistic way, and we might be tempted to blame donors or the aid system for allowing foreign aid to be spent in a way that is not purely altruistic. However as I emphasized in Chapters 2 and 3, excluding the government entirely is a Faustian bargain to make. All aid distribution modalities involve trade-offs, and involving the government in aid distribution is often the most efficient and effective trade-off that donors can make. Allowing governments to have some say in aid distribution ensures that governments care about foreign aid and have a stake in its success. Additionally, donors rarely have the capacity or information to work independently of governments. If giving governments a say in development means that sometimes aid goes to political supporters, that is perhaps a fair trade-off to make. I'll elaborate on some of these policy implications more in Conclusion.

What about the effects of political capture on democracy and electoral accountability? Here also the effects might not be as simple as they first appear. On one hand, we might rightly be concerned if donors have allowed poorly performing politicians to claim credit for the work and funding of donor organizations. Indeed, several scholars have made a compelling case that donors helped to keep President Daniel arap Moi in power despite Kenya's generally poor economic performance during his tenure.[47] However, as I show in Chapter 3, the fact of political influence is not necessarily bad for accountability–and may actually be

[47] Brown 2001; Jablonski 2014; Branch 2011.

good for accountability if it helps voters to identify those politicians that work hard for their interests. By giving politicians a stake in development, donors not only encourage politicians to partner effectively with donors but also provide voters with better information about what their government can and should do.

In Chapter 4, I will turn to an assessment of how foreign aid affects voting behavior.

# 5

# The Effects of Aid on Voter Behavior

> If someone who is campaigning on a platform of change is going around claiming that it was he that brought these projects to Sierra Leone, even in the face of such overwhelming evidence of Chinese financing, then this should be enough reason why Sierra Leoneans should not treat him and his recycled gang of politicians seriously.
>
> – Editorial criticizing APC officials in Sierra Leone of undeservedly claiming credit for Chinese financed projects.[1]

How does foreign aid change voting behavior? Most often, the answer to this question has been that foreign aid is good for incumbents and bad for challengers. Many also argue that this pro-incumbent bias is bad for electoral accountability and helps poorly performing leaders remain in power.[2] However, as highlighted in the above quote and as discussed in Chapter 3, there are good reasons to question whether incumbents consistently garner credit for foreign aid, or that these effects are always bad for electoral accountability.

This chapter reassesses the impact of aid on voting behavior through experimental and survey data collected from voters in Malawi. The outcomes align with the theory presented in Chapter 3, demonstrating that the effects of foreign aid on voting patterns are diverse and contingent upon the manner in which aid is delivered and the voters' perceptions regarding the government's involvement in aid distribution. Findings in this chapter challenge claims that foreign aid invariably benefits incumbents or undermines electoral responsibility.

1 Leeroy 2017.
2 Morrison 2014.

This chapter also examines what voters know about foreign aid, and about the composition of public spending generally. Using survey data with teachers and citizens in Malawi, I assess the likelihood that voters are aware of projects that donors or local governments have delivered to their community. Consistent with the arguments in other chapters, I show that voters are often familiar with projects in their community; however they frequently misattribute the source of funds. Projects that are delivered by local governments are misattributed to donors, and vice versa. These observations highlight the difficulties that many voters face in learning about government performance and holding politicians accountable.

This chapter starts with a review of the empirical evidence for a link between foreign aid and voting and a discussion of the challenges in interpreting this evidence. Next, I introduce the study which I and collaborators did with 2,323 Malawian voters and teachers in the catchment areas of 180 schools.[3] The main part of the study involved a survey conducted before and after the delivery of a foreign aid project from a international NGO to local primary schools. These surveys focused on measuring respondents' perceptions of incumbent performance and expected voting behavior. As is standard with aid projects in the education sector, the NGO consulted the incumbent councilor in the local ward prior to allocating the project. The NGO, which was a research partner in this study, collected information from politicians about where they preferred projects to be allocated. The final allocation of projects to schools was determined by the politicians' advice and a public lottery. Neither incumbents nor any government office provided funding to the project.[4]

This study is useful for assessing the theory in Chapter 3. Unlike with other studies of aid and voting, we can identify real variation in the extent to which incumbents influenced the allocation of foreign aid. Some schools receive aid because they were recommended by the incumbent. Other schools do not receive aid because they were *not* recommended

[3] The study was conducted with Brigitte Seim at the University of Minnesota and Johan Ahlback at the London School of Economics and Political Science. Research assistance was provided by Diane Jung, Inbok Rhee, Petra Matsi, Nonne Engelbrecht, Jimmy Mkandawire, and many friends and colleagues in Malawi. The study was preregistered at https://osf.io/zuxw6. Some results in this chapter overlap with a co-authored working paper (Jablonski, Seim, and Ahlback 2025).

[4] The NGO projects were wholly funded out of a research grant funded by USAID and the AidData Research Lab.

by the incumbent. A final group does not receive aid because it was not selected by the donor. If – as I argue in Chapter 3 – respondents condition their votes on beliefs about incumbent preferences and performance, we should see different effects of foreign aid across these three groups.

Additionally, we designed this study to identify how voter beliefs about incumbent lobbying and performance condition these effects. Between the baseline and endline surveys, the NGO, under our instruction, sent SMS messages to a random sample of communities informing them about the aid project and the role of the incumbent and donor in making the aid allocation decision. These messages were seen as credible to most recipients. By comparing recipients with nonrecipients, I can therefore assess how voter beliefs condition the effects of aid on voter behavior and perceptions of incumbent performance.

To preview the results, The data confirm that aid can be a mixed blessing for incumbents. Those who benefited from aid in this study became more supportive of the incumbent and became substantially more likely to vote for the incumbent. However, those who failed to benefit from aid sometimes blamed the incumbent for failing to deliver for their community, particularly when they were more informed about the politician's role in negotiating aid. It follows that foreign aid will most often affect election outcomes but can do so in a way that costs her or him support in some areas.

The results also confirm the important signaling role that foreign aid plays in helping voters make inferences about incumbent preferences and performance. I show that aid recipients positively update their views of incumbent effort and become more likely to believe that the incumbent works hard for their community. Nonrecipients become less likely to believe that the incumbent works for their community. Further, these effects are greater when voters receive SMS messages providing accurate knowledge of incumbents' role in influencing the donor.

The study also implies mixed effects of aid on electoral accountability and supports the visibility and uncertainty effects proposed in Chapter 3. On one hand, study participants were sophisticated in making inferences about the government from NGO projects: They reward incumbents who lobbied the NGO on their behalf and sanction incumbents they believe failed to work on their behalf. It follows that foreign aid can make it possible for well-informed voters to more accurately distinguish between incumbents who do and do not share their interests. In otherwise information-poor environments, foreign aid can therefore make incumbents *more*, not less accountable.

On the other hand, I show that study participants often have inaccurate and uncertain beliefs about the role that incumbents play in delivering foreign aid. In surveys, I ask study participants to describe all government and donor projects in their school. Using these data, I demonstrate that study participants often have highly inaccurate beliefs about the relative role that donors and incumbents plays in delivering development. It follows that voters in Malawi very likely make inaccurate inferences about the quality and performance of their elected officials, potentially harming accountability and helping to entrench poorly performing incumbents. Further, this uncertainty creates opportunities for poorly performing incumbents to manipulate the information environment in their favor, for instance by claiming credit for the work of donors.

## 5.1 WHAT DOES EXISTING EVIDENCE SAY ABOUT AID AND VOTING?

Does foreign aid affect election outcomes? If so, why? Much evidence and theory suggests that leaders who receive foreign aid stay in power for longer; however, the conditions under which this is the case remain contested.[5] Some studies suggest these effects primarily hold for autocratic leaders, or for leaders who were in power during the Cold War.[6] Other studies suggest that effects hold for both autocratic and democratic regimes, but to a different extent.[7] Some studies suggest that these effects depend upon donor intent and the extent of aid fungibility.[8]

There have been a few attempts to look directly at the effect of aid on election outcomes. Briggs 2015 estimates the effect of aid shocks on elections in African states and shows a positive correlation between aid in the year preceding an election and incumbent victory at the cross-national level. More recent work has tried to use subnational aid as a way to better identify these effects. Using a spatial difference-in-differences approach in three countries, Briggs 2019 shows that citizens near to foreign aid projects were *less* likely to support incumbents on average. Knutsen and Kotsadam 2020 conduct a similar analysis in a larger panel and estimates a 5 percentage point increase in support for incumbents as a result of being near aid projects. Cruz and Schneider 2017 examines specifically at one World Bank project in the Philippines and estimate that mayors who

[5] Bueno de Mesquita and Smith 2009.
[6] Bermeo 2016.
[7] Licht 2010; Yuichi Kono and Montinola 2009; Morrison 2014.
[8] Altincekic and Bearce 2014.

benefited from the project received a 12 percentage point jump in their vote share, despite the fact that mayors had no direct control over the allocation of the project. O'Brien-Udry 2021 looks at aid to minorities in Kosovo and concludes that such aid reduced trust in local and national governments.

In one of the few other experimental studies, Baldwin and Winters 2023 study the effects of randomly informing citizens in Uganda about the funding of a Japanese aid project. Respondents who learned about donor funding became less likely to vote for the incumbent in a survey; however, this negative effect dissipated when the government played more of a role in oversight. This study supports my contention that foreign aid can indeed be a mixed blessing for incumbents and that the consequences of aid on elections depend on voter beliefs.

One reason for divergent empirical findings may be that it is difficult to identify the effect of foreign aid on voting. For one, these effects are going to be conditional on how aid is delivered. As argued in Chapter 3, when politicians are seen to have limited influence over aid allocation, it is likely that aid will have no effect on voter behavior. In other cases, voters might blame politicians for ineffective decisions by donors or other actors.

Second, many attempts to estimate the effect of aid on elections rely on what might be unreasonable assumptions about the exogeneity of aid. If governments distribute aid based on anticipated voting behavior, or if aid is correlated with income or welfare shocks, then it might be hard to interpret correlations between aid and voting as an effect of one on the other. Likewise, if the timing of aid delivery is endogenous to election dates and electoral competitiveness, it may be hard to learn much by regressing election outcomes on aid.[9]

A final challenge is that the most credible evidence focuses on the effect of aid projects on localized voting behavior. While still informative, these local treatment effects don't necessarily tell us much about whether foreign aid helps incumbents remain in power. To see this, consider an aid project that goes to a school in a small rural town. The residents of that town may choose to credit a politician for that aid and reward her at the polls. However, residents of another village may blame that same politician for rewarding the first village rather than another. Thus, if we

[9] For instance, Faye and Niehaus (2012) note that aid spending increases around competitive elections, implying that it is election timing and competitiveness that sometimes drives aid spending rather than the other way around.

compare voting in the first village to the second, we might conclude that aid benefited the incumbent; however, in reality, the evidence is also consistent with positive, negative, or null effects of aid on election outcomes depending on scale of direct and indirect effects of aid and the way in which these effects are aggregated and compared in a particular analysis.

This study is specifically designed to address some of these measurement and identification challenges.

## 5.2 HYPOTHESES ABOUT AID ON VOTING

In Chapter 3, I develop a model of foreign aid and retrospective voting behavior. I assume that voters want to elect a politician who works hard for their own community, for instance, by lobbying on their behalf with donors. However – as is most often the case – voters do not observe what incumbents actually do. They only observe the welfare effects of the incumbent's actions. Voters use this welfare to make inferences about incumbent preferences and expected future behavior.

When incumbents have influence over donors' allocation of resources, I show that voters can make inferences about incumbents' effort and preferences from observing the welfare they receive from foreign aid. To illustrate this point, suppose you know that your incumbent politician can lobby a donor on your behalf. If you then benefit from the donor's aid, you might infer that the incumbent actually did lobby on your behalf and that he or she prefers your community over others. Likewise, if you did not benefit, then you might infer the incumbent prefers other communities to yours, or that he or she simply failed to work on your behalf. Similarly, if you know that an incumbent has little influence over donors, you might be able to infer little about a politician's preferences from observing patterns of aid spending.

Unlike other theories of aid politics, in this model, foreign aid only affects voting behavior by changing voter beliefs. The size and direction of these voting effects depend upon the welfare received by each voter and voters' beliefs about the incumbent's role in delivering aid (and these beliefs could be accurate or inaccurate). When voters believe that the incumbent is influential, then foreign aid will tend to increase support for the incumbent among those voters who benefit from aid. However, foreign aid will tend to decrease support for the incumbent among those voters who fail to benefit from aid.

One of the novel and testable implications of this model is that foreign aid will have heterogenous effects depending upon voter beliefs and the distribution of aid. When voters believe that the incumbent lobbies donors on their behalf, aid spending will cause aid recipients to have more positive perceptions of incumbent effort. Aid will also shift voting intention in the incumbent's favor. It predicts the opposite, however, for nonaid recipients. These voters will have worse perceptions of incumbent effort and will respond to aid by being *less* likely to vote for the incumbent. Further, aid will have no effect on voting when incumbents are not involved in aid distribution.

- H1 When incumbents are believed to be mediators in aid distribution, foreign aid will cause beneficiaries of that aid to (a) *positively* update their beliefs about incumbent effort, and to (b) become *more* likely to vote for the incumbent.
- H2 When incumbents are believed to be mediators in aid distribution, foreign aid will cause those who do not benefit from aid to (a) *negatively* update their beliefs about incumbent effort, and to (b) become *less* likely to vote for the incumbent.
- H3 When incumbents are not believed to be mediators in aid allocation, aid will have no effect on beliefs or voting.

The theory in Chapter 3 also implies that these effects should depend upon voter uncertainty. When voters are more uncertain about the role of donors and politicians in delivering public spending, then voters will struggle to make accurate inferences about politician performance and preferences. So, when voters are more uncertain, the effect of foreign aid on voting can be quite small. Additionally, in environments high uncertainty, voters might make incorrect inferences and improperly credit poor performing politician for what are, in fact, the actions of donors.[10]

In order to compare the effects of aid on voters with higher and lower levels of uncertainty, we conduct a parallel information experiment informing voters about the aid delivery process, and especially whether or not the voter's incumbent was responsible for delivering aid or not. By giving voters more accurate information about the role of politicians and donors in the aid delivery process, we expect that these treatments will reduce uncertainty and ameliorate bias in voter beliefs about incumbent lobbying.

According to my theory, these treatments will tend to reinforce the effects in Hypotheses H1-H3. Voters who both benefit from aid and

[10] For instance, see Proposition 5 and 6 in Chapter 3.

receive credible information that politicians are involved in the aid distribution should be more likely to positively update their beliefs about incumbent performance and preferences. Likewise, voters who do not benefit from aid and receive credible information that politicians are involved in aid distribution should be more likely to *negatively* update their beliefs about their incumbent. Finally, aid should have little effect among voters who learn that the politician was not responsible for aid delivery.[11]

- H4 Voters who receive credible information saying a politician was involved in aid distribution will be more likely to respond to foreign aid by updating their beliefs about politician performance.
- H5 Voters who receive credible information saying that a politician was not involved in aid distribution will be less likely to respond to foreign aid by updating their beliefs about politician performance.

## 5.3 STUDY CONTEXT

This study is focused on aid in the primary education sector of Malawi. This is one of the most aid-dependent sectors in one of the most aid-dependent countries. Between 2011 and 2016, donors directly funded projects in approximately 44 percent of primary schools, compared to 30 percent that received projects funded by the local government.[12] Donor branding is heavily visible to local communities, and more than 25 percent of schools are prominently branded with the names of one or more donors.[13]

Within Malawi, authority over primary schools primarily falls to local district councils.[14] Councils have an average budget of approximately $5 million, 11 percent of which is dedicated to education.[15] Councilors

[11] A key assumption underlying these hypotheses are that voters do not usually update adversely to the information. For instance, voters who are informed that the politicians are not involved in aid distribution should not become *more* likely to believe that politicians are involved in aid distribution. Since the treatment is binary (informing voters that politicians are or are not involved in aid distribution), this assumption is almost certainly true.

[12] These statistics are based on the survey of teachers in 311 schools across Malawi. See Appendix A.

[13] In our survey of teachers, we asked enumerators to note donor branding. See Appendix A for discussion.

[14] Within urban areas, these are called "town councils" or "city councils."

[15] These statistics are based on 2011–2012 budgets. An exchange rate of MK700 = $1 was used.

are elected in single-member constituencies (called "wards") every five years.[16]

The councils in our study were elected in 2014. This was the first time councils had been elected in Malawi in many years, so expectations of these incumbents were initially high. However, by the time of our survey, voters had become highly disillusioned. At baseline, over 70 percent of respondents to our survey said they would be unlikely to vote again for the incumbent and 66 percent said that their councilor was ineffective at getting things their village needs. This low support was reflected in the 2019 election: out of 462 council seats, only 82 (18 percent) were won by incumbents in 2019. The fact that voters had low expectations and little information implies that this was an environment in which voters were highly likely to respond to positive information about incumbent performance.

## 5.4 STUDY DETAILS

Our goal with this study was to identify the effects of foreign aid on voter beliefs and behavior. To do this, we conducted a panel survey with 2,019 citizens and 314 teachers in Malawi before and after the delivery of foreign aid to eighty-three schools by a small UK NGO donor.[17] In this survey, we specifically queried citizens' perceptions of local politician performance and voting intentions, allowing us a precise and individualized way to measuring the political effects of aid delivery. Because of the panel nature of the survey and a quasi-random allocation of goods, we can precisely estimate how receiving aid (and not) affected citizens' views of incumbents and beliefs about incumbent performance.

The way in which the aid in this project was allocated also provides a unique opportunity to study how voting effects are conditioned by politicians' interactions with donors. As is standard in Malawi, the NGO consulted local councilors prior to choosing which of the schools should receive aid. This consultative process means that politicians were explicitly involved in the aid allocation process and were (honestly) able to take credit for the spending decisions made by the donor. The structure of this consultative process was managed by the researchers and we recorded

[16] There are 462 wards in Malawi. On average, they are about 180 square kilometers in size and have approximately 15 primary schools.

[17] The aid project was branded by Tearfund NGO and all staff we identified were members of Tearfund. The project itself was funded by a USAID research grant which also funded this study.

details of all the schools recommended by the councilor. As discussed further, we provided information to citizens about this consultative process in a parallel SMS information experiment.

### 5.4.1 The Allocation of Foreign Aid

In this project, eighty-three primary schools in Malawi received one of three kinds of development goods. One good was a set of iron roofing sheets (N = 7 schools). Few schools in Malawi have adequate classrooms, and the rainy season often means that classes are often cancelled, so roofing sheets are a valuable good. The second development good was solar lamps (N = 19 schools). As few schools in Malawi have electricity, solar lamps can provide light for teacher preparation and student studying in the evenings. The third development good was a set of teacher supply kits (N = 32 schools) containing chalk, an eraser, pens, notepads, and a tote bag. While these were inexpensive goods, most of these communities are extremely poor, and these goods were valued by both politicians and recipients.[18] As I argue in Chapter 3, what should matter more than the size of an aid project is what voters learn from the project about incumbent preferences and behavior.

To select the recipients of these goods the donor (in cooperation with our research team) consulted with 333 out of the 462 local councilors in Malawi.[19] In meetings with donor-affiliated enumerators, each of these councilors selected one school in their ward to be eligible to receive *each* of these goods; so each councilor selected a total of three schools to be eligible to receive aid, one for each good.

Following the consultation process, the participating councilors' wards were entered into a public lottery.[20] Out of the 333 councilors

18 At endline, several teachers and citizens specifically mentioned these goods as something they remember that their councilor or a donor had delivered to their school. Likewise, a number of politicians participated in the lottery and the goods delivery process.

19 Councilors were excluded largely for data availability reasons. The sample of eligible schools is broadly representative of the population of schools. One exception is that the study tended to under-sample less populated areas, largely owing to data availability challenges in these areas.

20 Approximately one dozen government, NGO, and community representatives attended the lottery, which was held in the capital city of Lilongwe. The paper drawing-based random selection of constituencies (councilors) was prefaced by a brief speech read by the research manager explaining the study, the criteria for including schools in the study, and the reasons not all schools could receive development goods.

TABLE 5.1 *Experimental groups*

| Group | Treatment | Sampled schools | Description |
|---|---|---|---|
| A | School Recommended by Councilor + Aid Receipt | 60 | School was recommended by the councilor to receive aid. School received aid. |
| B | School Recommended by Councilor | 49 | School was recommended by the councilor to receive aid. School did not receive aid. |
| C | School Not Recommended by Councilor | 60 | School was not recommended by the councilor to receive aid. |

that recommended schools, the lottery randomly selected 83 councilors, for a selection rate of 25 percent.

For each incumbent chosen in the lottery, the NGO delivered goods to one of the schools the incumbent had selected. The decision regarding which of the incumbent's selected schools would receive goods was not random, but was made largely based on goods availability and delivery logistics.[21] Only schools that had been recommended by the councilor in the foreign aid recommendation experiment were eligible to receive development goods.

This allocation process created three categories of schools in each of these eighty-three wards: (A) schools that were eligible to receive foreign aid (by virtue of being selected by a councilor) and *did* receive foreign aid; (B) schools who were eligible to receive foreign aid, but *did not* receive foreign aid owing to NGO funding constraints; and (C) those schools that were ineligible to receive foreign aid because they were not selected by a councilor. We summarize these groups in Table 5.1, along with the number of schools sampled in the survey.

[21] For instance, constituencies in southern Malawi were more likely to receive iron roofing sheets due to the higher delivery costs in northern Malawi. Politicians were not aware of these logistical constraints and we see no evidence that they conditioned decisions on logistical constraints.

Schools in each of these groups were not necessarily equivalent or representative of the full population of schools in Malawi. Groups A and B were intentionally selected by the councilor and differ from Group C especially in their proximity to the councilor and their level of political support at baseline. Likewise Groups A and B differ from one another because of the differences in the aid delivery process.[22]

To identify the effects of aid, I will analyze *changes* in political preferences across these groups (in a difference-in-differences model). I do not have to assume that each group is equivalent in order to identify a causal effect of aid. Rather, the main identifying assumption in this study is that – absent any treatment – the trends in political preferences and beliefs would be equivalent across each of these groups.

### 5.4.2 Survey Sampling

Our goal with the survey was to obtain a representative sample of aid-eligible schools in each of the groups in Table 5.1. To accomplish this, we first randomly sampled sixty of the eighty-three councilors who won the lottery discussed above. Within each of these sixty wards, we sampled one school in Groups A, B, and C. That is, one school that received aid, one school that was selected but did not receive aid, and one school that was not recommended to receive aid. Our effective sample in Groups A, B, and C is sixty, forty-nine and sixty schools.[23] Further, we visited three additional schools per constituency and conducted interviews with teachers only.

This survey was conducted in two waves – baseline, in October 2016, and endline, in December 2016. The deliveries of development goods at the schools occurred in the intervening period.

Survey respondents were drawn from the catchment areas of each of the sampled schools. There were two groups of respondents. The first respondent at each school was always the head teacher (effectively, the

[22] Because of limited budgets, schools that were eligible to receive some types of goods were more likely to be selected by the donor to receive these goods. If politicians selected different kinds of schools to receive different kinds of goods, then this may create differences between Groups A and B schools.

[23] Because all recommended schools in eleven wards received aid, our sample in Group B is forty-nine instead of sixty. The reason for this is that in some small constituencies, there were not enough eligible schools for politicians to select more than one school to receive aid.

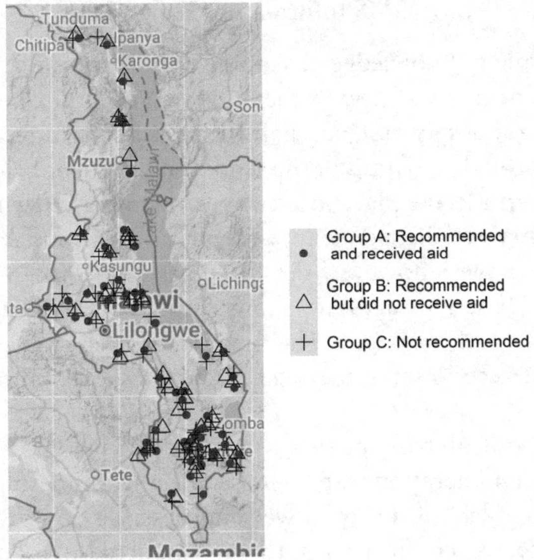


FIGURE 5.1 Map of surveys and groups
*Note*: This plot shows the location of all surveys by group.

school principal). Then, within the community surrounding each school, we used a random walk procedure to sample eligible voters in the area, alternating female and male heads of households.[24] This process resulted in a intended sample of thirteen people per school at three schools in sixty wards, or 2,340 people. Because of logistical issues such as particularly small communities or communities attending a funeral, we have 2,019 eligible voters and 314 teachers at baseline.

The goal was to contact the same respondents at baseline and endline. We were able to recontact 1,656 respondents from baseline (82 percent). This sample is reasonably balanced across each group in Table 5.1: 586 were in Group A, 467 were in Group B, and 603 were in Group C.[25]

We provide a map of the sample in Figure 5.1.

24 See further details in Appendix A.

25 Within school catchment areas, our baseline and endline samples do not differ to a significant degree on views of the incumbent or demographic variables. However, we do observe higher contact rates in communities with higher support for the incumbent. This attrition does not a major challenge to inference as we exclude all attritted respondents from the final analysis. All main estimates are also robust to using respondent fixed effects.

### 5.4.3 SMS Information Experiment

To assess the role of knowledge in shaping these effects, we conducted an SMS experiment in parallel with the survey. Within Groups B and C in Table 5.1, we randomly assigned half of the schools to receive reinforcing messages providing details of the school selection and aid receipt, and the other half to receive placebo messages thanking citizens for participating in the survey.[26] Respondents with phones in Group A also received reinforcing messages; however, the messages were not randomized in this group.[27] These messages are shown in Table 5.2. Each participant received two sets of messages. The first set of messages occurred after the lottery. The second set of messages occurred shortly after the aid was delivered.

For each school, all baseline survey participants who provided a phone number to our enumeration team were sent the set of messages randomly assigned to their school. In total, we sent messages to 671 phone numbers.[28] In order to confirm receipt, we conducted a follow-up phone survey with a random sample of sixty-two SMS recipients three to four weeks after the aid delivery.[29] Fifty-three percent of these (33) recall seeing a message. Almost all found the information useful $n=27$ and could accurately describe the content of the message $n=29$. We also asked respondents to comment on anything they discussed with others. Out of the 22 who did, 36 percent discussed the frequency or form of spending by the NGO. Twenty-three percent also discussed their disappointment that they were not chosen (sometimes mentioning the councilor specifically).

### 5.4.4 Analytical Strategy

We are interested in how perceptions of the incumbent changed from baseline to endline in each group. For the primary specification, I rely on a difference-in-difference estimator, comparing trends across groups.

26 Politicians were made aware that their decisions would be shared in advance of their decisions.

27 This decision was made this decision to maximize the power of the study to identify the effects of aid receipt.

28 The total number of recipients of this message is potentially much larger. Many phones are shared in rural Malawi, and we encouraged SMS recipients to share the messages (see Table 5.2). In a follow-up survey, almost all (73 percent) of recipients said they shared the message with at least one person.

29 We sampled 80, but 13 could not be reached by phone.

TABLE 5.2 *Treatment groups and messages*

| Group | N | Pre-aid message | Post-aid message |
|---|---|---|---|
| A | 378 phones<br>60 schools | Hello from Tearfund NGO. Thank you for telling us about education services in your community.<br>Your ward councilor recommended [school name] in your area to receive school materials from our NGO. We will deliver these materials shortly.<br>Please share this message with your neighbors. | Hello from Tearfund NGO. Your ward councilor recommended [school name] in your area to receive school materials from our NGO. We delivered these materials. |
| B | 166 phones<br>26 schools | Hello from Tearfund NGO. Thank you for telling us about education services in your community.<br>Your ward councilor recommended [school name] in your area to receive school materials from our NGO. However, your school was not among those selected for funding by Tearfund in this round.<br>Please share this message with your neighbors. | Hello from Tearfund NGO. Your ward councilor recommended [school name] in your area to receive school materials from our NGO. It did not receive funding. |
| C | 266 phones<br>30 schools | Hello from Tearfund NGO. Thank you for telling us about education services in your community.<br>Your ward councilor did not recommend [school name] in your area to receive school materials from our NGO. It will not receive school materials.<br>Please share this message with your neighbors. | Hello from Tearfund NGO. Your ward councilor did not recommend [school name] in your area to receive school materials from our NGO. |
| Placebo (all groups) | 328 phones<br>53 schools | Hello from Tearfund NGO. Thank you for telling us about education services in your community. | Hello from Tearfund NGO. Thank you for telling us about education services in your community. |

I estimate difference-in-differences effects via a two-way fixed effects estimator. Specifically, let $y_{ijt}$ be a respondent $i$'s assessment of their local council incumbent at time $t$ in school $j$. Let $a_j$ equal one if school $j$ received aid at time $t$ and zero otherwise. Let $m_i$ equal one if a respondent was eligible to receive a reinforcing message and zero otherwise. Per H4 and H5, this reinforcement message should magnify the effect of $a_j$.

I estimate the following linear model with time and school fixed effects ($s$ and $t$):

$$y_{ijt} = \beta_1 a_j m_i + \beta_2 a_j + t + s \tag{5.1}$$

In all equations, I cluster errors at the level of treatment (the school catchment area). The analysis sample includes only respondents who were contacted at both baseline and endline.

In Appendix D, I also estimate the direct effect of the SMS messaging under experimental assumptions. The estimates match closely with those shown in the main text.

### 5.4.5 Measuring Voting Intentions and Beliefs

I expect that these treatments will affect respondents' beliefs about politician performance and preferences, as well as their expected voting decisions. In Table 5.3, I summarize the questions that I use to measure these outcomes.[30]

In addition to measuring voting intentions and beliefs, I also examine whether respondent attribute aid to the incumbent. I also try to identify any respondents who observed the incumbent credit claiming for the project. To measure attribution, I use a question about whether the respondent believes the incumbent did something for the community. This variable allows confirm that respondents are attributing the aid delivery to the action of the incumbent as I assumed in the theory. To measure credit claiming, I measure whether respondents observed the incumbent visiting the community. If incumbents expect to gain votes from aid delivery they have incentives to claim credit for the work of donors by visiting the school.[31]

[30] In addition to this English language questionnaire, respondents had a choice to fill out the survey in Chichewa or Tumbuka.

[31] Incumbents occasionally chose to join with the NGO in handing over the aid (and often claimed credit and campaigned at the same time). The increase in incumbent visits at endline is partly explained by these handover ceremonies.

TABLE 5.3 *Outcome variables*

| Variable | Survey Question | Baseline Mean & SD | Endline Mean & SD |
|---|---|---|---|
| Will vote for incumbent | If an election were held today, how likely would you be to vote for your current councilor? 3 = Very Likely; 2 = Somewhat Likely; 1 = Unlikely | 1.33 (0.61) | 1.33 (0.59) |
| Incumbent is effective | How effective is your councilor at getting things that your village needs? 3 = Highly Effective; 2 = Somewhat effective; 1 = Not Effective | 1.40 (0.60) | 1.40 (0.59) |
| Incumbent works hard | Do you think your councilor works harder for your village or for other villages? 3 = Works harder for my village; 2 = Works about the same for my village and other villages; 1 = Works harder for other villages | 1.50 (0.50) | 1.33 (0.58) |
| Satisfied with incumbent | How satisfied are you with the work that your councilor has done since he or she was elected? 5 = Very satisfied; 4 = Somewhat satisfied; 3 = Neither satisfied nor dissatisfied; 2 = Somewhat dissatisfied; 1 = Very dissatisfied | 2.04 (1.32) | 2.10 (1.08) |
| Incumbent done anything | Are you aware of anything your councilor has done for [school name]? 1 = Yes; 0 = No | 0.09 (0.30) | 0.10 (0.29) |
| Incumbent visited community | How often has your councilor visited this village in the last six months? 5 = More than 5 times; 4 = 3 to 5 times; 3 = 1 to 3 times; 2 = 1 time; 1 = Never | 1.55 (1.06) | 1.48 (0.83) |

## 5.5 EXAMINING VOTER KNOWLEDGE

This study was also designed to assess what study participants know about donor and government activities in their community. One of the factors that make aid unique relative to other forms of public spending is voter uncertainty regarding the relationship between public welfare and government performance. Voters often lack the ability to obtain accurate information about who is responsible for public spending, and the relative role of the government, donors, and other stakeholders. I have argued that this uncertainty strongly influences the way in which voters respond to changes in their welfare.

During the baseline survey for this study, we surveyed both eligible voters within the catchment area of each school (N = 2,019) as well as the head teacher (or teachers) in each school (N = 314). In both surveys, we asked questions about respondent knowledge of education projects funded by the government and by donors in each school.[32] Since head teachers have intimate knowledge of the funding for their school, we can compare responses across the surveys to assess gaps in citizens' knowledge of government and donor spending on education.[33]

As shown in Figure 5.2, district councilors and donors have both invested widely in schools. According to the teacher data, councilors have invested in 30 percent of surveyed schools (N = 94 schools). Donors have invested in 44 percent of surveyed schools (N = 137 schools).[34]

Figure 5.2 shows the distribution of respondent knowledge of these projects. Respondents appear to have a relatively accurate picture of donor activities in their community: 83 percent of communities (56 percent of respondents) accurately note that a donor project had been delivered to their school. However, respondents highly *underestimate*

[32] Teachers were asked "Have there been any [government/donor] projects at this school in the last five years?" If so, they were asked to describe the government office, budget, timing and project type. Non-teachers were asked "Are you aware of anything that [your councilor/donors or NGOs] have done for [school name]?" If so, they were asked to describe the project.

[33] While head teachers are the people best placed to make assessments about school spending, it is certainly plausible that teachers likewise have incorrect beliefs about the relative role of the council and donors in education projects. Nonetheless it is reasonable to assume that teachers are much more accurate in their assessments than others in the community.

[34] Where teachers do not specifically name a government arm, I assume the project was provided by the council. Using a more conservative coding, councils have provided projects to 32 percent of schools. Note that some projects identified by teachers as being from councilors are still funded by donors through direct or indirect budget support (most often through the council's Local Development Fund).

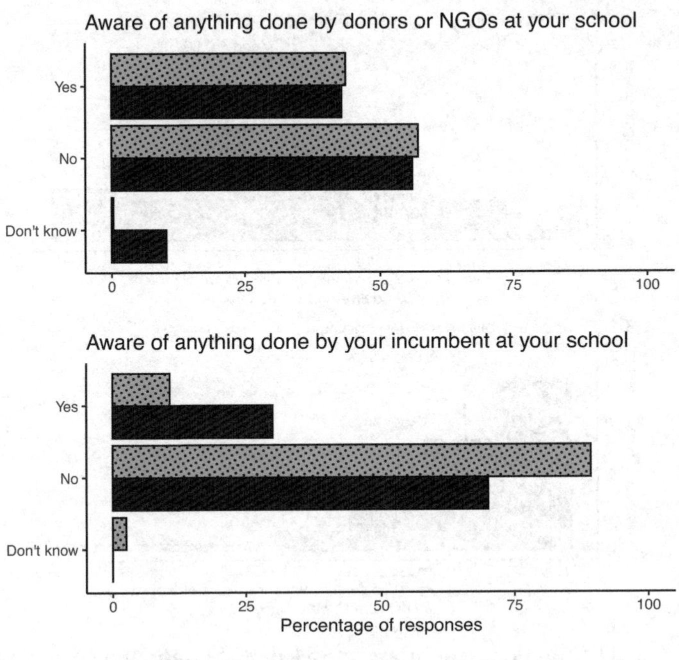


FIGURE 5.2 Citizen and teacher knowledge of donor and politician spending
*Note*: This plot shows the baseline level of knowledge held by teachers and other respondents of donor and politician spending at the local school.

what politicians are doing. Only 9 percent of respondents were aware of anything the incumbent councilor had done. Even among those who had benefited from a council project, only 14 percent were aware that the councilor had done anything.

To assess how frequently citizens have inaccurate beliefs, I create variables measuring the percentage of respondents around each school that have accurate beliefs about donor and council projects. In Figure 5.3, I plot histograms of these variables. The top panel shows the share of respondents in each surveyed community that could accurately identify at least one donor project. The bottom panel shows similar data for councilor projects.

It is clear that respondents have much more accurate beliefs about donor than councilor projects. Fifty-six percent of respondents accurately identify a donor project in their community. Only 13 percent accurately identify a councilor project in their community.

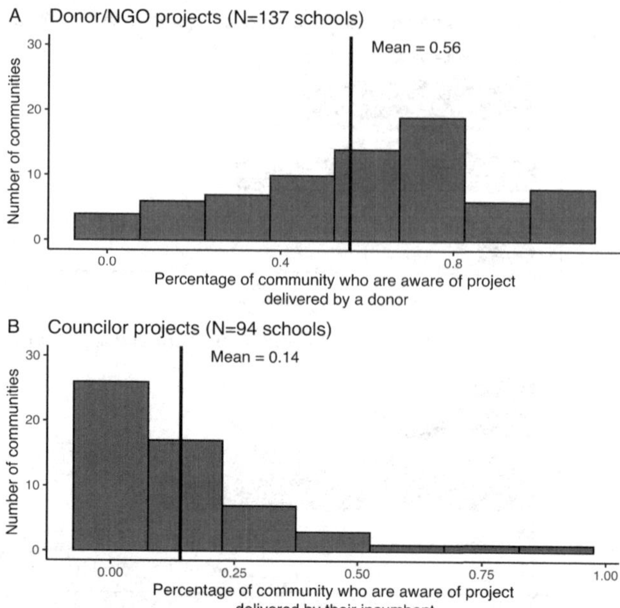


FIGURE 5.3 Distribution of accurate knowledge of donor and council projects
*Note*: This plot shows the distribution of accurate knowledge of donor (Panel A) and councilor (Panel B) projects delivered over the past five years. Vertical lines show the mean level of accurate knowledge in the respondent sample. Values exclude communities with no donor or councilor projects and don't know responses.

Why do citizens have inaccurate beliefs about who deserves credit? To shed light on this question, I examined in detail at all the council blocks (classrooms) built by the council in the prior five years. This is among the most frequent, visible, and costly council investments. Among the 126 nonteachers surveyed at these schools, 38 were aware of the school block construction. Twenty-five of these attributed the blocks to the councilor, and thirteen attributed the blocks to a donor or NGO. This suggests that even in cases where investments are highly visible and attributable to the government, recipients often struggle to accurately distinguish donor and government roles.

One reason why donors are given more credit may be the differences in the visibility of donor versus government activity. To examine this question, we asked our enumerators to make a note of any posters or signed from donors or from the government at each school they visited.

Twenty-six percent schools had clear branding from donors describing donor development projects. In contrast, there were notices from the government only at 7 percent of schools.

These respondent beliefs about donor and politician spending are also predictive of respondents' support for the incumbent. To illustrate this point, we can look at those communities that failed to benefit from a councilor project but did benefit from a foreign aid project. Those who attribute the project to the councilor are 47 percentage points *more* likely to say that they are "somewhat" or "very" likely to vote for the incumbent councilor compared to those who, more accurately, attribute the project to a donor.[35] While this correlation is not necessarily causal,[36] it lends credence to my argument that beliefs about attribution are important for understanding the effects of foreign aid.

## 5.6 EFFECTS OF FOREIGN AID

### 5.6.1 Effects among Aid Recipients

I now turn to an assessment of how study participants' views changed after the foreign aid was delivered. First, I examine the effects of receiving foreign aid. In Figure 5.4, I show how support for the incumbent councilor changed in communities that received aid compared to those who did not receive aid (Group A versus Groups B and C) by SMS treatment status.[37]

The estimates provide evidence in favor of H1. I estimate an increase of about 11 percentage points in the voting index among those who received aid. This corresponds to about 7 percentage point increase in votes for the incumbent (those who are "somewhat" or "very likely" to vote for the incumbent). Since respondents had quite low support for the incumbent

35 Among those who attribute aid to the councilor, 78 percent of them say they are "very" or "somewhat" likely to vote for the incumbent. Among those who attribute aid to a donor, 31 percent say they are "somewhat" or "very likely" to vote for the incumbent. The effect of respondent beliefs are similar if we look at communities that only benefited from councilor-led projects.

36 It is likely, for instance, that supporters of the incumbent will be more willing to believe that the incumbent played a role in aid spending.

37 The results are also consistent if we exclude Group C (since trends in Group C are likely related to treatment, the estimand differs across these specifications). I prefer this specification since the treatment estimate corresponds to the incumbent's net increase in votes.

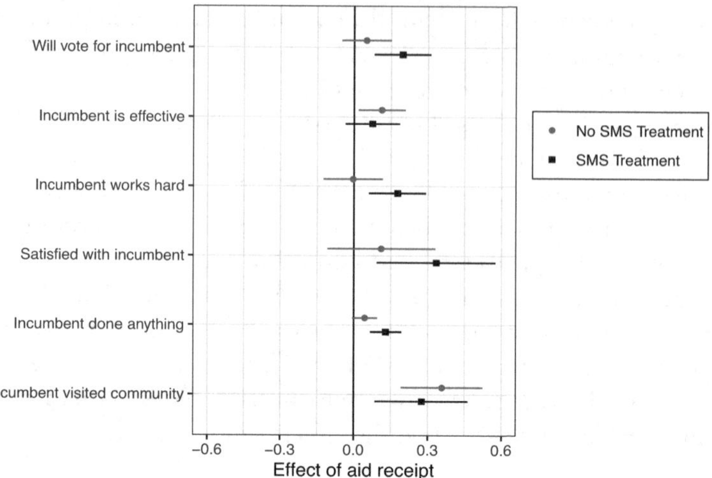


FIGURE 5.4 Effect of aid receipt on outcome variables (95 percent CI)
*Note*: This plot shows the change in survey responses from baseline among aid recipients compared to nonaid recipients (Group A versus Groups B and C). Reinforcement messages were not randomized in aid-receiving communities: All respondents who provided a valid phone number were sent reinforcement messages.

at baseline, this corresponds to quite a large effect in relative terms: nearly a 23 percent shift in votes. Consistent with H4, these results are largest when voters receive SMS messages informing them about the aid project and the incumbent's role in selecting their community.

I also examine the effects of aid on voters' beliefs. Consistent with my argument, respondents in schools that received foreign aid became more likely to believe the councilor is effective and works hard for their community. They were also more satisfied with the councilor's work overall. As with voting, these effects are substantially larger when respondents are well informed about the aid delivery and the role of the incumbent in the allocation of the project. Among recipients of the SMS, we estimate nearly twice the treatment effect in most outcomes: effects on voting intention increases to 15 percentage points and satisfaction increases by 21 percentage points.

We also see evidence that respondents saw aid as evidence that the incumbent had done something for their community. Aid delivery was also associated with visits from the incumbent. Respondents who benefited from aid saw a 35 percentage point increase in incumbent visits.

This evidence of incumbent visits is consistent with politicians attempting to claim credit for their role in aid delivery (in fact, many of these visits occurred during the delivery).

We sometimes observe this credit claiming activity directly. When politicians showed up during the aid delivery, we asked the delivery team to record politicians' actions. Councilors often claimed credit for the foreign aid. In the words of one of the delivery staff: "Councilors [use] the presentation ceremony as a political tool, talking too much about themselves." Consistent with my argument about retrospective voting, councilors frequently used this as an opportunity to talk – not about the project itself – but about what the project implied about their qualifications and their relationships with donors. For example, one councilor (stretching the truth) said that "[the NGO] conducted a competition," and that "the [elected officials] who did well" would receive development materials. He said he won the competition and that is why the school is receiving development materials. He added that he is the "right candidate in [the] coming elections," and he asked people to vote for him. He also added that he will "continue to work with [the NGO] in the future" and that he has a "strong relationship with [the NGO]" and he promised the community that he will "bring more development in the area through [the NGO]."

### 5.6.2 Effects among Nonaid Recipients

I next consider how citizens respond when they fail to benefit from foreign aid. First, in Figure 5.5, I compare respondents who were eligible and not eligible to receive foreign aid from the incumbent (Group C versus Group B).

Recall as I hypothesized in H2 that communities that failed to benefit from aid would punish the incumbent when the incumbent was known to be involved in aid distribution (Group C), but not when the incumbent was not involved in the decision (Group B). The results are broadly consistent with this hypothesis. On average, we see a mixed (but generally negative) trend in support for the councilor in Group C. This mixed effect is not particularly surprising given that respondents had little visibility into the aid delivery process and were unlikely to know that they were selected by the incumbent to receive aid.

The results change substantially when respondents received messages informing them that they were not selected by the incumbent (consistent with H5). Among these respondents, we observe a sizable backlash.

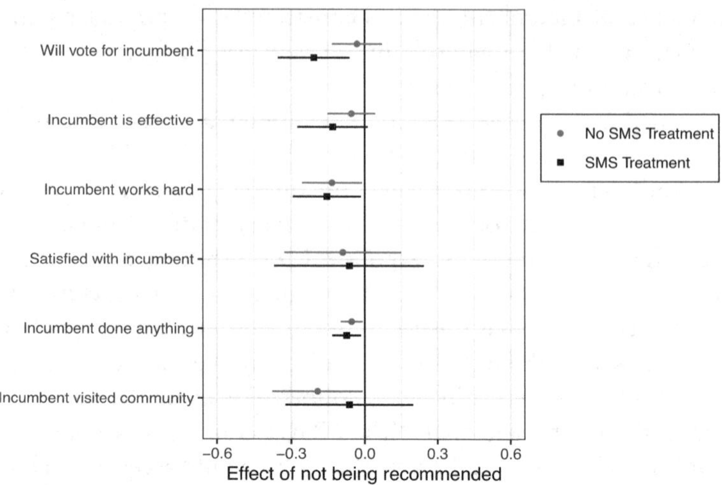


FIGURE 5.5 Effect of not being eligible for aid on outcome variables (95 percent CI)
*Note*: This plot shows the change in survey responses from baseline among communities that were not selected by the incumbent to receive aid. Sample only includes respondents who were not in communities receiving foreign aid. Reinforcement messages were randomized among respondents who provided a valid phone number at baseline.

In Group C, we observe a 16 percentage point drop in intention to vote. We also see a drop in perceptions of incumbent effectiveness and effort.

Finally, to test H3, I consider how respondents behave who were selected by the incumbent but did not receive aid. In Figure 5.6, we show a comparison of Group B versus Group C by SMS treatment status. Here, we observe no backlash against the incumbent. If anything, when respondents are informed about the fact that they were selected by the incumbent, they are more likely to have positive perceptions of the incumbent, even though they did not, in fact, benefit.

The contrast with the results in Figure 5.6 is stark. Even though both Groups B and C failed to benefit from aid delivery, respondents only punished those incumbents who were responsible for aid delivery decisions. In fact, politicians may have even benefited slightly from attempts to locate aid in Group B, even when these attempts were unsuccessful. This suggests that voters are quite sophisticated in how they interpret aid delivery and supports my argument that the electoral effect of aid works primarily by shifting perceptions of incumbent performance.

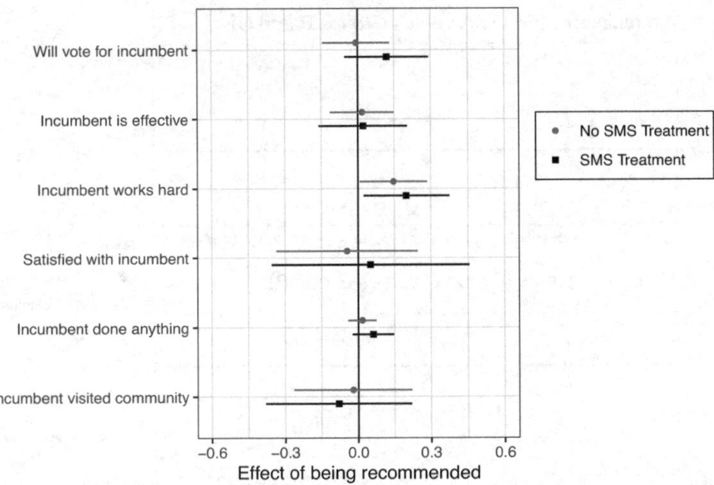


FIGURE 5.6 Effect of being selected (but not receiving) aid on outcome variables (95 percent CI)
*Note*: This plot shows the change in survey responses from baseline among those communities that were selected by the incumbent to receive aid. Sample only includes respondents who were not in communities receiving foreign aid. Reinforcement messages were randomized among respondents who provided a valid phone number at baseline.

### 5.6.3 Effects of Respondent Priors

The argument I present in Chapter 2 implies that foreign aid affects voting because it provides new information that helps voters learn about an incumbent's effort and preferences. Although it is difficult to observe learning directly, one additional implication of this argument is that the effects of foreign aid should be conditional on voters' prior beliefs about the incumbent. A voter who already believes that an incumbent works hard is unlikely to learn much from a foreign aid project and is unlikely to change their vote. Likewise, a voter that believes an incumbent does not work hard might not change their preferences much if they fail to benefit from aid.[38]

To test this mechanism, in Figure 5.7, I show how the effects of aid on voting intention vary by respondents' prior beliefs on councilor effectiveness. Indeed the effects of aid on voter behavior appear to be conditional on respondent beliefs about councilor effectiveness. Respondents who

[38] For discussion of how priors condition the effects of information on voting, see Arias et al. (2022); Izzo, Dewan, and Wolton (2018).

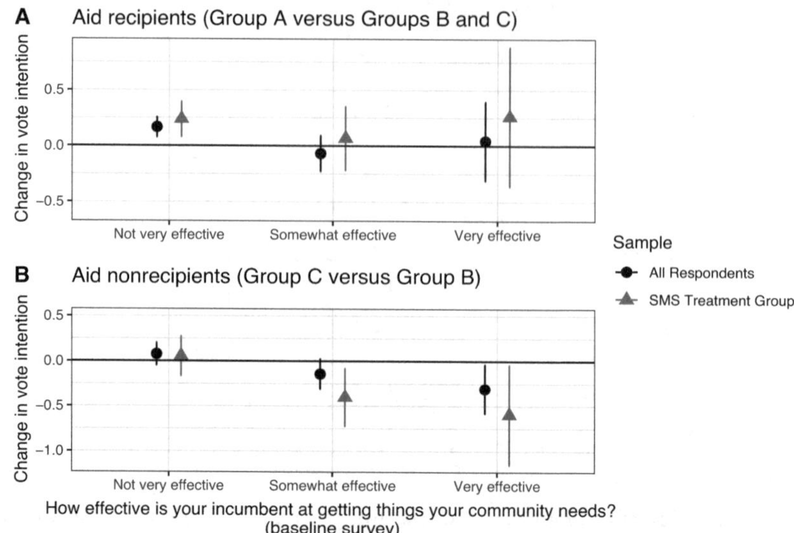


FIGURE 5.7 How respondent priors condition the effects of aid (95 percent CI)
*Note*: This plot shows the conditional effect of foreign aid among aid recipients (panel A) and among those who were not selected by the councilor (panel B). The effects are conditioned on baseline respondent beliefs about councilor effectiveness.

believed that the councilor was ineffective at baseline were particularly likely to respond to aid by changing their vote intention. Respondents who believed the councilor was very effective at baseline were particularly likely to sanction the incumbent for failing to deliver aid.

## 5.7 CONCLUSION

Scholars of foreign aid have often argued that foreign aid is a curse for democracy because it helps incumbents build undeserved reputations for public performance, facilitates patronage, and breaks links between taxation and accountability. As I argued here and in Chapter 3, these explanations do not adequately explain the electoral effects of foreign aid or account for the effects of aid on voting behavior.

Building on a framework of retrospective voting, I suggest a more nuanced account of the effects of aid on elections and accountability. Depending on voter priors, the distribution of aid and the effects of aid on voting will be heterogeneous across communities. Further, the net effects of aid on election outcomes are uncertain and depend on the distribution of aid and voter beliefs. Contrary to what is usually assumed, I also argue that foreign aid can be beneficial for electoral accountability.

I evaluate this argument with a panel survey and SMS experiment. I show that recipients of aid are more likely to vote for incumbents and perceive incumbent performance as high. Further, I document that politicians often attempt to claim credit for foreign aid delivery, and that voters often attribute aid delivery to government action. Finally, I document through an SMS experiment that these effects are strongest among those who can clearly attribute foreign aid to the actions of the incumbent.

However – and somewhat uniquely in the literature on aid – I also examine how perceptions of incumbent performance change among those who failed to benefit from foreign aid. The results among these respondents depend upon the involvement of politicians in aid delivery. Where politicians are responsible for not selecting a school, we document a sizable backlash against the incumbent. However when the NGO was responsible for not selecting a school, we see no backlash effect.

These findings help explain the heterogeneous effects of foreign aid on election outcomes. In contrast to what is often assumed, I estimate that the net effect of the project we study on incumbent votes would have been quite substantially negative if all respondents were well informed about aid delivery. Such negative effects are likely under-estimated in existing studies due to their inability to parse out geographical heterogeneity in aid benefits.

These results contest several tropes in discussions of aid politics. For one, they suggest the citizens are much more sophisticated in their voting decisions and understanding of aid than scholars often give them credit for. Voters neither always attribute aid to incumbents, nor do they always attribute aid to NGOs. Instead, they appear to correctly update their perceptions in response to information about the role of incumbents in aid delivery.

The results also challenge arguments that foreign aid is bad for electoral accountability. When respondents in our study were well-informed, they acted in ways that should enhance accountability. Respondents who learned that they were favored by the incumbent, were more likely to support the incumbent. Respondents who learned that they did not receive aid were less likely to support the incumbent; however this effect dissipated when respondents learned that this was due to the actions of the NGO rather than the politician. Thus the results imply that when voters are well-informed about the role of their government in aid delivery, foreign aid can enhance accountability.

# 6

# The Effects of Aid on Politician Spending Behavior

Sometimes I feel that the government officials are very busy. They are managing different donors, so it is like they run from one meeting to another... So maybe that is their job, but it feels too stretched. They cannot think, they do not have time.

– Portfolio coordinator for a bilateral donor in Malawi[1]

[Influence] goes the other way around. We present the things that we think are important and we hope to steer MPs to go in that direction.

– Portfolio coordinator for a multilateral donor when asked about the government's influence over donors.[2]

Much of this book has focused on ways in which politicians influence donor decisions; however, as the above quotes illustrate, donors also influence politicians' decisions. To better understand these effects, this chapter looks at the case of education spending decisions in Malawi. In a series of experimental interventions, I examine how foreign aid information and donor oversight change the way in which MPs and councilors in Malawi allocate resources to primary schools in their constituencies. I also examine survey data on what politicians know about donor activities in their constituencies.[3]

1 Interview A3, see Appendix B.

2 Interview A4, see Appendix B.

3 Much of the research described in this chapter was conducted in collaboration with Brigitte Seim and Johan Ahlbäck. Figures 6.1 and 6.2 are reprinted from *Journal of Development Economics*, vol. 146, Ryan Jablonski, Brigitte Seim, and Johan Ahlbäck, "How information about foreign aid affects public spending decisions: Evidence from a field experiment in Malawi", Copyright (2025), with permission from Elsevier. Versions

The results illustrate important ways in which donors change politicians' policy decisions. First, I demonstrate that politicians often lack policy-relevant information about what donors are doing in their constituencies. While most politicians meet donors and almost all claim to consider what they do, the scale, complexity, and opacity of donor activities make it hard for politicians to stay abreast of what donors are doing in their communities. Politicians especially struggle to identify funds from major donors and often know more about donor activities in more proximate and populous areas. Second, I show that what donors do affects policy incentives. When politicians are experimentally assigned more accurate information about donor activities, they alter their spending decisions. Politicians in this study reallocated resources away from those communities where donors have existing projects. I provide evidence that this displacement, is motivated by concerns about equity and efficiency.

I begin by describing three mechanisms by which donors might impact spending policy: through oversight, displacement, and information. I will then test each of these mechanisms in the empirical tests.

## 6.1 HOW DOES FOREIGN AID AFFECT SPENDING POLICY?

### 6.1.1 Donor Oversight

If you are a government minister in an aid-dependent democracy, you are probably very worried about what donors think. Your ability to get things done, or distribute resources to your supporters, is highly dependent on donors' willingness to provide resources. Knowing this, donors often condition the delivery of aid – particularly budget support – on governments' implementation of particular policies. Famously, this conditioning of aid has played a role in incentivizing several governments (including Hastings Banda's government in Malawi) to hold elections, and several scholars have argued for a general effect of aid conditionality or donor oversight on democratization.[4]

of figures 6.3, 6.5, 6.6, 6.7, 6.8, and 6.9 were originally published by Cambridge University Press in Jablonski and Seim (2023). They are republished here under Creative Commons License CC BY 4.0. A preanalysis plan (PAP) for the experiments described here is available at https://osf.io/kazfp.

4 Resnick and Van de Walle 2013; Dietrich and Wright 2015; Gibson, Hoffman, and Jablonski 2015.

But donor oversight also plays a role in more prosaic policy decisions. For instance, in 2014, most donors cut off budget support to Malawi due to the "Cashgate" scandal which involved the siphoning of millions of dollars from public budgets through fraudulent and hidden financial transactions. Since budget support had funded between 30 and 50 percent of government activities, this action was a severe blow to the government and likely contributed to the downfall of then incumbent Joyce Banda.[5] Since Cashgate, donors have used the promise of budget support as a way to coerce the government to make certain policy reforms, especially around public procurement.

Controversially, some of these proposed reforms have been contrary to the interests of the government. In 2016, for instance, President Peter Mutharika was purportedly planning to veto a freedom of information bill (the "Access to Information Bill") after it had been passed by Parliament out of concerns about the scope of its provisions. At this point, according to several reports, representatives of the European Union renewed threats to not resume budget support if the bill was not allowed to proceed. While denying that his decision had anything to do with donors, President Mutharika changed his opposition to the bill and signed it into law. In recent years, donors have also conditioned aid on reforms to Malawi's Farm Input Subsidy Program and various reforms to Malawi's financial management systems.[6]

It is often the case that these conditions do not have to be explicit. As I show earlier in this book, politicians' ability to deliver for their constituents depends a lot on the cooperation (and possibly friendship) of donors and NGOs. As a more senior official, having a good relationship with donors means that you have a seat at the table in a lot of important donor decisions that might affect your constituents. It also may mean that you can call on donors when you need support for a particular development initiative. This may mean that politicians are much less likely to act opportunistically when they know that donors are watching.

Politicians in Malawi often told us about their worries about offending donors. On the positive side, politicians sometimes talked about how donors put a check on mismanagement. One councilor told us: "If the donor is involved all the way, the greedy politicians become afraid to intervene in the project affairs, afraid of the donor and worried that can be exposed."[7]

[5] Seim 2015.
[6] Khamula 2016; Chilunga 2016.
[7] Appendix B, interview B5.

However, there is also a dark side to this oversight. In interviews, politicians sometimes discussed their reticence to question decisions that donors had made about development, even when those decisions were poorly made. One councilor said: "We cannot question or refuse development that comes into your area even if the type of development that the NGO is bringing is not what you are looking for."[8]

As these quotes illustrate, it is possible that donor oversight could be good or bad for development. On one hand, if donors use their influence to deter corruption and motivate more effective spending behavior, then this could incentivize more effective government performance, and indeed some evidence suggests that donor oversight reduces corruption and patronage.[9]

On the other hand, some have argued that these reputational concerns might cause politicians to be more interested and concerned about what donors want than what their constituents want.[10] As I noted in Chapter 2, it seems likely that politicians sometimes trade-off legislative or citizen-focused activity for investment in donor relations. As the anecdote above illustrates, it is also possible that politicians start to abrogate the responsibility to monitor development activities out of a concern about offending donors.

If indeed there is a trade-off between top-down (donor) accountability and (bottom up) citizen accountability, then it is quite possible that donor efforts to monitor and coerce politicians – even with the best of motivations – could undermine democratic accountability. Additionally, as I argued in Chapter 3, constraining politicians' decision-making is often bad for accountability. If voters believe politicians have very little agency vis-à-vis donors, this will make it harder for politicians to build a reputation for effective accountability. If so, donors may inadvertently fuel the very corruption and poor performance they try to deter.

### 6.1.2 Displacement and Fungibility

One of the more long-standing criticisms of foreign aid is that it has the potential to displace government spending, or be "fungible."[11] To

8 Appendix B, interview B6.

9 Gibson, Hoffman, and Jablonski 2015; Resnick and Van de Walle 2013; Wright and Winters 2010.

10 For example, Mkandawire (2010).

11 Fungibility refers more generally to the potential for revenue to be exchangeable. The displacement effects I study in the experiment are one manifestation of fungibility.

illustrate, consider what might happen if a donor invested in refurbishing school buildings in some politician's constituency. The politician might reason that at least some of the existing government budget for school refurbishment would be better spent on some other priority like teacher salaries and adjust the budget accordingly.

If so, the net effect of the donor's investment in school refurbishment might actually be a reduction in school quality. Once the displacement of the government's spending is taken into account, it is possible that the donor's project will have very little effect on the outcome the donor intends.[12] Consistent with this displacement effect, many empirical studies have shown that governments appear to shift their spending behavior away from sectors or areas that benefit from foreign aid.[13]

Politicians in Malawi indeed seem to consider what donors are doing when they make spending decisions. As noted in Chapter 2, more than 90 percent of surveyed politicians said they "consider what donors and NGOs have done for an area" when making decisions about development. In interviews, some officials note specific ways in which they adjust their policies. As one District Commissioner explained:

> [I]f a donor just says we want to come to village A or B and maintain teacher houses. The question would be to see if it falls under the District strategic plan .... The tricky bit about it is that we have needs but amongst the needs there are priority needs. The challenge now comes that we can't deny a project from a donor because it's not number one on our list.... if UNICEF say want to construct a toilet, we wouldn't say don't come because you will disturb our development plan. We would still let them come, say this was number 4 on the priority list then we knock it off the list and still seek to address 1, 2 and 3. In this way, they are not influencing for us to change but rather helping us address the problems that we have.[14]

The reason why many development scholars and practitioners worry about displacement and fungibility is that it might cause funds to be used ineffectively. To illustrate the problem: Suppose that this official instead of investing more in priorities 1, 2 and 3 instead decided to reallocate the government funds from toilets toward political patronage or corruption

[12] Alternatively, fungibility could go the other way: Some argue politicians may choose to spend in line with donors, either because they view donor spending as a kind of endorsement, or because of there are complementarities in government and donor investments (Hines and Thaler, 1995). These are sometimes called "flypaper" effects.

[13] Feyzioglu, Swaroop, and Zhu 1998; Walle and Mu 2007; Werker, Ahmed, and Cohen 2009; McGillivray and Morrissey 2000; Remmer 2004; Walle and Mu 2007; Seim, Jablonski, and Ahlbäck 2020.

[14] Appendix B, Interview D3.

– say building a new school in his home town. The official might rationalize this decision by saying that – with the help of donors – he does not need the toilet funds to deliver on his development plan. He might therefore decide that a politically or personally motivated spending decision is the best remaining option. If the official makes such a decision, then we might say that UNICEF, by funding a toilet, has actually funded corruption or political patronage.

If donors make it easier for politicians to spend in a politically motivated fashion, fungibility might also be bad for democracy. As discussed in Chapter 3, one of the main reasons why aid might lead to a political curse is the aid can allow ineffective or unaccountable leaders to redistribute more resources to their supporters without forcing them to raise taxes. A core assumption of these aid curse arguments is that governments can effectively do what they want with aid. Even if donors attempt to channel aid through NGOs, the fungibility effects mean that much of that aid can effectively be spent where and how politicians wish.[15]

Indeed, the predominant view of most economists and political scientists has been that fungibility is bad for development and democracy.[16] As the economist Dambisa Moyo put it in her popular book *Dead Aid*, "[Aid] monies set aside for one purpose are easily diverted toward another; not just any other purpose, but agendas that can be worthless, if not detrimental, to growth."[17]

However, as I will demonstrate further, the argument that the displacement of public spending is bad for development and democracy relies on assumptions that do not necessarily hold in practice. Because politicians often have better information than donors about the needs of their communities, they can also choose to adjust government spending in ways that result in a net improvement in welfare.

### 6.1.3 Information and Learning

Politicians face many barriers to learning about donor activities. One barrier is complexity. As the quote introducing this chapter illustrates,

[15] For instance, Mesquita and Smith (2009) assume in their model that "bilateral aid is largely fungible such that the recipient leader can spend the resources as she sees fit." Similarly, Morrison (2007) argues that "foreign aid is a highly fungible resource and acts similarly to oil in that it provides extra resources the government can use to distribute to its key constituencies without taxation."

[16] Easterly 2009; Gibson, Ostrom, and Shivakumar 2005; Remmer 2004; Morrison 2007; Moyo 2009; Feyzioglu, Swaroop, and Zhu 1998.

[17] Moyo 2009.

it can be quite taxing for politicians to stay abreast of all that donors are doing in a highly aid-dependent area. According to Malawi's Aid Management Platform, there are only about twenty-seven major donors working in Malawi (as of 2013).[18] However since most projects are channeled outside the government, and are implemented by NGOs and donor affiliates, this vastly underestimates the complexity most politicians face in tracking development. In our survey of teachers, for instance, we identify seventy-six separate organizations that have delivered projects to primary schools over a five-year period, and we estimate that at least 44 percent of primary schools have active donor-funded development projects (encompassing over 3,000 schools).[19] In total, there are over 1,200 registered NGOs doing development work in Malawi.[20] And even that does not encompass the many private contractors doing work on the behalf of donors and NGOs. The complexity in Malawi is not particularly unique: In Kenya, there are over 8,000 NGOs.[21] In Bangladesh, one study estimates over 90 percent of villages were home to at least one NGO.[22]

A second major barrier is a lack of transparency. While many governments require consultation between donors or NGOs and political bodies, compliance with these consultation rules are often mixed in practice. In Malawi, for instance, donors working in an area are required to consult with politicians sitting on Area Development Councils (ADCs) and District Commissioners (DCs); however in almost every interview, members of these bodies pointed out ways in which donors and NGOs had failed to comply with these rules or limited the flow of information.[23] As one Area Development Committee member pointed out:

> We don't have a productive relationship because the donors and NGOs just go straight to the schools and start the project without consulting the ADC who the main player in community development. This is a big a problem to us as because sometime we don't know which area they have donated and what they have donated and how much the donation is. If they asked we could have been

[18] Peratsakis, Christian, Joshua Powell, Michael Findley, Justin Baker, and Catherine Weaver 2012.

[19] See Appendix A Section A.3 for survey details and Chapter 5 for details on the coding of projects.

[20] NGORA Malawi 2022.

[21] Brass 2016.

[22] Brass et al. 2018.

[23] We also see this lack of compliance in formal statistics. For instance, as of 2016, less than 5 percent of NGOs in Malawi reported on their activities to the government. See discussion on page 54.

telling them which areas are the needy ones and what is needed within a particular area.[24]

The result is a situation where most politicians desire a lot more information and consultation from donors than they receive. To illustrate, I asked all interviewed officials to describe the "barriers to fulfilling their goals" as a politician or bureaucrat. After funding challenges, almost all officials mentioned some challenge in coordinating with donors and NGOs. One councilor said: "Even the NGOs' projects are projects which are decided somewhere in the office and they just brought the plans to [us] ... and [we] are told just to participate but all the decisions are made on paper somewhere."[25] A District Commissioner made a similar point, "[Donors] don't consult; they come with already framed projects. They come when they have already made a decision. In actual sense the District Executive Committee is there just to endorse what they have already planned."[26]

There are a number of ways in which these information gaps could alter public spending decisions in a detrimental way. Especially, we might observe more duplication and overinvestment in some areas relative to others.[27] The duplication of government and donor efforts may also overburden administrative systems and staff. Indeed, many scholars have noted such inefficiencies when donors fail to coordinate.[28] Less studied is how these coordination and information challenges might affect government policymaking.

When politicians struggle to make informed spending decisions, this can also have negative consequences for democracy. When politicians and donors coordinate effectively with one another, then politicians can accurately claim credit for changes in their constituent's welfare. However when spending is uncoordinated, voters may attribute a lot of politicians' effort to the work of donors. Indeed, as I showed in Chapter 5, the complex nature of development spending in Malawi has caused many voters to underestimate what their government does, and to attribute a lot of the development that does happen to donors. As I showed in Chapter 3, this

[24] ADC Interview C6, see Appendix B.
[25] Appendix B, Interview B5.
[26] Appendix B.
[27] Bourguignon and Platteau 2015.
[28] Gehring et al. 2017; Acharya, De Lima, and Moore 2006; Easterly and Pfutze 2008; Knack and Rahman 2007.

voter uncertainty about the activities of politicians can be bad for democracy and public spending because it helps poorly performing and corrupt politicians to remain in power despite doing little for their constituents.

## 6.2 THEORIZING THE EFFECTS OF AID ON SPENDING POLICY

To be more specific about these effects and their consequences, consider a simple extension of the theory discussed in Chapter 3. A donor plans to make an aid investment of size $a > 0$ to one out of $N$ communities. After observing the investment, the incumbent independently makes an investment $b > 0$ to one of these communities.

First consider the politician's decision: As discussed in Chapters 3 and 4, incumbents have to weigh a number of factors in making decisions about the distribution of resources. Two important factors will likely be the effects of the decision on citizen welfare and on votes. We can define the politicians returns in welfare and votes from spending in community $i$ as $d(a_i)$ and $v(a_i)$. For simplicity, we can define $d_i > d_{i+1}$ and $v_j > v_{j+1}$ for all $i$ and $j$. This implies that a vote maximizing politician will always invest in community $i = 1$, and a development maximizing incumbent will always invest in community $j = 1$.

If these voting and welfare effects are highly correlated across communities, the incumbent's decision is straightforward: She will simply spend on the community with the highest return in welfare and votes. But more often the spending decision requires a trade-off. Communities that are very pivotal in an election are very often not the same as those communities that are most deserving of funds. One reason for this trade-off is that impoverished or needy communities are often that way *because* they are not pivotal in the government's calculus.

I define the weight the politician places on $v_i$ versus $d_i$ in her decision as $\lambda$. So a politician is simply going to choose the community that maximizes the weighted sum of development and voting returns. That is,

$$\max_a \lambda(d_1 + d_2 \ldots d_N) + (1 - \lambda)(v_1 + v_2 \ldots v_N) \qquad (6.1)$$

How will this problem change in the presence of donor spending? If donors prioritize welfare, we might predict that they are always going to invest in the community with the highest return on development. So the donor should usually prefer to invest in community $i = 1$.

But this decision creates a problem for the incumbent. If a donor invested in community $i = 1$, the incumbent could reasonably infer that any investment in community $i = 1$ is going to have a smaller effect than an investment in a community $i = 2$ that has not benefited much from donor attention.[29] Additionally, the incumbent might worry that she will be criticized by voters or community leaders for investing additional funds in a community that has already seen investment when there are so many communities that have not seen any investment. A welfare maximizing incumbent might therefore rationalize spending on community $i = 2$ rather than community $i = 1$.[30]

Development economists, especially, have worried a lot about this kind of displacement. If politicians reallocate funds in response to their actions – regardless of how or why they do so – then this is often going to undermine the effectiveness of foreign aid. Note, for instance, that community $i = 1$ might even have been better off if donors had never got involved since donors have caused them to miss out on a substantial *government* investment. Moreover, even if foreign aid is quite effective at improving welfare, it may be hard for donors to identify any effect of aid on welfare outcomes since the direct effect of increasing aid may be outweighed by the secondary effect of decreasing government spending.

However, from the standpoint of citizens' welfare, the consequences of these displacement effects depend a lot on what we think about the incumbent's motivations. If the incumbent weighs welfare highly ($\lambda$ is large) she might deviate to the next neediest community ($i = 2$). While this will be worse for community $i = 1$, this will be better for the total welfare of the constituency than if she had invested in $i = 1$.

It is also possible that these displacement effects could decrease total welfare. If donors primarily target based on the welfare returns to spending ($d$), then foreign aid can increase the value to the incumbent of targeting based on nonwelfare-based considerations such as votes ($v$). If the incumbent knows that the donor has addressed the major needs in her constituency – even if she cares a lot about welfare – she might instead reason that spending on politically pivotal communities, or diverting funds to political supporters, makes more sense. If this political effect predominates, then foreign aid could crowd out public investment and

29 For instance because of decreasing marginal returns to investment: $\frac{\partial d_i}{\partial b_i}(a_i{>}0) < \frac{\partial d_i}{\partial b_i}(a_i{=}0)$

30 An incumbent might also rationalize that community $i = 1$ should receive more investment since teachers are going to make more effective use of resources when basic facilities are in place. This assumption of complementarity between donor and politician spending is sometimes called a "flypaper" effect (Hines and Thaler 1995; Remmer 2004; Walle and Mu 2007).

make public spending less efficient and more politically oriented. It might even encourage higher levels of corruption and negatively affect development.

How will these effect change if politicians lack knowledge of donor activities? Suppose donors invest but the incumbent fails to observe $a$, what will the consequences be for spending outcomes? In this case, the incumbent will spend the same way they would absent foreign aid. Thus they will invest in community $i = 1$ or $j = 1$.

This spending strategy will most often be a bad one for citizen welfare. In this scenario, both the incumbent and the donor will often invest in high need communities. Since there are often decreasing returns to development spending, this duplicative investment will almost always lower welfare relative a scenario where the incumbent has the option to deviate to another community with high need.[31] Moreover, since incumbents are unaware of the nature of donor spending, the incumbent will also be less able to take advantage of any complementarities that might exist between government and donor investments.

If incumbents are very likely to respond to foreign aid by spending on *less* needy communities, it is also possible that information could harm citizen welfare. However, this will always be a suboptimal scenario since citizens will always be better off if the incumbent can effectively allocate government resources.[32]

How might donor oversight change these outcomes? Suppose, for instance, donors condition their aid spending on the effectiveness of the incumbent (or incumbents worry that donors condition aid). If the incumbent cares about future revenues, donor oversight should therefore manipulate the weight that incumbents place on votes versus development ($\lambda$ in Equation 6.1). Independent of the donor's decision, donor oversight would therefore cause incumbents to spend more on needy communities.

Additionally, we might expect that donor oversight is going to make displacement less likely. If politicians believe that donors do not like fungibility, then greater donor oversight might cause them to be less likely to reallocate funds in a way suggested by fungibility arguments.[33]

31 It is suboptimal for welfare whenever $\frac{\partial d_{i=1}}{\partial b_{i=1}}(a_{i=1} > 0) < \frac{\partial d_{i=2}}{\partial b_{i=2}}(a_{i=2} = 0)$.

32 If the incumbent deviates from $i = 1$ to $j = 1$, then this will be negative for welfare whenever $\frac{\partial d_{i=1}}{\partial b_{i=1}}(a_{i=1} > 0) < \frac{\partial d_{j=1}}{\partial b_{j=1}}(a_{j=1} = 0)$ and positive for welfare otherwise.

33 For example, as suggested by Bermeo (2016) and Bermeo (2011).

## 6.3 HYPOTHESES

I summarize the competing hypotheses about the effects of aid on spending policy in the following list.[34]

**Displacement Effects**

H1 Foreign aid will cause politicians to spend *less* in areas targeted by donors.

H2 Foreign aid will cause politicians to spend *less* on the neediest communities and *more* on politically pivotal communities.

**Oversight Effects**

H3 Effective donor oversight will cause politicians to spend more on needy communities and less on politically pivotal communities

H4 Effective donor oversight will make it less likely that politicians adjust their spending in response to foreign aid.

**Information Effects**

H5 When politicians lack knowledge of donor activities in their constituency, there will be more duplication between politician and donor spending.

## 6.4 A STUDY OF AID AND POLICYMAKING

To test these hypotheses, my collaborators and I designed an experiment. Our intention with the experiment was to mimic politicians' discretionary development decisions. Specifically, we attempted to recreate a common way in which politicians advise donors and NGOs about development projects. To do this, we partnered with a small donor-funded UK-based NGO (Tearfund). Trained representatives of the NGO met in-person with 460 elected Local Councilors (LCs) and Members of Parliament (MPs) in Malawi and told them (truthfully) about a development project that would deliver supplies to schools in their constituency. The NGO then asked the politician to assist them by recommending schools to receive these goods. Following the experiment, each politicians' constituency was allocated school supplies in accordance with the incumbents' preferences and the outcome of a public lottery.[35]

34 The hypotheses for this study were preregistered at https://osf.io/kazfp.

35 The way goods are distributed in this study mirrors in many ways the study described in Chapter 5. They are however different studies. The experiment described in this chapter was fielded after the other experiment. While this study was informed by many of the lessons from the earlier study, this study focuses on different questions and has a broader study sample.

We use this experiment to test these hypotheses about the displacement effects of foreign aid. To do so, we randomly assigned politicians to receive information about foreign aid projects at the schools in their constituency. We then compared politicians' allocation decisions in an environment where they learned, or not, about foreign aid in their communities. Because the information about aid is randomly assigned and allocation decisions are precisely attributable, we can identify how learning about foreign aid changes politicians' spending decisions.

We also use this experiment to assess whether donor oversight shapes public spending. We informed half of the incumbents (accurately) that their names and the decisions that they made would be shared in a report to all major donors in Malawi. We informed others that their decisions would remain private. If politicians indeed worry about their reputation among donors, we would expect that this report would cause politicians to be more circumspect in their decisions and avoid spending on close family members or political supporters. We also predicted that this treatment would cause more spending on objective measures of need.

Finally, we also use survey and interview data to assess politicians' gaps in knowledge about donor activities in their constituencies. We asked each official to complete a quiz assessing their knowledge of activities in a random sampling of schools. As discussed further, we document sizeable gaps in politicians' knowledge of donor activities, particularly in the far reaches of their constituencies.

The use of experiments to study the effects of foreign aid on policy is rare. Most commonly, scholars have studied the effect of aid on spending by looking at observational data on foreign aid and public budgets at the national and cross-national levels. However, the findings from such analysis have been heterogeneous across contexts. Most studies conclude that governments indeed respond to foreign aid by changing the composition of public spending.[36] Yet, estimates from these studies are surprisingly disparate. Some studies document a large *negative* effect of aid on public spending.[37]. Other studies find "flypaper" effects in which foreign aid *increases* public spending.[38] Still others find no evidence of fungibility.[39]

36 World Bank 1998; Chatterjee, Giuliano, and Kaya 2012; Marć 2017; Feyzioglu, Swaroop, and Zhu 1998; Werker, Ahmed, and Cohen 2009.

37 Marć 2017; Feyzioglu, Swaroop, and Zhu 1998; Werker, Ahmed, and Cohen 2009; World Bank 1998.

38 Walle and Mu 2007; Morrissey 2015; Remmer 2004.

39 Pack and Pack 1990.

Estimates of the scale of fungibility similarly vary from nearly the entirety of the aid budget to more marginal effects.[40]

This analysis has failed to resolve a lot of the debates about aid and spending policy. For one, it is quite difficult to determine causal precedence: We don't know whether foreign aid is affecting spending or whether spending is affecting foreign aid. After all, we know donors often tailor aid conditionality provisions in anticipation of fungibility. Additionally, demand for foreign aid is related to shocks in public spending and income, making it challenging to show that one causes the other.[41] There are also a number of measurement challenges in existing studies of aid and public spending.[42]

Additionally, existing studies have also been largely unable to disentangle who benefits from the displacement of public spending, or what motivates politicians' decisions to reallocate development. As discussed earlier, many arguments imply more public spending among political supporters or in less deserving communities. Yet, there have been few attempts to validate these assumptions.[43] The research in this chapter addresses many of these challenges, and I believe that it provides a more credible and detailed explanation for the effects of aid on spending policy.

### 6.4.1 Context of the Study

We began this research project by reaching out to all the MPs and LCs in Malawi, the majority of whom (70 percent) agreed to meet with us. In total, we recruited 125 in-office Members of Parliament (MPs) and 335 in-office Local Councilors (LCs).[44] We show a map of sampled constituencies in Figure 6.1. The officials were elected in 2014 and the study took place in 2016 and 2017.

40 Werker, Ahmed, and Cohen 2009; Chatterjee, Giuliano, and Kaya 2012; Sijpe 2013; Walle and Mu 2007.

41 For instance, aid may target a budget shortfall. See Werker, Ahmed, and Cohen 2009 for discussion and evidence of bias.

42 Among other problems, there is no easy way to determine how much donors intended to be spent in a particular sector in most cases, and distinguishing between on-budget and off-budget aid is not trivial (Sijpe 2013). Also, public spending data in aid-dependent states is often unreliable or potentially even strategically biased (Morrissey 2015).

43 Morrissey 2015; Wagstaff 2011.

44 The sample is broadly representative of the larger population of politicians in Malawi. See further details on recruitment and sample statistics in Appendix A and Appendix E.

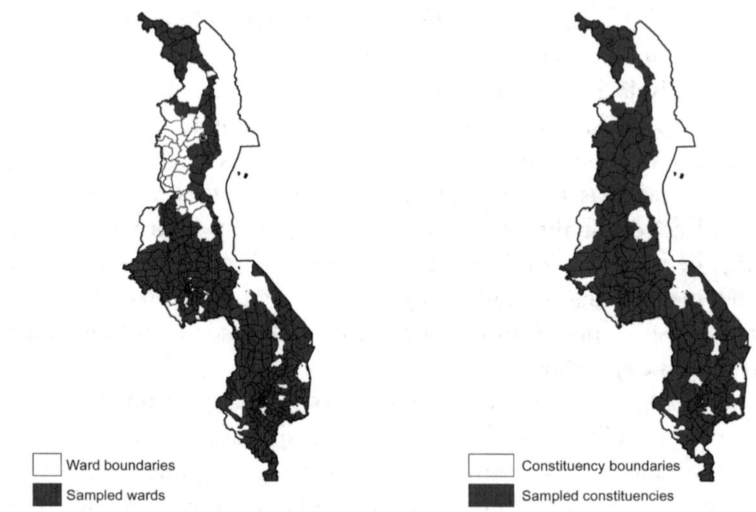


FIGURE 6.1 Sampled constituencies
*Note*: This figure shows the constituencies of politicians in the sample.

## 6.5 POLITICIAN KNOWLEDGE OF DONOR ACTIVITIES

I will begin with an examination of what politicians in the study know about donor activities in their constituencies. To answer this question, we designed a quiz for all interviewed officials. During our meetings, we gave each a list of three randomly selected primary schools in their constituencies. We then asked the politicians to tell us which of the three schools "received the most projects sponsored large donors" in the past five years. We also asked each politician to name the major international donor(s) that had invested in that school. Since district governments (and to a lesser extent MPs) have statutory authority over the funding and management of primary schools, this is a question that should not have been particularly difficult.[45]

To assess the accuracy of these responses, we also need an objective measure of donor activities in each school. To this end, we approached all major donors active in Malawi's education sector and asked them for details on the schools they had invested in over the last five years (from 2011 to 2016). In total, 3,151 primary schools received 4,566 foreign aid projects from this set of donors between 2011 and 2016. This constitutes

[45] Most primary education resources are managed by Local Councils (LCs) and Area Development Committees (ADCs) in Malawi. MPs often sit as observers on both LC and ADC meetings, and often have substantial informal authority, partly due to their control over Constituency Development Funds (CDFs).

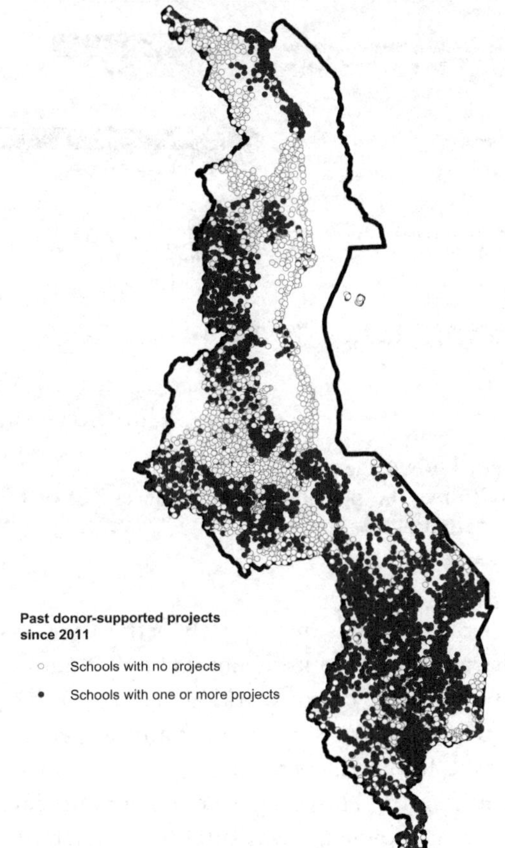


FIGURE 6.2 Primary schools and foreign aid projects

about 57 percent of the primary schools in Malawi. The number of foreign aid projects in each school varied from 0 to 4. Figure 6.2 displays the total sample of primary schools in Malawi with no projects supported by donors (in white) versus those with at least one project (in gray).[46] While this dataset does not encompass smaller donors or NGOs, it represents the vast majority of donor funding going to the Malawi education sector.

I summarize responses to the quiz in Figure 6.3. The results present a mixed picture of donor knowledge. Responding politicians did not do particularly well in describing the geography of education aid in their constituency: Only 24 percent of MPs and 21 percent of local councilors (LCs) were able to provide a correct answer about the number of projects

[46] For further details on the data collection and coding, see Appendix E.

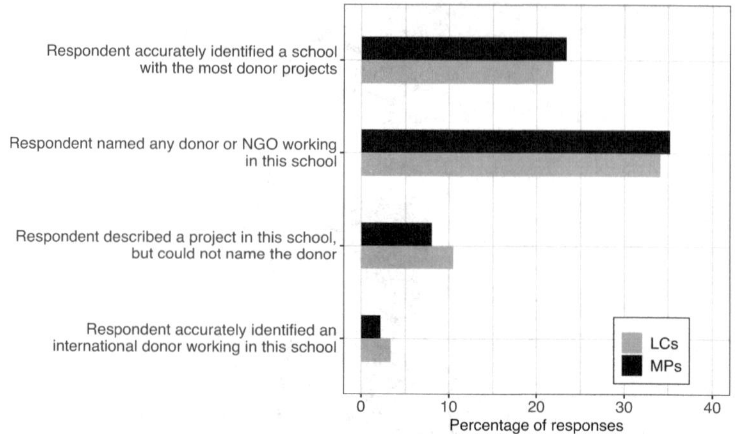


FIGURE 6.3 Donor knowledge quiz
*Note*: The x-axis shows the percentage of responses out of the 335 councilors and 125 MPs participating in the survey.

in each school: a rate which is only slightly better than random chance.[47] That said, politicians do often know about some donor activities. When asked to describe a specific donor working in a school: 35 percent of MPs and 34 percent of councilors were able to name a specific donor working in a school. An additional 8 percent and 10 percent could describe a project but not a donor.[48] However, even when politicians knew about a specific project, that knowledge was often incomplete. It was quite rare for politicians to name the main international donor providing funding to a school. Less than 3 percent of politicians were able to do so. Most often politicians would instead provide the name of an NGO or implementing partner.

The results from this quiz imply that politician knowledge is incomplete and heterogeneous: While politicians are often familiar with some donor activities in their area, the knowledge is incomplete. Politicians are especially less knowledgeable about international donors and the formal funding arrangements for particular projects. This pattern of responses is consistent with the observation in Chapter 2 that politicians outside the

[47] Respondents had the choice of selecting school A, B, or C, all schools, or no schools. Additionally, they could say they didn't know.

[48] Often in this case, politicians would describe a project but say they could not remember the donor.

central government are more likely to meet with NGOs rather than the direct representatives of major donors.

To more thoroughly explore the causes of heterogeneous knowledge, I look at the characteristics of those schools where politicians provide more accurate answers.[49] The results of this regression in Table 6.1 suggest that the complexity of monitoring donor activities indeed may play a role in these knowledge gaps. Politicians especially struggle to answer questions about more remote communities. A one standard deviation increase in the distance between a councilor's home town and a school decreases the probability of a correct quiz answer by about 4 percent. The effects of school size and population density are more mixed. A one standard deviation increase in a school's enrolment decreases the probability of a correct quiz answer by about 5 percent, perhaps reflecting the more complex funding arrangements at larger schools. MPs are also unlikely to know about donor activities in less populous areas of their constituency.[50]

### 6.5.1 Politician Spending Decisions

During each meeting, politicians were also asked to make decisions about which schools in their constituency should receive development goods from the NGO. Specifically, they were presented with several maps of their constituency, each showing three primary schools. The three schools that appeared on each map were randomly selected from the government's list of primary schools in the constituency. The politician was then asked to decide which of the three schools should be allocated school supplies from the NGO donor. Specifically, the decision prompt was: "When you are ready, please tell me which school you would like to choose to receive a set of [*school supply*]. Please take your time in making this decision." The maps, examples of which are shown in Figures 6.4 and 6.5, were shown to the politician on portable tablets and could be studied in detail before the spending decision was made.

49 That is, for each politician, I created a variable indicating whether the politician correctly answered at least one of the quiz questions. I then regress the characteristics of the school with the most donor projects (i.e. the correct answer) on that variable. Since the schools that get the most attention from donors are representative of all the schools in Malawi, these estimates are likely a biased measure of politicians' true knowledge of all schools.

50 For discussion of how politicians in Malawi learn about their constituencies and the role of geographic distance in shaping knowledge, see Jablonski and Seim (2023).

TABLE 6.1 *Correlates of donor knowledge*

| Variable Name | All Politicians (1) | Councilors (2) | MPs (3) |
|---|---|---|---|
| Log Distance from Hometown | −0.042** | −0.049*** | −0.023 |
| | (0.017) | (0.018) | (0.067) |
| Incumbent Percent | −0.005 | −0.002 | −0.022 |
| | (0.019) | (0.025) | (0.032) |
| Pop Density at School | 0.019 | −0.005 | 0.153** |
| | (0.024) | (0.026) | (0.060) |
| School Enrollment | −0.061** | −0.078** | −0.065 |
| | (0.027) | (0.031) | (0.057) |
| Poverty at School | −0.001 | −0.046* | 0.017 |
| | (0.013) | (0.026) | (0.016) |
| Constant | 0.206*** | 0.204*** | 0.269*** |
| | (0.025) | (0.027) | (0.071) |
| Observations | 349 | 309 | 40 |
| $R^2$ | 0.027 | 0.044 | 0.181 |

*Note:* *p<0.1; **p<0.05; ***p<0.01.
This table shows the results of a linear regression of normalized school covariates on the proportion of correct answers about donor-funded education projects in each school. The outcome variable is the share of correct questions about each school.

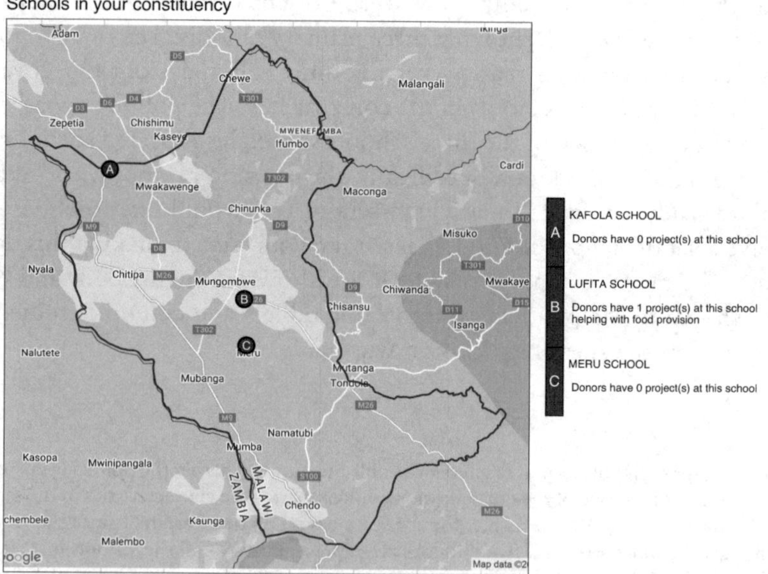


FIGURE 6.4 Example treatment map with aid information

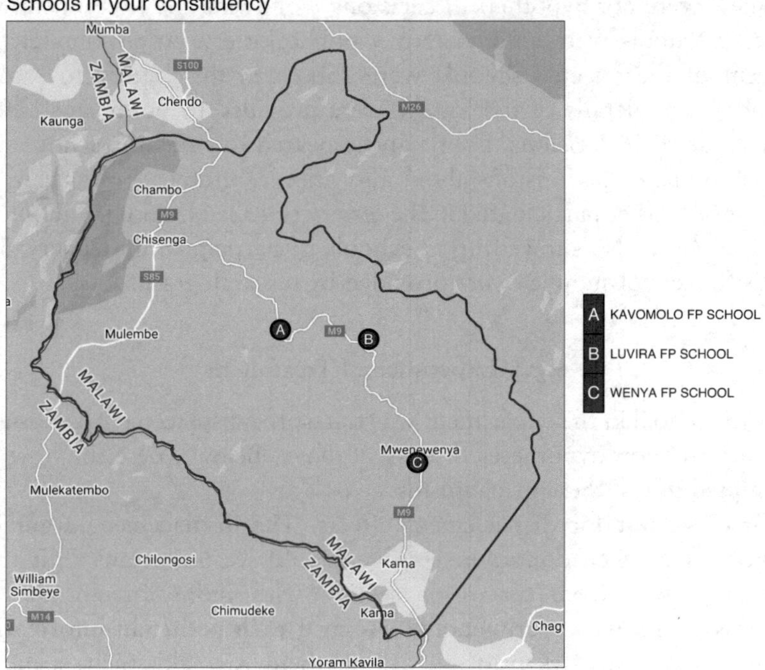


FIGURE 6.5 Example control map with no information

Each politician repeated the decision process three times, so they each saw three maps and selected three schools out of nine to receive school supplies.[51] Each decision involved the allocation of a different type of school supplies – either a set of ten solar lamps, ten teacher supply kits, or ten English dictionaries. Our focus group discussions with project stakeholders suggest that these school supplies are valued by politicians and schools. The portable, stand-alone solar lamps are useful in allowing students and teachers to work after dark. The dictionaries are helpful in lesson planning and studying. The teacher supply kits consisted of a box of chalk, rubbers, pens, notebooks, and a tote bag – basic supplies considered necessary for teachers to carry out their work. The ordering of maps, supplies, and schools was random.

[51] Because of the small number of schools in some constituencies, some politicians (21 percent) received fewer than three maps.

These were not hypothetical decisions. Following the experiment, the selected schools were entered into a public lottery. Approximately 20 percent of the selected schools were chosen in this lottery to receive supplies. The details of the lottery were provided to politicians before they made their decisions. Politicians appeared to value the school supplies and make the decisions about allocation carefully. About a third of our sample either participated in the lottery or called to inquire about the results. Many also showed up at schools to participate in delivery. The funds for school supplies were provided by research grants.

### 6.5.2 Experimental Treatments

A primary goal in the experiment was to test the displacement, oversight, and information hypotheses discussed above. Below I describe how we attempted to test these mechanisms.

First, we test for displacement effects. The displacement argument suggests that when donors invest, we should see politicians shift their spending away from places or sectors with more foreign aid. To test this claim, we experimentally assigned each politician information about donor activities prior to asking them to make their spending decisions.

On a randomly assigned half of the maps shown to politicians, we included information from donors about foreign aid at schools in their constituency over the last five years (using the data described in Section 6.5).[52] Specifically, the information detailed how many donor-supported projects had been carried out at each individual school and the type of donor support provided at that school. An example map for the treatment group is shown in Figure 6.4. It contains a side panel with information about foreign aid projects. An example control map is shown in Figure 6.5. It contains no information about foreign aid projects.

Our expectation was that the aid information treatment would cause politicians to update their beliefs about the number and type of foreign aid projects in the mapped schools. As a consequence, by comparing politicians' decisions when they receive treatment versus control maps,

[52] Since we're looking at within respondent treatment effects, the maps were randomized within respondent-level blocks. In addition to the aid information treatment, politicians also received information about school needs and voting in a cross-factorial treatment design. For details on the additional treatments and their effects, see Jablonski and Seim (2023).

we can isolate the causal effect of learning about foreign aid projects on the allocation decisions of politicians.[53]

We create two variables to measure aid at the school level: *Aid Project Count* equalling the log(+1) of the number of projects in each school and *Aid Good Types* equalling the log(+1) of the number types of project. Aid project types include capacity building, construction, health services, food provision, community support, gender issues, and teacher training. Some aid projects encapsulate several project types. Since politicians might care both about the number of foreign aid projects and the scale of donors' involvement in a school, and since both types of information were provided in the aid information treatment, we predicted that both variables would have similar effects on spending outcomes. Seventy-three (73 percent) of our treatment maps contained variation across schools in the number of foreign aid projects.

To test for oversight effects, we attempted to increase the perceived risk that donors would observe (and potentially sanction) politicians' spending decisions. Specifically, we told a random half of the politicians in the study (truthfully) that their decisions would be compiled in a report to major donors. Prior to making any spending decisions, the interviewer told the politician the following:

> Please note that Tearfund will distribute a report about your choices today. This report will be provided to major donors in Malawi, and will include your name and a description of the schools you have selected today. The report will also explain the lottery. I have brought with me a copy of the letter that donors will receive.

The politicians were then provided with an example of the report that would be shared with donors (see the example in Appendix E). As promised in the survey, we sent a report to all major donors working in the Malawi education sector at the conclusion of this study. The report contained information about the decisions that politicians made about where to allocate funding.

If politicians believe that donors have strong preferences and condition aid on politician performance, then it should be the case that politicians spend differently when they know that this report will be shared with donors.[54]

[53] We cannot identify updating directly, so our estimand is an intention to treat (ITT) effect in which we assume that politicians update their priors about foreign aid projects in the expected direction in response to information.

[54] Additionally, some politicians received information telling them that their choices would be announced on community radio. We see little evidence that this radio treatment had an effect on politician spending decisions. See discussion in Jablonski and Seim (2023).

### 6.5.3 Identifying School Characteristics

I hypothesized that displacement and oversight might also change the way in which politicians weigh need and politics in their spending decisions. To test whether this is the case, we need a way to measure how needy and politically pivotal a particular school is.

To identify how needy a school is, I rely on official school-level statistics from the Education Management Information System (EMIS) at the Malawi Ministry of Education Science and Technology.[55] Though not an exhaustive assessment of school need, these data allow me to identify three highly visible characteristics of need. First, I measure structural overcrowding using the ratio of students per classroom. Structural overcrowding is among the more severe problems facing schools in Malawi: On average, primary school classrooms have 138 students each, though some have more than 300. Second, I measure teacher overcrowding using the number of students per teacher. Due to chronic problems of low or unpaid salaries, teachers in Malawi are often heavily overcommitted and underpaid. Primary school teachers are expected to teach 75 students on average, though some have more than 200. (The global average is twenty-three students per teacher.[56]) Third, I measure the quality of existing classrooms by looking at the ratio of temporary classrooms to permanent classrooms. The quality of temporary classrooms varies in Malawi, but they are often of extremely poor quality–sometimes a lean-to or a borrowed residence.

These measures generally align with the priorities of teachers themselves. In our survey of teachers,[57] we asked head teachers to name, in order of priority, the important needs of the school. The highest priority issues by far (named by over 60 percent of head teachers and citizens) were overcrowding in classrooms or teachers' houses. Teachers also frequently mentioned needing more staff, various facility improvements including electricity, and learning materials. Additionally, in our interviews with politicians about their development decisions in the education sector, they most frequently mentioned enrollment levels, the number of classrooms, and the number of teachers houses. That said, there are some

[55] These data are from 2014 and encompass over 99 percent of all schools in Malawi. They are collected approximately biannually by district education offices through the support of local headmasters. These data have been collected and refined over multiple years and independent assessment exercises on these data suggest a high level of reliability (Bernbaum and Moses 2011).

[56] World Bank 2024.

[57] See Appendix A.

need-based characteristics that these data do not capture: For instance, several politicians also mentioned that they use measures of school quality and achievement, such as the passing rate, or that they simply examine the "look of the infrastructure," or "just see the nature of the school."

To simplify the analysis, I used these data to create an overall index of school need, *School Need*, which is equal to the sum of the z-scores of the three measures of school need.[58]

In order to measure the political characteristics of communities, I collected polling station-level data from the Malawi Electoral Commission on the votes received by all candidates for council and MP seats. A large proportion (68 percent) of the schools in our sample were also polling stations, allowing us to directly measure political support in those communities. For those schools in our sample (32 percent) which were not used as polling stations, measure political support by using the geographically nearest polling station to the school.

As discussed in Chapter 4, there are good reasons to believe that politicians in Malawi bias spending in favor of communities where they have a large number of supporters.[59] To measure the targeting of core supporters, I create a variable *Incumbent Percent*, which equals the percentage of votes received by the incumbent politician in the nearest polling station to a school.

In addition to changing the probability that politicians target political supporters, displacement and oversight might change the extent to which politicians attempt to gain personally from foreign aid. As one measure of such corruption, I identify whether a politician's family member attended a particular school, since these schools might be particularly likely to benefit from networks of patronage. I coded this by asking the politicians to indicate which schools their children or their family's children attend.

### 6.5.4 Spending Behavior in the Control Group

I begin by considering spending patterns in the control group: when politicians did not receive information about the schools in their constituency. In Figure 6.6, I show the coefficients from eight different

58 *School Need* $= \frac{x-\mu_1}{\sigma_1} + \frac{x-\mu_2}{\sigma_2} + \frac{x-\mu_3}{\sigma_3}$ where $\mu_i$ and $\sigma_i$ indicate the within ward/constituency means and standard deviations of students per teacher, students per classroom, and proportion of temporary classrooms for all available primary schools in Malawi.

59 Jablonski and Seim 2023; Dionne, Kramon, and Roberts 2013; Brazys, Heaney, and Walsh 2015.

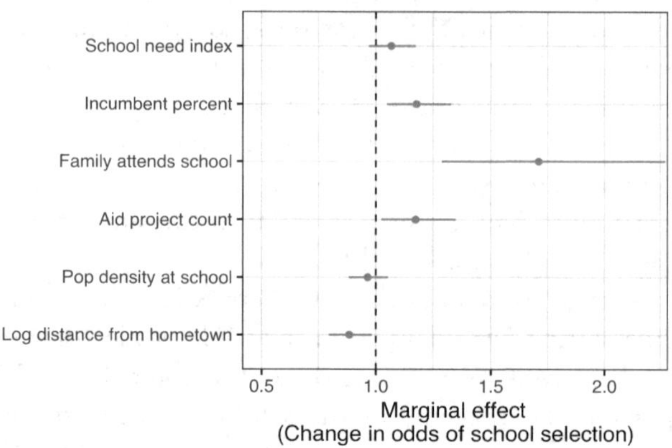


FIGURE 6.6 Effects of school characteristics on the school selection
*Note*: This figure shows the coefficients of separate conditional logistic regressions of school selection on baseline variables. The sample is limited to maps that do not contain treatment information related to the school characteristic. Ninety-five percent confidence intervals are shown in the horizontal lines. Standard errors are clustered on politician. Continuous variables are normalized for comparison purposes. Control variables include *Log Permanent Classrooms, Log Temporary Classrooms, Log Teacher Houses Permanent, Log Teacher Houses Temporary, Opposition Percent Votes (for MP and LC), Log Enrollment, Number of Aid Projects, Family Attends School, Incumbent Percent at Polling Station, and School Need Index.*

conditional logit regressions of school selection on school characteristics.[60]

The results suggest that politicians do take need *and* politics into account when making spending decisions. A one standard deviation increase in a school's need index increases the odds that a school is selected by 1.07. Likewise, schools in electorally supportive communities are also more likely to be selected–as we would expect if politicians weigh the electoral consequences of their actions. A standard deviation increase in percent votes for a politician (21 percentage points) is associated with a 1.18 increase in the odds of a school being selected. Politicians also appear to prefer to spend on close family networks: The odds that a school with a family member is selected are nearly double (1.7 times) the odds that a school without a family member is selected.

[60] Regressions are conditioned on each choice set (map). In each regression, we subset the data to include only maps in the relevant control group: Those maps without information about that school characteristic (e.g., the regression of school selection on Aid Project Count excludes maps with the Aid Information Treatment).

It is worth noting that this strong effect of electoral returns is consistent with the theoretical expectations and observations in Chapters 3 and 4, and implies that politicians indeed seek to lobby donors to achieve electoral gains.

Schools in the control group are *more* likely to be selected when they have received more projects or types of projects from donors. Given the weak preexisting knowledge surrounding foreign aid projects, I do not interpret this to mean that politicians in the control group target schools with more aid spending: rather, I see this as evidence that donors and politicians often have overlapping spending priorities. This is also suggestive evidence that the challenges that politicians face in coordinating with donors and learning about donor activities indeed result in a more inefficient allocation of resources.

### 6.5.5 Displacement Effects

I argued that foreign aid would cause politicians to invest less in areas targeted by donors (Hypothesis 1). The results of the aid information experiment suggest that this is indeed the case. In Figure 6.7, I show estimates of how providing aid information changed the odds that a school with aid projects would receive funding from a politician.[61]

The results suggest that foreign aid indeed crowds out a significant share of public spending. On average, Aid Information decreases the odds of a school with one foreign aid project being selected by 0.21 ($p = 0.05$).[62] Within our sample, these estimates suggest that each aid project reduces the probability of additional funds being allocated to a school by about 8 percent. While this is certainly a meaningful effect, it is also worth noting that this effect is much smaller than what many have assumed. Several influential studies based on more correlational data have suggested that upward of 50–70 percent of public spending is displaced by foreign aid.[63] Our data suggest that these extreme scenarios are unlikely.

In addition to the number of aid projects, we consider the effect of information about the number of donor-provided goods types (*Aid Good*

[61] Specifically, I regress school choice on the interaction between the *Aid Information Treatment* and *Aid Project Count* or *Aid Good Types*. I use a conditional logit estimator conditioned on each choice set (map). Errors are clustered on politician. See further discussion of estimation in Appendix E.

[62] On average, schools have 0.9 aid projects.

[63] Marć 2017; Feyzioglu, Swaroop, and Zhu 1998; Chatterjee, Giuliano, and Kaya 2012.

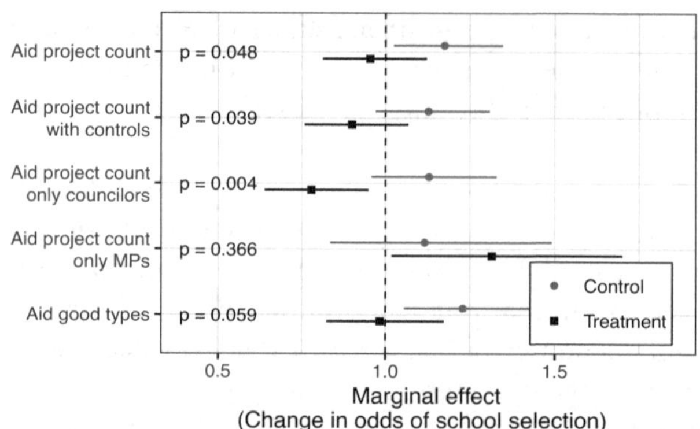


FIGURE 6.7 Effects of aid information on the school selection
*Note*: Circles indicate estimated effects of *Aid Project Count* or *Aid Good Types* on the odds of a school being selected in the control group (those appearing on maps without the Aid Information Treatment). Triangles indicate estimated effects in the treatment group (those appearing on maps with the Aid Information Treatment). Horizontal lines indicate 95 percent confidence intervals. The p-values on the left indicate the probability our treatment estimate is consistent with a null effect.

*Types*). We find that when a politician learns from the Aid Information Treatment that there are three types of goods being delivered by donors at a school (the average is 2.6), the odds of the politician allocating to that school decrease by 0.91 ($p = 0.05$).

We also see that the fungibility effect is much larger among councilors than MPs. This was unexpected. One possible explanation may be that councilors were less confident that they knew what was going on in their constituency. We find, for instance, that 81 percent of LCs claim that they find the information useful compared to 64 percent of MPs. However, these differences should be interpreted with caution due to the small sample of MPs.

### 6.5.6 Consequences of Displacement

I next consider how the aid information treatment changes the way in which politicians chose to distribute funds. As I discussed earlier, many worry that the displacement of spending will increase the tendency for politicians to spend money on corruption or patronage, or that politicians will spend more on richer areas, making the poor increasingly dependent upon donors for their welfare. To test these claims, I interact the aid information treatment with school-level variables intended to

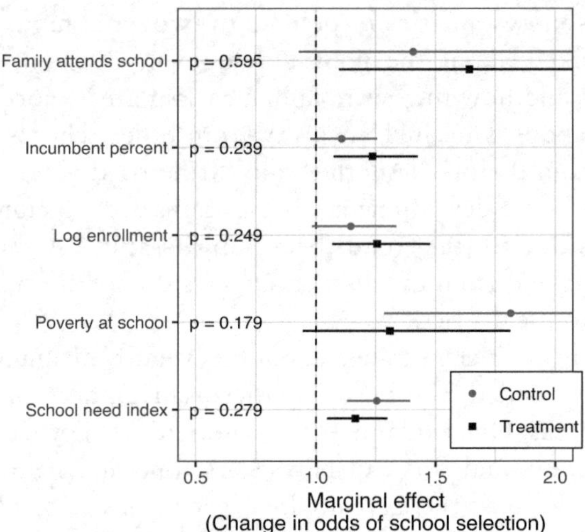


FIGURE 6.8 Effects of school characteristics on the school selection for politicians in the aid information treatment
*Note*: This figure shows the coefficients of separate conditional logit regressions of school selection on baseline variables by treatment status with 95 percent confidence intervals. Standard errors are clustered on politician. Continuous variables are normalized for comparison purposes. On the left side we include p-values for whether the observed difference between treatment and control is consistent with the null hypothesis.

measure corruption, patronage, and need. By comparing the effects of these variables on spending between treatment and control groups, we can determine whether the aid information treatment caused politicians to make significantly different spending decisions.

In Figure 6.8, we see that spending decisions in treatment and control groups are similar. Aid information appears to result in slightly fewer goods being allocated to overcrowded schools, as well as to schools where politicians' family members attend. However, these differences are small and mostly not statistically significant.[64]

To gain more insight into why foreign aid changes politicians' spending decisions, we also asked the politicians in our study for a brief explanation regarding the choices they made. These explanations suggest causal mechanisms to explain the displacement effects we observe.

[64] There may also be small differences which cannot be identified with our sample. This is particularly true for identifying treatment effects on the selection of family members' schools since this represents only a small proportion of schools in our sample (5 percent).

In their responses, politicians pointed to two main motivations. First, politicians talked about the poor development decisions that donors were making, and how they were failing certain areas. For instance, one said, "This school is located far away from other schools and there is no support from donors." Another said "[t]he road is far away... and no access and some development organizations are reluctant to support those schools due to [the] road [being] impassable." A third said "the school is in far end from the district. Donors do not consider this when they come into the district."

Additionally, politicians talked about the welfare advantages of investing in areas excluded by donors or the disadvantages of spending in overlapping areas. One explained "the school [does] not receive any support from donors and this can be the first one and help the school." Another said "Because there are no donors in some areas, it has given me influence to do more." In total, 17 percent of politicians specifically discussed concerns about overlapping with donor projects and 16 percent specifically mentioned concerns about fairness or need.

This qualitative and quantitative evidence presents a challenge to aid critics who argue that the displacement of public spending has large negative effects on welfare, development, and democracy. While we might challenge whether the effects in this study are true universally, the data here suggests that politicians are mostly responding to foreign aid in a way that they think improves public welfare. We don't see any evidence that politicians weigh personal or political considerations more highly as a result of donor investments.

### 6.5.7 Consequences of Oversight

Finally, consider whether politicians who learned about the donor report made different decisions during the experiment. As I discussed earlier, donors often pressure politicians to put in place particular policies, and politicians often act as if they are worried about displeasing donors. What is less clear is whether such oversight shapes local politicians' decisions about the distribution of public spending.

The results in Figure 6.9 are not consistent with Hypotheses 3. Politicians who knew about the report were no more likely to spend on needy

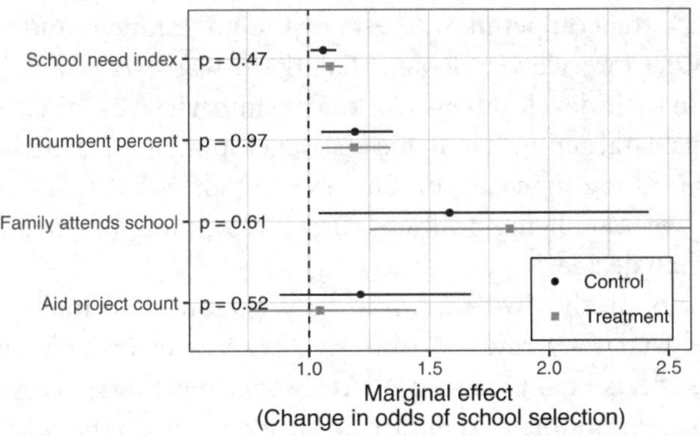


FIGURE 6.9 Effects of school characteristics on the school selection for politicians in the donor report treatment

*Note*: This figure shows the coefficients of separate conditional logit regressions of school selection on baseline variables by treatment status with 95 percent confidence intervals. Standard errors are clustered on politician. Continuous variables are normalized for comparison purposes. On the left side, I include p-values for whether the observed difference between treatment and control is consistent with the null hypothesis.

schools, or to refrain from spending on political supporters or family members.[65]

Why were politicians in our study not more worried about donor oversight? It is possible that this was a weak treatment. Politicians may not have believed that we would indeed share this information with donors. However, our research team recorded that politicians almost universally read the example report carefully. Alternatively, there might be something unique about the decision environments, and it's possible that politicians would have been more susceptible to this treatment if they were making a decision in a legislative context.

However, I think the most likely explanation is that donors lack the information – and perhaps the interest – to sanction distributional decisions which are not entirely focused on need. To assess whether this is the case, I later asked representatives of five major education donors in Malawi the following question: "When working with donors, government officials sometimes prioritize political or personal interest over the development needs of a community. When this is the case, how do

[65] Some politicians also received a parallel treatment telling them that their decisions would be announced on local radio. This treatment also had null effects.

you balance the competing interests of the government and the community?"[66] One interviewee denied that there was ever space for political influence in their development work. Two interviewees said they observed that political targeting often harms development in Malawi, but said there was nothing they can do. One explained: "[W]e can't do anything, otherwise we start being political. Us, development partners, we just go by what they decide."

Only two of the five discussed any action they might take. Both mentioned that they refer to objective criteria in order to validate the politicians' decisions. One said, "[At district meetings] everybody wants to take the programme to their area. But when we do the objective analysis of the data, we defeat their decision." Another said, "To manage risk: we make the process as transparent as possible. We develop criteria with them with objective indicators. For example, we want to identify schools with specific characteristics (as example, school should have a pass rate of X%, be in sufficiently hard-to-reach area, etc." Neither mentioned any specific action they would take to sanction officials who failed to make effective development decisions. In contrast, every donor was able to name specific actions they would take to sanction an official who stole from a donor-funded project.

These interviews suggest that donors do care about the politicization and misuse of development, but often feel they have little capacity to do much about it.

## 6.6 CONCLUSIONS

In order to deliver effective policies, politicians in aid-dependent democracies have to coordinate with a range of donors, NGOs, and their agents. The challenges and costs of effective coordination potentially have a number of distortionary effects on policymaking. In this chapter I discuss the only large scale field experiment yet to study these effects. From this Malawi evidence, I make several arguments about how foreign aid–and aid dependence generally–can shape policy.

First, politicians in Malawi demand more information and consultation than they in fact receive. Despite saying they consider what donors are doing, almost all interviewed officials complain about the frequency and form of their consultations with donors and NGOs. This lack of consultation, combined with a high level of complexity and fragmentation,

[66] See Appendix B.

leads to systemic gaps in what politicians know about donor activities in their constituencies. Data from a quiz I administered to politicians suggests that politicians especially struggle to learn about the activities and funding arrangements of major international donors, especially in more remote areas of their constituency. These findings are consistent with the observation in Chapter 2 that international donors are less likely to consult with politicians than are NGOs.

I also establish that these gaps in information can meaningfully change spending policy. When politicians in Malawi know more about the activities of international donors, they are more likely to spend in areas that are neglected by donors. This finding suggests that politicians' information gaps also contribute to *distortions* in public spending. If politicians were better informed, it is plausible that we would see less duplication and a more equal allocation of spending.

These findings also provide nuance to debates over the political and economic consequences of displacement and fungibility. Consistent with evidence from other contexts, we find that foreign aid indeed crowds out other forms of spending. However, the study challenges those who claim that these displacement effects will make it easier for politicians to spend in ways that might be distortionary or politically biased. While we find strong evidence that politicians consider politics and family connections in their spending decisions, we mostly fail to reject the null hypothesis that the kinds of schools that benefit from politician spending are systemically different in treatment versus control. If anything, qualitative evidence from politicians appears to suggest that displacement is motivated by concerns about donor neglect and citizen welfare.

Finally, the study informs debates about the role of donor oversight. On one hand, it is clear from donor and politician interviews that politicians in Malawi are sensitive to the opinions of donors. Further, we have many accounts in Malawi and elsewhere of donors successfully pressuring for meaningful policy reforms. Given this, we were surprised to find no evidence that informing major donors about politician spending decisions had any effect on what politicians did.

However, these null effects are less surprising in light of two facts. The first is that politicians are quite dismissive of donors' ability to assess community needs, and frequently complain in interviews about the way donors fail to consider development plans or idiosyncratic school characteristics. Given this, politicians were likely skeptical (probably rightly so) that donors would be capable of assessing their decisions. Second, from interviews, it is clear that donor staff find it very difficult to intervene in response to policy decisions that are politically motivated but not obviously corrupt (see also the discussion in Chapter 4 on this point).[67] Together these findings suggest that donor oversight is unlikely to have much of an effect on the misallocation or politicization of development funds where there is no explicit corruption involved.

It is also worth noting some parallels between the findings in this chapter and my argument about voter behavior in Chapter 3. Like with voter behavior, one of the main ways in which donors distort decisions is by changing politicians' information environment, and making it harder for politicians to make accurate inferences about what development activities are happening in their areas. Likewise, these adverse outcomes are not inherent to aid, and instead have more to do with the ways in which the complexity of development decisions in Malawi raise politicians' costs of information and policy coordination. As discuss in Chapter 7, some of these adverse effects might be avoided by changing modes of aid delivery.

[67] This conclusion is also consistent with Swedlund (2017a). In a survey experiment with 114 donor officials, Swedlund notes that political transgressions only increase support for aid suspension if the transgression directly affects the donor aid portfolio.

# 7

# Conclusions

## *Understanding Democracy in Aid-dependent Countries*

The Malawian economist Thandika Mkandawire, coined the term "choiceless democracies" to describe the Third Wave of aid-dependent democracies. He pointed out that, at the same time donors were funding electoral reforms in the 1990s, they were eroding sovereignty and electoral accountability by creating major alternative, off-budget, and non-transparent sources of finance and public spending that were insulated from parliamentary oversight and control. He argued that the result was that "fear of donor demands rather than citizens' wishes" were shaping government policy with the result that politicians were more accountable to foreign than domestic publics.[1]

Mkandawire's description of choiceless democracy, in many ways, still reflects politics in aid-dependent democracies today. Foreign aid continues to erode political choice and circumvent parliamentary sovereignty. Evidence from surveys and interviews in Malawi especially demonstrates the limited scope politicians have to shape constituent welfare without the support and goodwill of donors. Likewise, the evidence in Chapters 5 and 6 demonstrates that voters and politicians often lack sufficient information needed to effectively monitor what donors are doing in their area or to hold donors accountable for their actions. This erosion of choice is further fuelled by the unwillingness of many donors or Non-governmental organizations (NGOs) to meaningfully consult with elected public officials or report on their actions, particularly outside the halls of ministry offices.

[1] Mkandawire 1999, 2010.

Nonetheless, this book also demonstrates some ways in which politicians have retained choice. Despite declining budget support and government ownership over aid, politicians and governing officials are still able to bargain favorably with donors and NGOs as a way to shape service delivery and earn political credit for improvements in public welfare. These bargaining efforts shape where and how foreign aid is delivered and help politicians attract votes and win elections. The consequences of aid for elections also imply that voters retain some agency in determining how aid is spent. Nonetheless, this reliance on donors has, in a real way, transformed what democratic governance means. Despite politicians having little institutional authority over donors, many politicians see their role more in terms of influencing and monitoring donors and NGOs than affecting legislative action. For example, I show in Chapter 2 that, when asked about their responsibilities and achievements, many interviewed councilors and MPs in Malawi spoke more about monitoring donors and delivering donor-funded projects than about legislative actions. While there is considerable variation, some politicians claim to work and meet with donors more than they meet with citizens or other parliamentarians. Even in making more traditional governance decisions, I demonstrated in Chapter 6 that politicians consider what donors do, and try to balance the effects of donor and government spending on citizen welfare.

The role of donors in service delivery has also changed how *voters* think about governance. Many likewise see meeting with and lobbying donors as part of a politician's role and as something that should matter for their assessment of politician performance. For instance, the evidence from Chapter 5 demonstrates that voters in Malawi condition their views of politician performance on what foreign NGOs do in their community. These estimated effects of donors on voter beliefs and behavior are large enough to change election outcomes in many aid-dependent democracies.

In light of this, I propose an alternative conceptualization of elections and accountability in aid-dependent democracies. Donors – much like parliaments and more traditional democratic actors – are an important, and sometimes the most important, means for politicians to deliver resources to citizens in highly aid-dependent democracies. Because of this, voters condition their assessments of incumbent performance not just on legislative action, but on how foreign aid is spent in their community and on their beliefs about the role that politicians have played in influencing that spending.

I argue that there are two features of foreign aid that make these voter assessments particularly challenging. The first is a lack of transparency. Much donor spending is not formally budgeted and does not go through parliamentary appropriations. This, combined with a high degree of complexity in budgeting, procurement, and delivery, means that voters and politicians often lack credible sources of information about how foreign aid is spent or about the role of government offices in shaping that spending. The second feature is coproduction. Many decisions about foreign aid spending (and indeed government spending) result from bargaining between government officials, donors, NGOs, and bureaucrats. This means that voters cannot easily make inferences about politician performance and preferences from observing development spending.

In Chapter 3, I show how electoral behavior changes when these features are included in models of retrospective voting. Specifically, I reconceptualize the problem of electoral accountability in aid-dependent democracies as an agency problem with incomplete information and co-production. Like in any democracy, citizens try to reelect those incumbents that work hard for their interests; however, they lack information about the terms of aid projects and the relative role of politicians, donors, and other stakeholders in making development decisions. I show how this implies that voters will often make inaccurate inferences about politician performance from aid, and that the effect of foreign aid on electoral outcomes will depend upon the gap between voters' expectations of politician performance and aid spending outcomes.

This uncertainty and bias in voter beliefs can indeed be bad for accountability. Foreign aid can cause citizens to vote against their interests and to undeservedly credit or punish politicians for what are in fact the actions of donors. This uncertainty can also give politicians scope and incentives to mislead voters about their role in aid delivery. These adverse effects are greater the less information voters have about aid spending and the less control politicians have over the aid spending process. Evidence from panel surveys and experiments in Chapter 5 confirms that voters make inaccurate inferences about politician effort and that the effects of aid on voting are conditional on voter beliefs.

At the same time, foreign aid can improve accountability by increasing the visibility of politician effort. One of the greatest challenges politicians in fiscally constrained settings face is simply doing anything for their constituents. Budgets for nonrecurrent expenses are scarce, especially for politicians who are lower in the political hierarchy. This means that politicians, however, noble their ambitions, can struggle to campaign on any accomplishments. Surveys with Malawian voters in Chapter 5 illustrate how extreme this problem can be: Only 9 percent of respondents who had benefited from a council project were aware that the incumbent councilor had done anything at all. However imperfectly, foreign aid is therefore an important tool for many politicians to signal to voters that they are, in fact, working on their behalf, and politicians often point to NGO and donor projects as main accomplishments when they are talking to voters.

The scale of these uncertainty and visibility effects will depend a lot on how foreign aid is delivered. When voters are well-informed about politician effort, and foreign aid provides a strong signal of that effort, then foreign aid should generally be good for accountability. When voters are misinformed, and foreign aid spending decisions do not reliably signal politician effort, foreign aid can make it harder for voters to hold politicians accountable.

## 7.1 POLITICS BEYOND MALAWI

Much of the evidence in this book comes from Malawi. While in some ways the situation faced by politicians, voters, and donors in Malawi is similar to other aid-dependent democracies, there are also ways in which these circumstances are more unique. The budgetary situation faced by the Malawi government is especially dire and donor dependent. Malawian ministries are largely reliant on unstable revenue from agricultural taxation and foreign budget support for delivering services. Donors have historically played a critical role in filling the gaps left by government service provision. Among other consequences, this gives donors considerable bargaining power over the government. Malawi is also somewhat unique (though certainly not alone) in the fragmentation and decentralization of the aid environment. Due to donor concerns about corruption, donors have empowered NGOs in the aid delivery process and limited government ownership. How might the effects of aid on electoral behavior differ in other aid-dependent democracies?

This is a difficult question to answer; however, the theory in this book suggests a couple important scope conditions for the argument. First, the argument requires that politicians have a say in the distribution of aid funds – and are recognized to have a say by voters. Further, when we see variation in government ownership, this will affect the direction and scale of the electoral effects of aid. When voters are less likely to believe that politicians influence aid delivery, we will tend to see smaller electoral effects of aid. When voters are more likely to expect politician influence, we should see larger effects.

I have provided some evidence that incomplete government ownership is a norm in most of the world's poorest democracies. Both donors and governments have explicit requirements for government consultation and oversight. Moreover, survey evidence from a wide variety of contexts confirms that voters see politicians as playing a key role in the delivery of foreign aid funds.[2] There is nonetheless variation on the extent to which donors give politicians control and ownership over aid.[3] Voter beliefs about government ownership will also be affected by the modality of aid. In the case of programmatic, or budgetary aid, for instance, voters may assume more government ownership than when aid is delivered as independent projects or through NGOs.

A second scope condition for the argument is that voters have incomplete knowledge of the relative role of donors versus politicians in development. It is difficult to assess cross-country variation in voter knowledge of government involvement in aid; however, given the complexity of donor ecosystems in many aid-dependent countries, it is reasonable to assume this as a general truth. Indeed several country-level studies document that aid recipients most often struggle to identify the source of aid funds.[4] That said, voter knowledge will likely depend a lot on how foreign aid is delivered. In contexts like Malawi or Zambia, where much aid is delivered through NGOs, for instance, voters are likely to have less knowledge about the source of aid funds than in contexts where aid delivery is more centralized. Where citizens have more knowledge, we would expect voters to be able to make more reliable inferences about politician performance. This could make aid more politically valuable and reduce adverse effects on accountability.

I am aware of only one cross-country survey that attempts to get at voter beliefs about the relationships between governments and

[2] Jablonski 2014; Springman 2023; Guiteras and Mobarak 2015; Baldwin and Winters 2023; Ijaz 2025; Briggs 2012; Cruz and Schneider 2017; O'Brien-Udry 2021.

[3] Dietrich 2021; Swedlund 2017b.

[4] Dietrich, Mahmud, and Winters 2018; Cruz and Schneider 2017; Blair and Roessler 2021; De Juan, Hofman, and Koos 2023.

international donors. In 2008, Afrobarometer asked citizens across 20 African countries whether international donors and NGOs had "too little, too much, or about the right amount of influence" over their government. While not a perfect measure, this question should offer an indication of how much power their government has over donors. Additionally, Afrobarometer asked respondents how much international donors and NGOs "help your country." Responses to this question should give us an indication of citizen beliefs about their country's and government's dependence on donors.

The results suggest that citizens in Malawi are about average in terms of their beliefs about donor influence and dependence. I summarize the data in Figures 7.1 and 7.2. Malawians are more likely than Kenyans, Nigerians, or Botswanans to say they have too much influence. However, if we look at countries at the more extreme end of donor dependence – Lesotho, Zambia, Madagascar, and Mozambique – citizens are more likely than Malawians to say that donors have too much influence. Likewise, Malawians are about average among African countries in how they view the scale of donor help to their country.

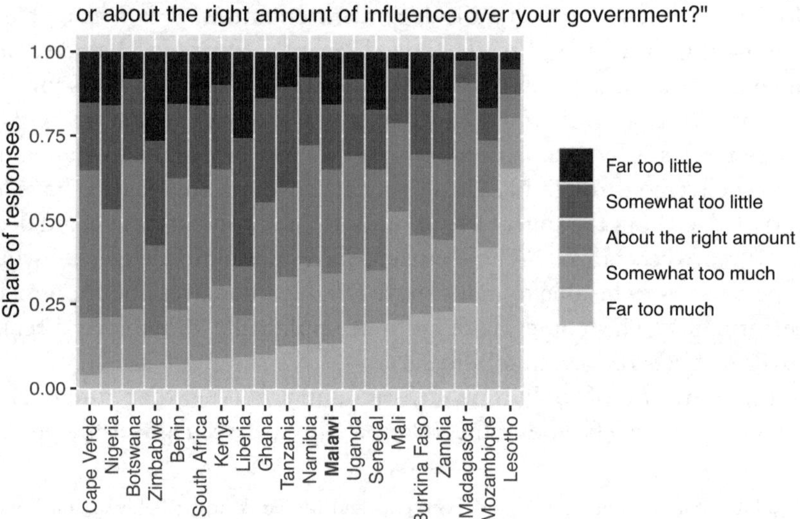


FIGURE 7.1 Citizen beliefs about donor influence
*Note:* This figure shows average responses to the question "Do you think that each of the following has too little, too much, or about the right amount of influence over your government: International donors and NGOs" in round 4 of Afrobarometer (2008). Excludes "don't know" and "refused" responses.

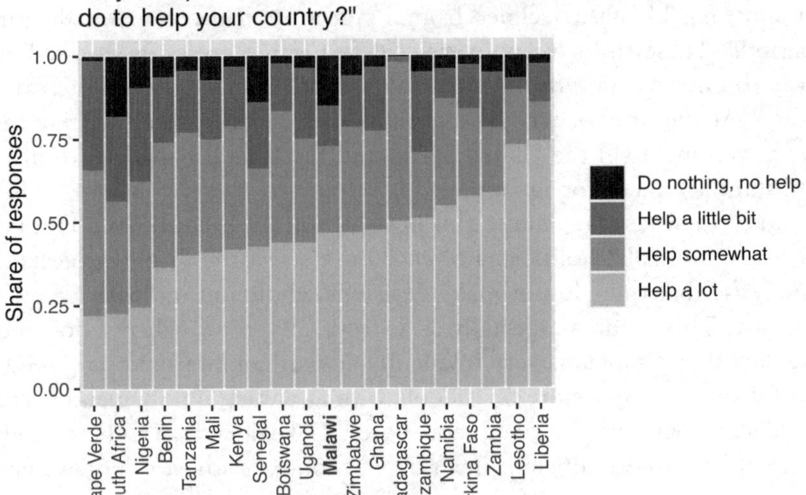


FIGURE 7.2 Citizen beliefs about donor help
*Note:* This figure shows average responses to the question "In your opinion, how much do each of the following do to help your country, or haven't you heard enough to say: Other international donors and NGOs (apart from the United Nations)?" in round 4 of Afrobarometer (2008). Excludes "don't know" and "refused" responses.

## 7.2 POLICY IMPLICATIONS

Sometimes officials at donor organizations see working with politicians as a sort of necessary evil: important for building capacity and sustaining development, but often a source of corruption and mismanagement. For instance, a senior official at a major international charity in Malawi said the following when asked about balancing political interests in development:

> What I have seen in campaigns is that Constituency Development Fund (CDF) projects become more of a concern [than foreign aid]. [Politicians] do not use it usually for the right projects. I think it is not a good thing. A politician is not a development practitioner. It has no strong monitoring system. The money would be better with an NGO.[5]

Similar concerns about misuse have contributed to a decline in government ownership over aid. The amount of aid channeled through the public sector in low-income countries has declined from an estimate high

[5] Interview A6; see Appendix A.

of 54 percent of aid in 2010 to 41 percent in 2021. The amount of budget support has likewise declined from 9 percent to 7 percent over the same period.[6] These shifts away from local ownership are often justified as a way to improve aid effectiveness and reduce mismanagement or corruption.[7] At the time of writing, concerns over misuse are also being used by governments in the United States and the United Kingdom to justify substantial cuts to foreign aid.

In some ways, the data in this book affirm these concerns about government control.[8] Politicians often do not select the "right projects" in the sense that they do not make decisions wholly on the basis of public welfare. This point is especially clear from Chapter 6, where I document the fact that politicians very frequently advised an international NGO to spend substantially more on schools with attending family members and in places where they received more votes. The evidence in Chapter 4 likewise affirms that politicians in a range of contexts advise donors to favor their (often more well-off) copartisans.

Yet this book also highlights the costs of going with an NGO rather than the government. While there might be short-term welfare gains from limiting government ownership, there are potentially longer-term consequences for electoral accountability. When governments have more ownership over aid spending, aid spending will be more reflective of politician preferences and effort. As long as voters are well-informed about how aid is delivered, this can decrease the ability of politicians to mislead voters through credit claiming and can improve voters' ability to assess and sanction politician performance.

In Chapter 6, I also highlight another cost of limiting government ownership. In aid-dependent democracies, effective policymaking requires coordination with donors. Yet I show that Malawian politicians do not receive enough information and consultation from donors and NGOs to coordinate effectively. Further, I show evidence that these information gaps are large and contribute to less equitable policymaking. What this means is that even if limiting government ownership improves the effectiveness of aid, it may come at the cost of less effective coordination and government policy effectiveness.

[6] OECD 2024.

[7] Winters 2014; Dietrich 2013; Gibson, Ostrom, and Shivakumar 2005.

[8] For discussion of some of the debates over government ownership see Honig (2018), Armon (2007), Gibson, Ostrom, and Shivakumar (2005), Easterly (2014), and Swedlund and Lierl (2020).

That said, this argument does not necessarily favor involving more government stakeholders into the aid decision-making process. Involving more governmental (or nongovernmental) stakeholders in the aid delivery process without also centralizing oversight and control risks exacerbating some of the attribution and visibility challenges discussed in Chapter 3 by making the chains of attribution more complex and varied. From the standpoint of electoral accountability, what is important is to clarify responsibility for development decision-making, not adding new layers of authority. To improve democratic accountability, this argument favors forms of aid delivery that provide formal and transparent decision making power to politicians, parliaments, and councils. This could, but does not have to, involve forms of aid delivery like budget support and programmatic aid that are centrally managed and formally in-budget.

This book also challenges the idea that international development policy is ever truly apolitical. Many donors have an explicit policy of not interfering in domestic politics. For instance, The World Bank's articles of agreement state: "The Bank and its officers shall not interfere in the political affairs of any member; nor shall they be influenced in their decisions by the political character of the member or members concerned."[9] Likewise, influential studies have argued that the political effects of aid depend on donor intent or fungibility.[10] While not denying the importance of donor intent, the findings in this book suggest that foreign aid will almost always have consequences for political behavior and elections. Even when aid is channeled away from the government, there remains considerable scope for voter uncertainty about the role of the government. To some extent, by trying to avoid politics and corruption, donors may do particular harm to democracy by decreasing the visibility of politician effort and increasing voter uncertainty about the role of the government in public welfare.

9 World Bank 2012.

10 Bermeo 2016, 2011; Morrison 2014; Altincekic and Bearce 2014.

# Appendix A

## Survey Details

### A.1 SURVEYS WITH POLITICIANS IN MALAWI

I conducted three separate surveys with politicians in Malawi. All surveys were codesigned and fielded by Brigitte Seim at the University of Minnesota. Jimmy Mkandawire (Malawi Ministry of Labour and Statistics) and Johan Ahlbäck (LSE) were responsible for on-site management of these surveys. Additional assistance was also provided by Petra Matsi and Nonne Engelbrecht. The survey firm, rtSurvey, assisted with the technology for displaying the survey and managing survey output for most of these studies. The enumeration itself was always conducted by a trained and local enumeration team.[1]

First, in 2015 and 2016, we conducted an in-person survey with 333 elected councilors. The purpose of this survey was to collect information about councilor spending decisions and to pilot the experimental protocol we describe in Chapter 6. I especially draw on this study to assess the effects of foreign aid on voting in Chapter 5. This was an in-person survey with trained Malawian enumerators. Further details on this survey can be found at Jablonski and Seim (2018). A full survey instrument can be found on the preregistration statement at http://egap.org/registration/1588.

Second, following this survey, we randomly sampled 101 of these councilors for a follow-up phone survey. This phone survey asked the politicians to describe in more detail how they get information about constituents and donor activities. It also asked politicians to describe their recent interactions with donors. I draw on this survey in Chapter 2

[1] Jimmy Mkandawire, Bright Chimatiro, Francis Kamungu, Frank Sulamoyo, Richard Ganiza, Frazier Mkwaila, Hector Honde, and Felix Chauluka.

to explain how frequently politicians interact with different kinds of donors.

Third, in spring of 2017, we conducted a third survey with 125 in-office Members of Parliament (MPs) and 335 in-office Local Councilors (LCs) in Malawi, or 63 percent and 73 percent of each population, respectively. The purpose of this survey was to collect information about what politicians know about their constituencies, as well as to field the experiment described in Chapter 6. We also collected additional information about politicians' interactions with donors as described in Chapter 2. Further details on this survey can be found in Jablonski and Seim (2023). All original survey instruments can be found on the dataverse at https://doi.org/10.7910/DVN/HS5R5S. I draw on data from this survey to describe heterogeneity in politician-donor relationships in Chapter 2. I also draw on these data to assess the effects of the experimental treatments described in Chapter 6.

No politicians refused to participate in these surveys. The main reason for sample attrition was the difficulty of reaching some politicians (particularly MPs) due to their frequent travel schedule. Some politicians were also excluded for data availability reasons. See attrition statistics in Appendix A. All participants were offered compensation for their time.

These surveys were funded by AidData at the College of William and Mary and the United States Agency for International Development (USAID) Global Development Lab through cooperative agreement AID-OAA-A-12-00096, by The Suntory and Toyota International Centres for Economics and Related Disciplines, and by the London School of Economics and Political Science.

These studies were reviewed and approved by the London School of Economics Research Ethics Committee and the Malawi National Commission on Science and Technology of Malawi. Participants provided verbal consent prior to participating in all studies. Per agreement with interviewees and ethics bodies, all identifying information is redacted.

### A.1.1 Politician Sample Characteristics

We have 460 politicians included in the main politician survey referred to in the text. Out of 462 Local Councilors (LCs), 335 were included in the sample. Out of 193 MPs, 125 were included in our sample. Politicians were excluded largely due to missing data on key variables (e.g., due to by-elections) or because there were not enough schools to make the treatment protocol feasible. Additionally, a few MPs were excluded

TABLE A.1 *Local councilor sample statistics*

| Variable | In_Sample | Out_of_Sample |
|---|---|---|
| Mean School Enrollment | 938.859 (411.212) | 1566.974 (964.155) |
| Mean Number of Teachers | 13.26 (5.631) | 20.948 (12.028) |
| Mean Student to Teacher Ratio | 72.946 (18.749) | 77.365 (26.933) |
| Number of Aid Projects | 11.03 (10.836) | 4.681 (7.567) |
| Number of Schools | 12.94 (6.226) | 6.447 (5.295) |
| Turnout | 0.699 (0.086) | 0.678 (0.129) |
| Incumbent Victory Margin | 0.259 (0.193) | 0.172 (0.148) |
| Registered Voters | 18090.91 (7642.809) | 15736.553 (14056.628) |
| Incumbent Percent | 0.49 (0.143) | 0.436 (0.12) |
| DPP Incumbent | 0.334 (0.471) | 0.468 (0.504) |
| UDF Incumbent | 0.036 (0.186) | 0.021 (0.146) |
| MCP Incumbent | 0.232 (0.422) | 0.234 (0.428) |
| PP Incumbent | 0.104 (0.306) | 0.043 (0.204) |
| Independent Incumbent | 0.069 (0.253) | 0.064 (0.247) |
| Average School Population Density | 11.356 (15.838) | 39.7 (63.663) |

because they were travelling or otherwise unavailable. No politicians refused to participate.

Our sample is reasonably representative of the country as a whole. In Tables A.1 and A.2, we show variable means for included and excluded wards and constituencies with standard deviations in parentheses.

Across both groups, population characteristics (turnout and number of registered voters) are well balanced. Since we were forced to exclude some smaller wards, our LC sample includes, on average, more schools and lower average enrolment. We generally see good balance on political characteristics of MPs and LCs. It is perhaps noteworthy that we sampled fewer ruling party (DPP) MPs. This is likely due to the fact that ruling party MPs are more likely to travel on a regular basis and were therefore harder to contact.

See also Appendix E for analysis of the relationship between experimental treatment variables and attrition.

## A.2 SURVEY WITH CITIZENS IN MALAWI

In October 2016 I conducted an in-person panel survey with citizens in Malawi to assess the views of recipient teachers and citizens about

TABLE A.2 *MP sample statistics*

| Variable | In_Sample | Out_of_Sample |
|---|---|---|
| Mean School Enrollment | 938.859 (411.212) | 1566.974 (964.155) |
| Mean Number of Teachers | 13.26 (5.631) | 20.948 (12.028) |
| Mean Student to Teacher Ratio | 72.946 (18.749) | 77.365 (26.933) |
| Number of Aid Projects | 11.03 (10.836) | 4.681 (7.567) |
| Number of Schools | 12.94 (6.226) | 6.447 (5.295) |
| Turnout | 0.699 (0.086) | 0.678 (0.129) |
| Incumbent Victory Margin | 0.259 (0.193) | 0.172 (0.148) |
| Registered Voters | 18090.91 (7642.809) | 15736.553 (14056.628) |
| Incumbent Percent | 0.49 (0.143) | 0.436 (0.12) |
| DPP Incumbent | 0.334 (0.471) | 0.468 (0.504) |
| UDF Incumbent | 0.036 (0.186) | 0.021 (0.146) |
| MCP Incumbent | 0.232 (0.422) | 0.234 (0.428) |
| PP Incumbent | 0.104 (0.306) | 0.043 (0.204) |
| Independent Incumbent | 0.069 (0.253) | 0.064 (0.247) |
| Average School Population Density | 11.356 (15.838) | 39.7 (63.663) |

foreign aid and relationships with politicians. This survey was codesigned and fielded by Brigitte Seim at the University of Minnesota. Jimmy Mkandawire (Malawi Ministry of Labour and Statistics) and Johan Ahlbäck (LSE) were responsible for on-site management of the survey. The survey firm, rtSurvey, assisted with the technology for displaying the survey and managing survey output.

The survey was designed to overlap with a set of decisions that politicians in Malawi made over the allocation of goods to schools in Malawi. We utilized a hierarchical sampling procedure in order to select the schools to be included in this survey. We began with the sample of 333 wards which were involved in piloting activities. From these, we then randomly selected 60 wards, stratified by region, to be involved in the survey.

This process resulted in a total intended sample of 13 people per school at three schools in 60 wards, or 2340 people at 163 schools. Because of logistical issues in sampling from some communities, the total sample was 2019.

Within the community surrounding each school, we used a random walk procedure to sample potential voters in the area. A team of two Malawian enumerators first located the school and recorded its GPS coordinates. Then, they spun a bottle and walked in the direction of the bottle opening. They sampled the male head of household at the first house, skipped two houses, and then sampled the female head of household at the next (fourth) house. They then continued until they had sampled six heads of households in that direction, at which point they returned to the school and repeated the process in a different direction, sampling a female head of household the second time. There were almost no instances of participants refusing to participate, but where this occurred or where the head of household was not home, the house was skipped, and the sampling procedure simply ignored this house in the random walk pattern.

All participants gave verbal consent to participate and were given between MK200 ($0.25) and MK1000 ($1.25) as a token of appreciation for their time (the payment was greater for head teachers and greater at baseline).

As described in Chapter 5, the survey was a panel. In December 2016, we attempted to recontact all individuals involved in the original survey. We successfully interviewed 1,502 of the same individuals at endline.

Further details on this survey, including the survey instrument can be found in the preregistration statement at https://osf.io/zuxw6.

## A.3 SURVEY WITH TEACHERS IN MALAWI

Our survey of head teachers focused on the same schools as those used for the survey of citizens (as described above). At each sampled school, enumerators were instructed to contact the head teacher. In total, they were able to contact 314 head teachers at 311 school. The survey covered a number of topics, including the condition of the school, the investments of donors and politicians in the school, and perceptions of politician performance.

We also contacted 119 teachers again at endline. The lower number of respondents is due to the fact that we only visited those schools that had both teacher and citizen surveys at baseline.

Further details on this survey, including the survey instrument can be found in the preregistration statement at https://osf.io/zuxw6.

# Appendix B

## Interview Details

In this book, I draw on a number of interviews with politicians, bureaucrats, donors, and citizens. In Tables B.1–B.4 and Section B.5, I describe all the interviews cited in the text. Per agreement with ethical oversight bodies and interview subjects, the identity and constituency of all interview subjects are redacted or fictionalized. Interviewees were asked for verbal consent prior to participating in the interviews. Most public officials and voters were compensated for their time.

Unless otherwise mentioned, all interviews were conducted in person by the author or a research assistant. Interviews were conducted in English or the respondent's native language (Chichewa or Tumbuka). When non-English languages were used, the enumerator translated the response when transcribing the interview.

Interviews were not recorded, but enumerators were asked to write the interviewee's responses as closely as possible. Where quotes from these interviews are provided in the main text, I correct obvious spelling errors, grammatical errors, and missing words in the original transcript. I also replace acronyms and abbreviations to ease clarity of understanding.

### B.1 DONOR INTERVIEWS

Most interviews with donors were conducted in the summer of 2023. The intention of these interviews was to obtain as comprehensive a sample as possible of all the major donors involved in education provision in Malawi. At each organization, we asked to speak with the main official (program manager or task team leader) involved in the provision of education. Since education provision is both highly aid-dependent and

TABLE B.1 *Interviews of donors and NGO officials*

| ID | Date | Location | Interviewee | Description |
|---|---|---|---|---|
| A1 | November 2017 | Phone Interview | Programme officer working for a bilateral donor on public health service delivery in Malawi. | This interview discussed corruption in public health service delivery in Malawi and the effectiveness of different anti-corruption institutions. |
| A2 | July 2023 | Lilongwe | Programme officer for major bilateral donor working on education-related issues. | This interview discussed interactions between the donor various government institutions and policies. |
| A3 | July 2023 | Lilongwe | Portfolio coordinator for a national government's development finance initiative. | This interview discussed interactions between the donor various government institutions and policies. |
| A4 | July 2023 | Lilongwe | Person in charge of education projects (in Malawi) for an international organisation. | This interview discussed interactions between the donor various government institutions and policies. |
| A5 | July 2023 | Lilongwe | Manager of education projects for a bilateral aid agency. | This interview discussed interactions between the donor various government institutions and policies. |
| A6 | July 2023 | Lilongwe | Senior technical advisor for the Malawi office of an international charity focused on child welfare. | This interview discussed interactions between the donor various government institutions and policies. |
| A7 | February 2017 | Lilongwe | Portfolio coordinator for a national government's public health finance initiative. | This interview discussed corruption in public health supply chains. |

TABLE B.2 *Interviews of elected officials*

| ID | Date | Location | Interviewee |
|---|---|---|---|
| B1 | August 2015 | Southern Region, Malawi | Councilor |
| B2 | September 2016 | Southern Region, Malawi | MP |
| B3 | August 2016 | Central Region, Malawi | MP |
| B4 | September 2016 | Central Region, Malawi | MP |
| B5 | August 2016 | Southern Region, Malawi | Councilor |
| B6 | July 2016 | Southern Region, Malawi | Councilor |
| B7 | September 2016 | Central Region, Malawi | Councilor |
| B8 | August 2016 | Southern Region, Malawi | Councilor |
| B9 | July 2016 | Central Region, Malawi | Councilor |
| B10 | August 2016 | Central Region, Malawi | Councilor |
| B11 | August 2015 | Southern Region, Malawi | Councilor |
| B12 | August 2015 | Southern Region, Malawi | Councilor |
| B13 | August 2015 | Southern Region, Malawi | Councilor |
| B14 | August 2015 | Southern Region, Malawi | Councilor |
| B15 | September 2016 | Central Region, Malawi | MP |
| B16 | September 2016 | Southern Region, Malawi | MP |
| B17 | September 2016 | Southern Region, Malawi | MP |
| B18 | August 2016 | Southern Region, Malawi | MP |
| B19 | September 2016 | Southern Region, Malawi | MP |

TABLE B.3 *Interviews with ADCs*

| ID | Date | Location | Interviewee |
|---|---|---|---|
| C1 | July 2016 | Central Region | Member, ADC |
| C2 | May 2016 | Southern Region | Member, ADC |
| C3 | September 2016 | Central Region | Member, ADC |
| C4 | July 2016 | Central Region | Member, ADC |
| C5 | August 2016 | Southern Region | Member, ADC |
| C6 | August 2016 | Southern Region | Member, ADC |

TABLE B.4 *Interviews of bureaucrats*

| ID | Date | Location | Interviewee |
|---|---|---|---|
| D1 | September 2016 | Northern Region, Malawi | District Commissioner |
| D2 | October 2016 | Southern Region, Malawi | District Commissioner |
| D3 | September 2016 | Central Region, Malawi | District Commissioner |
| D4 | August 2016 | Northern Region, Malawi | District Commissioner |
| D5 | July 2016 | Southern Region, Malawi | District Commissioner |
| D6 | August 2016 | Southern Region, Malawi | District Commissioner |

decentralized in Malawi, this allowed me to identify the ways in which donors interact with varying kinds of officials. Since many questions posed to teachers and public officials focused on the education sector, this sampling strategy allows cross-comparison.

## B.2 POLITICIAN INTERVIEWS

Enumerators were provided with an interview script assessing (1) the relationship between politicians and other actors involved in development, including donors, NGOs, and citizens; (2) the oversight MPs face from these actors; (3) the relationship between politicians and donors; (4) politicians' perceived job responsibilities and role in development; (5) gaps politicians face in fulfilling their job responsibilities.

## B.3 AREA DEVELOPMENT COMMITTEE (ADC) INTERVIEWS

Enumerators were tasked to ask questions about (1) how ADCs perceive their role in development; (2) the nature of relationships between ADCs, donors, and politicians; (3) ways in which ADCs provide oversight to development; (3) how ADCs might react to development decisions that they disagree with; and (4) how different kinds of officials (councilors, TAs, MPs, DCs, NGOs, and donors) influence decisions made by ADCs.

## B.4 INTERVIEWS WITH BUREAUCRATS

Interviews were focused on District Commissioners (DCs), who are the senior civil servants at the district level in Malawi. Enumerators were tasked to ask questions about (1) how DCs perceive their role in development; (2) the relationship between donors, NGOs, DCs, and politicians; (3) ways in which DCs provide oversight to donors, councilors, and MPs; (3) how DCs might react to development decisions that they disagree with; (4) how different kinds of officials (councilors, TAs, MPs, ADCs, NGOs, and donors) influence decisions made by DCs.

## B.5 FOCUS GROUP INTERVIEWS

Trained local enumerators conducted focus groups with thirty citizens in four wards in southern Malawi. In each ward, the interviewee was instructed to go to the largest trading center nearby and recruit ten subjects from the area. These subjects were not randomly selected but were recruited from different parts of the trading center and were not already in a discussion together at the time of recruitment. We asked that the participant list be balanced on gender, age, and profession. All participants were asked for consent and were compensated for their time.

The enumerator then asked, in a group setting, the respondents to discuss in depth three separate issues: (1) perceptions and knowledge regarding the roles and responsibilities of ward councilors in allocating development aid; (2) beliefs about potential mechanisms of electoral and horizontal accountability; (3) perceptions of the role of donors and civil society groups in their communities.

# Appendix C

## Further Details, Chapter 4

### C.1 FOREIGN AID DATA

Testing the hypotheses in Chapter 4 requires historical data on the subnational distribution of foreign aid projects in Kenya, Malawi, and Sierra Leone.

In the case of Malawi, I rely on data from the Malawi Government's Aid Management Platform.[1] This dataset provides spatial coordinates for approximately 80 percent of all international development financing reported to the government from 2000 to 2012. In the case of Sierra Leone, I rely on data from the government's Development Assistance Database. This database tracks donor commitments across 856 projects affecting 2,314 locations from 1992 to 2014.[2]

The Kenyan government has not systematically tracked donor activities. However, both the World Bank and the African Development Bank publish reports on all committed projects in Kenya.[3]

I and a team of research assistants read all relevant reports from 1992 to 2010. I then coded each project with a geographic coordinate (or set of coordinates) representing its location (or locations), as well its geographic scope.[4] Additionally, for projects that were complete as of 2011,

1 Peratsakis, Christian, Joshua Powell, Michael Findley, Justin Baker, and Catherine Weaver 2012.

2 AidData (2017)

3 World Bank Project Database, available at http://worldbank.org/projects, accessed March 1, 2011; African Development Bank Projects and Operations, available at http://afdb.org/en/projects-and-operations, accessed March 1, 2011.

4 In coding these data, I relied on a coding scheme designed by Findley et al. (2011).

I rely on existing data from the AidData project.[5] Using these data, I am able to estimate the total value of allocated aid going to each of Kenya's constituencies. This provides a dataset of 3,780 constituency-years (210 constituencies × 18 years), representing over $7 billion in committed aid. These data were originally used in Jablonski 2014, 2013.

### C.1.1 Matching Aid to Constituencies

There are many challenges in identifying how much foreign aid goes to a particular location that are somewhat unique. Unlike other spatial data, foreign aid project locations can rarely be uniquely placed in space. And even where this might be possible, donors are unable or unwilling to track projects at a highly disaggregate level of precision. For example, a donor might target a country or district for spending, but then hand off the implementation of the project to an NGO or government in ways that are difficult to track. Or a donor might also spend on something like a road that borders multiple administrative areas. In some cases, donors will report each district or location affected by such a project. In other cases, a donor might only report the entire region affected by the project.

A related problem arises in trying to code the amount of money targeted to a particular geographic area. Even in cases where donors report the precise geographic locations affected by a project, they will rarely report the precise share of funding allocated to each geographic location.[6]

Thus, in order to analyze the relationship between aid and voting, it is necessary to rely on some assumptions. In the main analysis, I assume that project funding is distributed in proportion to population.[7] So if a project crosses a constituency boundary, I assume that the funds are distributed in proportion to each constituency's population. Likewise, if a project can only be geolocated to a district rather than to a specific constituency, I assume that each constituency receives aid in proportion to its share of the population.

An alternative assumption is that projects are distributed in proportion to number of constituencies regardless of population. So if a project crosses a boundary, we could assume that both constituencies equally

[5] Tierney et al. 2011.

[6] The Sierra Leone and Malawi platforms do not report any location-specific funding. In the case of Kenya, it is sometimes possible to infer from project documents how funding was distributed across project locations. I do this where possible.

[7] Following the approach used in Jablonski (2014).

benefit. If we reestimate the results under this assumption, the size and magnitude of the treatment effects remain similar.

## C.2 ELECTORAL DATA

### C.2.1 Kenya

Kenya holds elections every five years in December for the president and 210 constituency-level members of the National Assembly. The president is elected by a plurality rule, with the contingency that he must obtain 25 percent of the vote in five of Kenya's seven provinces. MPs are similarly elected by a plurality rule in single-member districts. While a number of parties contest each of these elections, in practice almost all votes go to the two leading parties in each election.

Using data from Kollman, Ken, Allen Hicken, Daniele Caramani, David Backer, and David Lublin (2020) supplemented with data from the Electoral Commission of Kenya, I code the percentage of support the incumbent party received in National Assembly elections in each of the 210 constituencies only from 1992 to 2010. Since I am interested in the effect of electoral politics and Kenya has only held multiparty elections since 1992, I look at the allocation of aid after this date.[8]

From 1992 to 2002, I assume that the allocation of aid was influenced by the regime of Daniel arap Moi and the Kenya African National Union (KANU) party.[9] In 2002, Moi stepped down, and Kibaki and the National Alliance of Rainbow Coalition (NARC) came to power in a contested election. Thus from 2002 until the election in 2007, I assume that the Kibaki regime influenced the allocation of aid.

Coding the decision rules from the December 2007 election to the end of my study period in 2010 is less straightforward. The 2007 election in Kenya was highly contested and resulted in widespread violence. In the

[8] While Kenya held elections prior to 1992, they were widely considered to be a referendum on the ruling regime rather than a competitive election.

[9] One might object to this coding on the grounds that Daniel arap Moi was term limited after 1997 and so had few incentives to bias aid in the KANU's favor. However, despite being term limited, Moi appears to have been invested in the KANU victory. This is due in part to Moi's intention to retain control over the KANU government behind the scenes. In addition to appointing Uhuru Kenyatta as his chosen successor, Moi appointed himself the chairman of the new KANU party with veto power over policy decisions and cabinet appointments. As an additional incentive, Moi faced the very real (though largely unrealized) threat that he and his family would be prosecuted if the KANU were to lose the election, see Steeves (2006) and Branch (2011).

aftermath, the United Nations brokered a power-sharing arrangement between the two front-runners, Kibaki (now Party National Unity [PNU]) and Raila Odinga (Orange Democratic Movement [ODM] Party). The provisions of this agreement included joint heads of state, unanimity rules, and a shared cabinet. This joint arrangement makes it difficult to determine a clear decision rule. However, most ministries involved in aid delivery were held by the ODM, potentially giving it more influence. I therefore code the ODM as the incumbent. For further discussion and evidence on this assumption, see Jablonski (2014).

### C.2.2 Malawi

Malawi holds national elections every five years for 193 single-member parliamentary constituencies. Due to limited scope of Malawi's aid management platform, I can code aid to constituencies only from 2000 to 2013. Data on election results come from Kollman, Ken, Allen Hicken, Daniele Caramani, David Backer, and David Lublin (2020), supplemented by data from the Malawi Election Commission in the case of missing data.

From 2000 to 2004 and again from 2004 to 2009, the government was held by the United Democratic Front. In 2009, the government was controlled by the Democratic Progressive Party (DPP), though under the same president, Bingu wa Mutharika.

### C.2.3 Sierra Leone

Sierra Leone holds national-level elections every five years. I focus on parliamentary elections and code support for the ruling party in Sierra Leone's 112 single-member constituencies. I focus on elections from 2002 to 2013. 2002 was the first election in which an incumbent (Ahmed Tejan Kabbah of the SLPP) had largely uncontested control over the government. I only include up to 2013 due to limitation on the scope of data on foreign aid. Obtaining accurate election results at the constituency level prior to 2002 is also difficult. Data on election results come from Kollman, Ken, Allen Hicken, Daniele Caramani, David Backer, and David Lublin (2020).

Throughout this history, Sierra Leone has been dominated by two main parties: the Sierra Leone People's Party (the SLPP) and the All People's Congress (the APC). These parties tend to split the vast majority of votes between them. From August 2007 to November 2012, and again from November 2012 to March 2018, the government was held by the APC under Ernest Koroma. From May 2002 to August 2007, the government was held by the SLPP under Ahmad Kabbah.

One challenge in coding the 2002 election is that the election commission never released constituency-level voting data. To address this challenge, I use voting data from the 2007 election as a proxy for the support that the SLPP received in the 2002 election. Since the same parties contested the 2007 election, this assumption is mostly reasonable. However, it should be noted that the SLPP lost a significant share of voters between the 2002 and 2007 elections, so this assumption may underestimate SLPP support, particularly in more contested areas.

# Appendix D

## Further Details, Chapter 5

### D.1 SMS AVERAGE TREATMENT EFFECTS

In the main text, I show difference-in-differences estimates comparing the effects of foreign aid on changes in incumbent support. This estimate does not necessarily identify the effect of providing the SMS treatment because (1) not all respondents were eligible to receive SMS messages, and (2) the treatment effect on the treated could have plausibly spilled over onto untreated individuals.

To estimate the effect of the SMS message directly and independently of the effect of aid, we use the following estimation approach:

$$y_{ijt} = \beta_1 m_j + \beta_2 y_{ijt-1} + \epsilon_{ij} \tag{D.1}$$

Here, $m_j = 1$ if a respondent was sent an SMS treatment message and 0 if a respondent was sent an SMS placebo message. Standard errors are clustered at the school level (the level of treatment assignment).

Since $m_j$ was randomly assigned, $\beta_1$ should identify the causal effect of receiving an SMS message within each aid-eligible group in Table 5.1.

One important thing to note is that, for power reasons, we did not randomize the SMS treatment within the aid-recipient group (Group A). So for this group, we estimate the following equation:

$$y_{ijt} = \beta_1 m_i^* + \beta_2 y_{ijt-1} + \epsilon_{ij} \tag{D.2}$$

Unlike above, $m_j^*$ equals one if a respondent was eligible to receive an SMS message (i.e., provided a valid phone number). It equals zero if a respondent was ineligible. Since there was no random assignment and

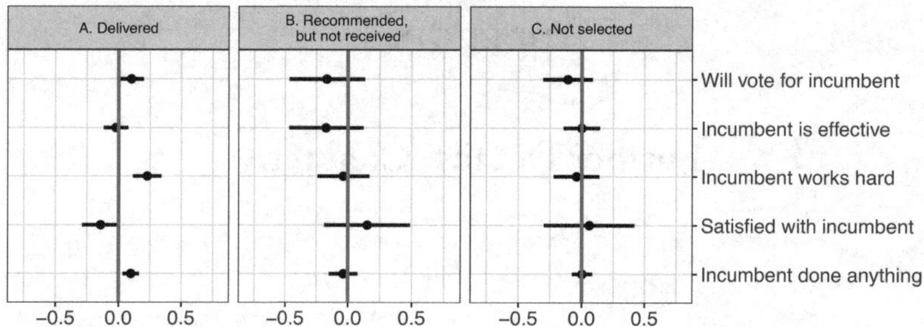


FIGURE D.1 Effect of SMS messages on outcome variables (95 percent CI)
*Note*: This plot shows the change in survey responses from baseline among those receiving an SMS treatment message compared to those receiving an SMS placebo message (except in the delivery group as described above).

respondents with phone numbers differ in important ways from those without, there are reasons to doubt that this is a causal estimate. For one, the SMS treatment effect is only identified under the assumption of parallel trends in outcomes across eligible and noneligible respondents. As I discuss in the main text, this is a plausible assumption; however, it cannot be confirmed directly. Additionally, since SMS recipients often communicated with others in their community, it is likely that estimates for this group violate the stable unit treatment value (SUTVA) assumption. This spillover likely biases the treatment effect estimate downward.

The results in Figure D.1 are consistent with the predictions in the main text. We have comparatively weak statistical power in these tests (Ns = 575, 155, and 255 for Groups A, B, and C); so the 95 percent confidence intervals overlap with the null for some outcomes. However, in Group A, we can reject the null that the messages had no effect on voting intention or beliefs about incumbent performance. In Group C, we observe a negative effect on voting intention, though the estimate does not reach standard levels of statistical significance ($p = 0.13$). Consistent with the predictions, the results in Group B are consistent with the null.

# Appendix E

## Further Details, Chapter 6

### E.1 ESTIMATION

To test my hypotheses, I estimate how Aid Information change the odds a politician allocates to a school with certain traits.

Formally, let $P(Y_{nsi} = 1)$ indicate the probability politician $n$ chooses school $i$ in map $s$. In the absence of any information treatment, I expect that this probability will vary depending on the levels of *School Need Index*, *Aid Project Count*, *Aid Good Types*, and *Percent Votes*. Let these characteristics of each school equal $z_{is}$. Let $X_{is}$ be a vector of school-specific controls.

To estimate aid information treatment effects, I evaluate how the effects of $z_{is}$ vary with treatment assignment. Let $t_s \in [0, 1]$ be the randomly assigned treatments of information at the map level. The treatment equals one if map $s$ has been assigned to a treatment group and zero if it is in a control group. To estimate the effects of treatment, I interact $t_s$ with $z_{is}$ as in equation E.1.

$$P(Y_{nsi} = 1) = \phi(\beta_1 z_i + \beta_2 t_s z_i + \gamma X_{is} + e_{nsi}). \tag{E.1}$$

I estimate $\phi$ using a conditional logit model (conditioned on map $s$). The conditional logit is an extension of the logit model for discrete choice experiments in which individuals make decisions between more than two outcomes.[1] The estimates from a conditional logit estimator are generally less biased than alternative estimators in this setting.[2] I also see

[1] McFadden 1973.

[2] For discussion of trade-offs in the estimation of discrete choice experiments, see Clark et al. (2014) and McFadden (1973).

consistent estimates using a linear probability model with fixed effects for each $s$. The conditional logit model averages the odds of a school being selected for allocation within each choice map, so variables that do not vary within $s$ drop out of the estimating equation (such as $t_s$). Since politicians each make more than one choice, I cluster our errors at the politician level. Conservatively, I use two-tailed hypothesis tests throughout.

I am also interested in estimating how the aid information treatment effects varies across politicians who were assigned the donor transparency treatment. I estimate these conditional average treatment effects using a triple interaction term. That is, for each conditioning variable $w_i$, I estimate the following equation and then analytically calculate the treatment effect and standard error conditional on $w_i$.

$$P(Y_{nsi} = 1) = \phi(\beta_1 z_i + \beta_2 w_i + \beta_3 t_s z_i + \beta_4 t_s w_i + \beta_5 z_i w_i + \beta_6 t_s z_i w_i + \gamma X_{is} + e_{nsi}). \tag{E.2}$$

I include estimates with and without control variables. The prespecified controls include *Log Permanent Classrooms, Log Temporary Classrooms, Log Teacher Houses Permanent, Log Teacher Houses Temporary, Opposition Percent Votes (for MP and LC), Log Enrollment, Number of Aid Projects, Family Attends School, Incumbent Percent at Polling Station*, and *School Need Index*.

I normalize continuous variables in the analysis: so coefficients can be interpreted as the effects of a standard deviation change in a continuous variable (or a one-unit change in a count variable) on the odds or log odds of a school being selected for allocation by the politician. We also discuss within-sample predictions on a probability scale.

## E.2 ATTRITION STATISTICS

### E.2.1 Sample Attrition

In order to participate in the experiment, politicians had to be active in office and accurate data had to be available on all information treatments. By these criteria, 353 LCs and 187 MPs were eligible for participation in the experiment. Of these, we were able to contact 335 LCs and 125 MPs. Subjects were excluded primarily because they were out of town at the time of the study. Since the information treatments were blocked on respondent, attrition is unrelated to treatment by design.

However, attrition also raises concerns about generalizability. In Tables A.1 and A.2, I show that there is little systematic difference between included and excluded subjects. Additionally in Table E.1, below, I conduct a regression of available covariates on attrition. An F-test easily fails to reject the null that these variables help explain patterns of attrition. We conclude that our subject pool is not biased to any large extent by attrition.

TABLE E.1 *The effect of covariates on survey attrition*

| Variable Name | MP Survey (1) | Councilor Survey (2) |
|---|---|---|
| Aid Good Types | −0.423* | −0.059 |
| | (0.246) | (0.082) |
| Aid Project Count | 0.570 | 0.074 |
| | (0.357) | (0.115) |
| Councilor Party AFORD | 2.172 | −0.101 |
| | (1.550) | (0.263) |
| Councilor Party DPP | 0.129 | −0.061 |
| | (0.156) | (0.045) |
| Councilor Party Independent | 0.501** | −0.036 |
| | (0.222) | (0.062) |
| Councilor Party MCP | −0.007 | −0.012 |
| | (0.157) | (0.047) |
| Councilor Party Other | 0.823* | −0.093 |
| | (0.471) | (0.171) |
| Councilor Party PP | 0.113 | −0.064 |
| | (0.196) | (0.055) |
| Councilor Party UDF | – | – |
| Frequency of Donor Interaction | 0.003 | 0.017 |
| | (0.039) | (0.013) |
| Incumbent Percent at Poll Station | −1.693 | 0.106 |
| | (2.310) | (0.237) |
| Incumbent Percent Votes in Ward | 0.020 | 0.468 |
| | (1.149) | (0.401) |
| Incumbent Votes at Poll Station | 0.0002 | −0.0001 |
| | (0.0004) | (0.0001) |
| Log Area | −0.003 | 0.032 |
| | (0.099) | (0.027) |
| Log Enrollment | −0.111 | −0.070** |
| | (0.119) | (0.033) |
| Log Permanent Classrooms | 0.097 | 0.101 |
| | (0.282) | (0.086) |

*(continued)*

TABLE E.1 *(continued)*

| Variable Name | MP Survey (1) | Councilor Survey (2) |
|---|---|---|
| Log Permanent Houses | −0.100 | 0.016 |
| | (0.153) | (0.044) |
| Log Population | 0.035 | 0.011 |
| | (0.165) | (0.049) |
| Log School Count | −0.101 | −0.067 |
| | (0.154) | (0.046) |
| Log Teachers | 0.030 | −0.078 |
| | (0.214) | (0.065) |
| Log Temporary Classrooms | −0.018 | −0.008 |
| | (0.203) | (0.059) |
| Log Temporary Houses | 0.211 | −0.038 |
| | (0.146) | (0.047) |
| Log Votes at Poll. Station | −0.046 | 0.159** |
| | (0.263) | (0.063) |
| MP Party AFORD | −0.411 | −0.045 |
| | (0.499) | (0.137) |
| MP Party DPP | −0.093 | 0.046 |
| | (0.144) | (0.045) |
| MP Party Independent | −0.019 | 0.045 |
| | (0.117) | (0.039) |
| MP Party MCP | −0.011 | 0.013 |
| | (0.140) | (0.048) |
| MP Party Other | −0.154 | −0.013 |
| | (0.179) | (0.061) |
| MP Party PP | −0.001 | −0.002 |
| | (0.130) | (0.042) |
| MP Party PPM | −0.039 | −0.018 |
| | (0.213) | (0.070) |
| MP Party UDF | – | – |
| Opposition Percent at Poll Station (LC) | −0.440 | −0.362 |
| | (0.771) | (0.271) |
| Percent Votes at Poll Station (MP) | 2.033 | 0.240 |
| | (2.326) | (0.183) |
| Percent Votes in Constituency | −0.023 | 0.014 |
| | (0.261) | (0.090) |
| Pop Density | – | – |
| Pop Density at School | 0.0001 | −0.002 |
| | (0.004) | (0.001) |

*(continued)*

TABLE E.1 *(continued)*

| Variable Name | MP Survey (1) | Councilor Survey (2) |
|---|---|---|
| School Need Index | −0.205 | −0.059 |
| | (0.197) | (0.041) |
| School Need Index | – | 0.015 |
| (constituency) | – | (0.025) |
| School Need Index (ward) | 0.251 | – |
| | (0.196) | – |
| Victory Margin at Poll Station | 1.772 | 0.135 |
| (MP) | (2.255) | (0.096) |
| Victory Margin in | 0.078 | 0.004 |
| Constituency | (0.243) | (0.077) |
| Victory Margin in Ward | −0.106 | −0.588** |
| | (0.925) | (0.298) |
| School Need Index (ward) | 0.897 | −0.951* |
| | (2.073) | (0.497) |
| Observations | 187 | 353 |
| $R^2$ | 0.212 | 0.096 |
| F-statistic | 1.050 (df = 38; 148) | 0.879 (df = 38; 314) |

*Note:* *p<0.1; **p<0.05; ***p<0.01

### E.2.2 Post-treatment Attrition

No politicians refused to participate in the study or answer questions about schools; however, we excluded some maps from the final analysis for technical reasons. The main reason for this is that politicians sometimes contested whether one or more schools were actually in their constituency.

Since politicians never select schools which they believe (rightly or not) to be outside their constituency, we exclude these contested maps from our analysis. We also excluded one map that was not correctly displayed on an RA tablet. These issues affect 83 out of 1,169 maps, and we exclude these 83 maps from our analysis.

To test whether this post-treatment attrition is related to treatment assignment, in Table E.2, we estimate whether attrited maps are more likely to be in one or more treatment groups. We do not find evidence that this is the case.

TABLE E.2 *Effect of treatment on attrition due to politician contesting a school location*

| Variable Name | (1) | (2) | (3) | (4) |
|---|---|---|---|---|
| Need Treatment | −0.014 | – | – | −0.013 |
| | (0.013) | – | – | (0.013) |
| Aid Treatment | – | −0.010 | – | −0.010 |
| | – | (0.013) | – | (0.013) |
| Voting Treatment | – | – | −0.018 | −0.017 |
| | – | – | (0.013) | (0.013) |
| N Maps | 1252 | 1252 | 1252 | 1252 |
| Pseudo-$R^2$ | 0.001 | 0.0004 | 0.001 | 0.002 |

*Note:* *p<0.1; **p<0.05; ***p<0.01
This table shows the results of a linear regression. The outcome variable is one if a map is attritted due to politicians contesting map boundaries and zero if the map remains in the analysis sample. Estimates are clustered on respondent.

## E.3 FOREIGN AID DATA

To collect information on foreign aid used for the aid information treatment, we focused the data collection on the main foreign donors active in the primary education sector in Malawi, and the projects these donors had carried out in individual primary schools in the past five years (since 2011). Following consultations with local stakeholders and practitioners active within the aid sector in Malawi, we identified the main donors whose project activities included the primary education sector. When approaching each of these donors, we asked them to provide detailed data on their project activities since 2011, including the type of intervention and the name and location of the recipient school. Donors were also asked to cross-validate our list of active donors in the sector and to suggest organizations that were not on the list.[3] As we discuss further,

[3] The organizations from which data on aid projects were obtained include Department for International Development (DFID), Deutche Gesellschaft fur Internationale Zusammenarbeit (GIZ), German Development Cooperation (KFW), Norwegian Embassy, Save the Children, United States Agency for International Development (USAID), United Nations Children's Fund (UNICEF), United Nations Development Programme (UNDP), Volunteer Service Overseas (VSO), World Food Programme (WFP), and the World Bank. Organizations that were identified as active in the education sector, but that failed to respond to our queries, include the Japan International Cooperation Agency (JICA), OXFAM, United Nations Population Fund (UNFPA), and World Vision.

the politicians in our experiment had little or no knowledge about most of these foreign aid projects and were not involved in their allocation. Like most of the Malawian aid portfolio for these donors, these education projects were almost entirely off-budget and implemented by donors or nongovernmental implementing partners. Government ministries were consulted on some projects. However, we could find no evidence that council authorities or parliamentary representatives in benefiting constituencies had influence or insight into the process of allocating these projects.

In total, 3,151 primary schools received 4,566 foreign aid projects from this set of donors between 2011 and 2016. This constitutes 57 percent of the 5,438 primary schools in Malawi for which we had location data. The number of foreign aid projects in each school varied from 0 to 4. Figure 6.2 displays the total sample of primary schools in Malawi with no projects supported by donors (in gray) versus those with at least one project.

The total number of primary schools included in the school maps presented to the 125 sampled MPs was 1,109. Of these, 683 (62.03 percent) contained at least one foreign aid project. The average number of projects per school was 0.95, ranging from 0 to 4. For the 335 sampled LCs, the total number of primary schools presented in the maps was 2,646, of which 1,545 (58.39 percent) contained at least one foreign aid project. The average number of projects was 0.88, again ranging from 0 to 4.

## E.4 EXAMPLE DONOR OVERSIGHT TREATMENT REPORT

The following Figure E.1 is an example of the oversight report shared with politicians during the experiment described in Chapter 6.

**DONOR REPORT**

**PRIMARY SCHOOL DEVELOPMENT MATERIALS PROJECT**

Prepared for:

USAID, DFID, GIZ, World Food Program, UNICEF, Save the Children, World Vision

June 2017

In the first half of 2017, Tearfund NGO initiated a project to provide development materials to primary schools across Malawi. The first phase of this project involved meeting with elected officials to give them the opportunity to select schools in their areas to receive materials. The schools recommended by these officials will be entered into a public lottery to determine which schools will receive materials. This report provides information about the decisions of the officials and the characteristics of the schools they selected that you may find helpful as you plan projects in the future.

Member of Parliament ***John Banda***, representing ***Nyasa Constituency***, selected the following schools to receive materials:

***Selected to Receive Teacher Kits***

**Mkuku Primary School**
**Location of School:** Mbeta Village, Chizwe Ward
**Number of Students:** 872
**Number of Classrooms:** 7
**Number of Teachers:** 12
**Number of Donor Projects:** 1
**% Votes MP Received in Community:** 35 percent

***Selected to Receive Dictionaries***

**Mpenga Primary School**
**Location of School:** Mwai Village, Chipeza Ward
**Number of Students:** 963
**Number of Classrooms:** 5
**Number of Teachers:** 10
**Number of Donor Projects:** 0
**% Votes MP Received in Community:** 16 percent

***Selected to Receive Solar Lamps***

**Nkhande Primary School**
**Location of School:** Mapeto Village, Nkhozwe Ward
**Number of Students:** 450
**Number of Classrooms:** 8
**Number of Teachers:** 15
**Number of Donor Projects:** 2
**% Votes MP Received in Community:** 68 percent

*Please note that, because of our project guidelines, not all schools in the constituency were eligible for selection.*

FIGURE E.1 Example donor oversight report

# References


"90% of aid to NGOs can't be traced" (2016). *The Nation*, September 8.

Acharya, Arnab, Ana T. F. De Lima, and Mick Moore (2006). "Proliferation and fragmentation: Transactions costs and the value of aid." *The Journal of Development Studies* 42.1, pp. 1–21.

Ahmed, Faisal Z. (2012). "The perils of unearned foreign income: Aid, remittances, and government survival." *American Political Science Review* 106.1, pp. 146–165.

(2019). *The Perils of International Capital.* Cambridge University Press.

AidData (2017). *Sierra Leone AIMS Geocoded Research Release v1.0 geocoded dataset.* Accessed June 2023. https://aiddata.org/research-datasets.

Albers, Thilo N. H., Morten Jerven, and Marvin Suesse (2023). "The fiscal state in Africa: Evidence from a century of growth." *International Organization* 77.1, pp. 65–101.

Ali, Murad (2009). "US foreign aid to Pakistan and democracy: An overview." *Pakistan Journal of Social Sciences* 29.2, pp. 247–258.

Altincekic, Ceren and David H. Bearce (2014). "Why there should be no political foreign aid curse." *World Development* 64, pp. 18–32.

Alwy, Alwiya and Susanne Schech (2004). "Ethnic inequalities in education in Kenya." *International Education Journal* 5.2, pp. 266–274.

Anaxagorou, Christiana, Georgios Efthyvoulou, and Vassilis Sarantides (2020). "Electoral motives and the subnational allocation of foreign aid in sub-Saharan Africa." *European Economic Review* 127, p. 103430.

Andersen, Jørgen Juel, Niels Johannesen, and Bob Rijkers (2022). "Elite capture of foreign aid: Evidence from offshore bank accounts." *Journal of Political Economy* 130.2, pp. 388–425.

Arias, Eric et al. (2022). "Priors rule: When do malfeasance revelations help or hurt incumbent parties?" *Journal of the European Economic Association* 20.4, pp. 1433–1477.

Armon, Jeremy (2007). "Aid, politics and development: A donor perspective." *Development Policy Review* 25.5, pp. 653–656.

Ashworth, Scott (2012). "Electoral accountability: Recent theoretical and empirical work." *Annual Review of Political Science*, 15, pp. 183–201.

Ashworth, Scott, Ethan B. de Mesquita, and Amanda Friedenberg (2018). "Learning about voter rationality." *American Journal of Political Science* 62.1, pp. 37–54.

Auerback, Adam, Shikhar Singh, and Tariq Thachil (2024). "Who knows how to govern? Procedural knowledge in India's small-town councils." *American Political Science Review* 119.2, pp. 1–19. https://doi.org/10.1017/S0003055424000297.

Baldwin, Kate (2013). "Why vote with the chief? Political connections and public goods provision in Zambia." *American Journal of Political Science* 57.4, pp. 794–809.

Baldwin, Kate and Matthew S. Winters (2023). "Foreign aid and political support: How politicians' aid oversight capacity and voter information condition credit-giving." *World Politics* 75.1, pp. 1–42.

Banerjee, Abhijit et al. (2011). "Do informed voters make better choices? Experimental evidence from urban India." Unpublished manuscript, Harvard University.

Bangladesh Ministry of Finance (2024). *Bangladesh Economic Review 2024*. Government of Bangladesh. https://bit.ly/4jvExMK.

Barkan, Joel D. et al. (2010). "The African legislatures project: First findings." http://hdl.handle.net/11427/19858.

Bechtolsheimer, Götz (2012). "Breakfast with Mobutu: Congo, the United States and the Cold War, 1964–1981." PhD thesis. London School of Economics and Political Science.

Berliner, Daniel and Joachim Wehner (2022). "Audits for accountability: Evidence from municipal by-elections in South Africa." *The Journal of Politics* 84.3, pp. 1581–1594.

Bermeo, Sarah B. (2011). "Foreign aid and regime change: A role for donor intent." *World Development* 39.11, pp. 2021–2031.

(2016). "Aid is not oil: Donor utility, heterogeneous aid, and the aid-democratization relationship." *International Organization* 70.1, pp. 1–32.

Bernbaum, Marcia and Kurt Moses (2011). *EQUIP2 lessons learned in education: A guide to education project design, evaluation, and implementation based on experiences from EQUIP2 projects in Malawi, Uganda, and Zambia education management information systems*. Technical Report. USAID. https://bit.ly/4qgAN4v.

Blair, Robert A and Philip Roessler (2021). "Foreign aid and state legitimacy: Evidence on Chinese and US aid to Africa from surveys, survey experiments, and behavioral games." *World Politics* 73.2, pp. 315–357.

Blair, Robert A and Matthew S Winters (2020). "Foreign aid and state-society relations: Theory, evidence, and new directions for research." *Studies in Comparative International Development* 55, pp. 123–142.

Blattman, Christopher, Mathilde Emeriau, and Nathan Fiala (2016). "Do anti-poverty programs sway voters? Experimental evidence from Uganda." *Review of Economics and Statistics* 100.5, pp. 891–905.

Bommer, Christian, Axel Dreher, and Marcello Perez-Alvarez (2022). "Home bias in humanitarian aid: The role of regional favoritism in the allocation of international disaster relief." *Journal of Public Economics* 208, p. 104604.

Bomprezzi, Pietro et al. (2024). "Wedded to prosperity? Informal influence and regional favoritism."

Bourguignon, François and Jean-Philippe Platteau (2015). "The hard challenge of aid coordination." *World Development* 69, pp. 86–97.

Branch, Daniel (2011). *Kenya: Between hope and despair, 1963–2010*. Yale University Press.

Brass, Jennifer N (2012a). "Blurring boundaries: The integration of NGOs into governance in Kenya." *Governance* 25.2, pp. 209–235.

(2012b). "Why do NGOs go where they go? Evidence from Kenya." *World Development* 40.2, pp. 387–401.

(2016). *Allies or adversaries: NGOs and the state in Africa*. Cambridge University Press.

Brass, Jennifer N et al. (2018). "NGOs and international development: A review of thirty-five years of scholarship." *World Development* 112, pp. 136–149.

Brautigam, Deborah, Odd-Helge Fjeldstad, and Mick Moore (2008). *Taxation and state-building in developing countries: Capacity and consent*. Cambridge University Press.

Bräutigam, Deborah A and Stephen Knack (2004). "Foreign aid, institutions, and governance in sub-Saharan Africa." *Economic Development and Cultural Change* 52.2, pp. 255–285.

Bräutigam, Deborah A and Monique Segarra (2007). "Difficult partnerships: The World Bank, states, and NGOs." *Latin American Politics and Society* 49.4, pp. 149–181.

Brazys, Samuel, Peter Heaney, and Patrick Paul Walsh (2015). "Fertilizer and votes: Does strategic economic policy explain the 2009 Malawi election?" *Electoral Studies* 39, pp. 39–55.

Briggs, Ryan C (2012). "Electrifying the base? Aid and incumbent advantage in Ghana." *The Journal of Modern African Studies* 50.4, pp. 603–624.

(2014). "Aiding and abetting: Project aid and ethnic politics in Kenya." *World Development* 64, pp. 194–205.

(2015). "The influence of aid changes on African election outcomes." *International Interactions* 41.2, pp. 201–225.

(2019). "Receiving foreign aid can reduce support for incumbent presidents." *Political Research Quarterly* 72.3, pp. 610–622.

(2021). "Why does aid not target the poorest?" *International Studies Quarterly* 65.3, pp. 739–752.

Brollo, Fernanda and Tommaso Nannicini (2012). "Tying your enemy's hands in close races: The politics of federal transfers in Brazil." *American Political Science Review* 106.4, pp. 742–761.

Brollo, Fernanda et al. (2013). "The political resource curse." *American Economic Review* 103.5, pp. 1759–96.

Broockman, David E and Christopher Skovron (2018). "Bias in perceptions of public opinion among political elites." *American Political Science Review* 112.3, pp. 542–563.

Brown, Stephen (2001). "Authoritarian leaders and multiparty elections in Africa: How foreign donors help to keep Kenya's Daniel arap Moi in power." *Third World Quarterly* 22.5, pp. 725–739.

(2005). "Foreign aid and democracy promotion: Lessons from Africa." *The European Journal of Development Research* 17, pp. 179–198.

Bueno de Mesquita, Bruce and Alastair Smith (2009). "A political economy of aid." *International Organization* 63.2, pp. 309–340.

Buntaine, Mark T, Patrick Hunnicutt, and Polycarp Komakech (2021). "The challenges of using citizen reporting to improve public services: A field experiment on solid waste services in Uganda." *Journal of Public Administration Research and Theory* 31.1, pp. 108–127.

Buntaine, Mark T. et al. (2018). "SMS texts on corruption help Ugandan voters hold elected councillors accountable at the polls." *Proceedings of the National Academy of Sciences* 115.26, pp. 6668–6673.

Burgess, R. et al. (2015). "The value of democracy: Evidence from road building in Kenya." *The American Economic Review* 105.6, pp. 1817–1851.

Bussell, Jennifer (2019). *Clients and constituents: Political responsiveness in patronage democracies*. Oxford University Press.

Chasukwa, Michael and Dan Banik (2019). "Bypassing government: Aid effectiveness and Malawi's local development fund." *Politics and Governance* 7.2, pp. 103–116.

Chatterjee, Santanu, Paola Giuliano, and Ilker Kaya (2012). "Where has all the money gone? Foreign aid and the composition of government spending." *The BE Journal of Macroeconomics* 12.1.

Chilunga, Zawadi (2016). "Malawi: Goodall upbeat on budgetary support resumption in Malawi, world bank gives glimmer of hope – reports." *Nyasa Times* September 28, 2016. https://allafrica.com/stories/201609290010.html.

Chinsinga, Blessings (2011). "Seeds and subsidies: The political economy of input programmes in Malawi." *IDS bulletin* 42.4, pp. 59–68.

Clark, Michael D et al. (2014). "Discrete choice experiments in health economics: A review of the literature." *Pharmacoeconomics* 32.9, pp. 883–902.

CONGOMA (2016). "90% of aid to NGOs cannot be traced?" https://congoma.mw/90-of-aid-to-ngos-cannot-be-traced/. Accessed August 2024.

Cox, Gary W. (2010). "Swing voters, core voters, and distributive politics." *Political Representation*. Ed. by Ian Shapiro et al. Cambridge University Press, pp. 342–357.

Cruz, Cesi, Philip Keefer, and Julien Labonne (2021). "Buying informed voters: New effects of information on voters and candidates." *The Economic Journal* 131.635, pp. 1105–1134.

Cruz, Cesi and Christina J Schneider (2017). "Foreign aid and undeserved credit claiming." *American Journal of Political Science* 61.2, pp. 396–408.

De Juan, Alexander, Paul Hofman, and Carlo Koos (2023). "More information, better knowledge? The effects of information campaigns on aid beneficiaries' knowledge of aid projects." WIDER Working Paper.

de la Cuesta, Brandon et al. (2019). "Oil and aid revenue produce equal demands for accountability as taxes in Ghana and Uganda." *Proceedings of the National Academy of Sciences* 116.36, pp. 17717–17722.

de la Cuesta, Brandon et al. (2022). "Owning it: Accountability and citizens' ownership over oil, aid, and taxes." *The Journal of Politics* 84.1, pp. 304–320.

Dietrich, Simone (2013). "Bypass or engage? Explaining donor delivery tactics in foreign aid allocation." *International Studies Quarterly* 57.4, pp. 698–712.

(2021). *States, markets, and foreign aid.* Cambridge University Press.

Dietrich, Simone, Minhaj Mahmud, and Matthew S Winters (2018). "Foreign aid, foreign policy, and domestic government legitimacy: Experimental evidence from Bangladesh." *The Journal of Politics* 80.1, pp. 133–148.

Dietrich, Simone and Matthew S Winters (2021). "Foreign aid and quality of government." *The Oxford Handbook of the Quality of Government*, p. 449.

Dietrich, Simone and Joseph Wright (2015). "Foreign aid allocation tactics and democratic change in Africa." *The Journal of Politics* 77.1, pp. 216–234.

DiLorenzo, Matthew (2023). "International politics and the subnational allocation of world bank development projects." *Political Studies Review* 21.2, pp. 400–411.

Dionne, Kim Yi (2017). *Doomed interventions: The failure of global responses to AIDS in Africa.* Cambridge University Press.

Dionne, Kim Yi, Eric Kramon, and Tyson Roberts (2013). "Aid effectiveness and allocation: Evidence from Malawi." *ASA 2013 Annual Meeting Paper.* Conference Research Frontiers in Foreign Aid at Princeton University. https://ssrn.com/abstract=2237356.

Dipendra, KC (2020). "Which aid targets poor at the sub-national level?" *World Development Perspectives* 17, p. 100177.

Dixit, Avinash and John Londregan (1996). "The determinants of success of special interests in redistributive politics." *The Journal of Politics* 58.4, pp. 1132–1155.

Djankov, Simeon, Jose G Montalvo, and Marta Reynal-Querol (2008). "The curse of aid." *Journal of Economic Growth* 13.3, pp. 169–194.

Dreher, Axel et al. (2019). "African leaders and the geography of China's foreign assistance." *Journal of Development Economics* 140, pp. 44–71.

(2022). *Banking on Beijing: The aims and impacts of China's overseas development program.* Cambridge University Press.

Duarte, Raúl et al. (2019). *Brokering votes with information spread via social networks.* Technical Report. National Bureau of Economic Research.

Dunning, Thad and Janhavi Nilekani (2013). "Ethnic quotas and political mobilization: Caste, parties, and distribution in Indian village councils." *American Political Science Review* 107.1, pp. 35–56.

Dunning, Thad et al. (2019). *Information, accountability and cumulative learning.* Cambridge University Press. https://doi.org/10.1017/9781108381390.

Dynes, Adam M and Lucy Martin (2021). "Revenue source and electoral accountability: Experimental evidence from local US policymakers." *Political Behavior* 43.3, pp. 1113–1136.

Easterly, William (2009). "Can the west save Africa?" *Journal of Economic Literature* 47.2, pp. 373–447.

(2014). *The tyranny of experts: Economists, dictators, and the forgotten rights of the poor.* Basic Books.

Easterly, William and Tobias Pfutze (2008). "Where does the money go? Best and worst practices in foreign aid." *The Journal of Economic Perspectives* 22.2, pp. 29–52.

Ejdemyr, Simon, Eric Kramon, and Amanda Lea Robinson (2018). "Segregation, ethnic favoritism, and the strategic targeting of local public goods." *Comparative Political Studies* 51.9, pp. 1111–1143.

Ensminger, Jean and Jetson Leder-Luis (2025). "Detecting corruption: Evidence from a world bank project in Kenya." *World Development* 188, p. 106858.

Eubank, Nicholas (2012). "Taxation, political accountability and foreign aid: Lessons from Somaliland." *Journal of Development Studies* 48.4, pp. 465–480.

Faye, Michael and Paul Niehaus (2012). "Political aid cycles." *American Economic Review* 102.7, pp. 3516–30.

Fearon, James D (1999). "Electoral accountability and the control of politicians: Selecting good types versus sanctioning poor performance." *Democracy, Accountability, and Representation.* Vol. 2. Cambridge University Press.

Ferraz, Claudio and Frederico Finan (2008). "Exposing corrupt politicians: The effects of Brazil's publicly released audits on electoral outcomes." *The Quarterly Journal of Economics* 123.2, pp. 703–745.

Feyzioglu, Tarhan, Vinaya Swaroop, and Min Zhu (1998). "A panel data analysis of the fungibility of foreign aid." *The World Bank Economic Review* 12.1, pp. 29–58.

Findley, Michael G et al. (2011). "The localized geography of foreign aid: A new dataset and application to violent armed conflict." *World Development* 39.11, pp. 1995–2009.

(2017). "Who controls foreign aid? Elite versus public perceptions of donor influence in aid-dependent Uganda." *International Organization* 71.4, pp. 633–663.

Francken, Nathalie, Bart Minten, and Johan FM Swinnen (2012). "The political economy of relief aid allocation: Evidence from Madagascar." *World Development* 40.3, pp. 486–500.

Gadenne, Lucie (2017). "Tax me, but spend wisely? Sources of public finance and government accountability." *American Economic Journal: Applied Economics*, pp. 274–314.

Gehring, Kai et al. (2017). "Aid fragmentation and effectiveness: What do we really know?" *World Development* 99, pp. 320–334.

Gibson, Clark C, Barak D. Hoffman, and Ryan S. Jablonski (2015). "Did aid promote democracy in Africa? The role of technical assistance in Africa's transitions." *World Development* 68, pp. 323–335.

Gibson, Clark C, Krister Andersson, Elinor Ostrom, and Sujai Shivakumar (2005). *The samaritan's dilemma: The political economy of development aid.* Oxford: Oxford University Press.

Gottlieb, Jessica (2016). "Greater expectations: A field experiment to improve accountability in Mali." *American Journal of Political Science* 60.1, pp. 143–157.

Grossman, GM (2001). *Special Interest Politics.* The MIT Press.

Grossman, Guy and Janet I Lewis (2014). "Administrative unit proliferation." *American Political Science Review* 108.1, pp. 196–217.

Grossman, Guy, Jan H Pierskalla, and Emma Boswell Dean (2017). "Government fragmentation and public goods provision." *The Journal of Politics* 79.3, pp. 823–840.

Grossman, Guy, Melina R Platas, and Jonathan Rodden (2018). "Crowdsourcing accountability: ICT for service delivery." *World Development* 112, pp. 74–87.

Grossman, Guy and Tara Slough (2022). "Government responsiveness in developing countries." *Annual Review of Political Science* 25, pp. 131–153.

Guiteras, Raymond P and Ahmed Mushfiq Mobarak (2015). "Does development aid undermine political accountability? Leader and constituent responses to a large-scale intervention." National Bureau of Economic Research Working Paper.

Gulzar, Saad, Zuhad Hai, and Binod Kumar Paudel (2021). "Information, Candidate selection, and the quality of representation: Evidence from Nepal." *The Journal of Politics* 83.4, pp. 1511–1528.

Harris, J Andrew and Daniel N Posner (2019). "(Under what conditions) do politicians reward their supporters? Evidence from Kenya's constituencies development fund." *American Political Science Review* 113.1, pp. 123–139.

Hawkins, Darren G et al. (2006). *Delegation and agency in international organizations*. Cambridge University Press.

Heckelman, Jac C and Stephen Knack (2008). "Foreign aid and market-liberalizing reform." *Economica* 75.299, pp. 524–548.

Hicken, Allen, James Atkinson, and Nico Ravanilla (2019). "Pork and typhoons: The influence of political connections on disaster response in the Philippines." *Building Inclusive Democracies in ASEAN*. World Scientific, pp. 74–101.

Hines, James R and Richard H Thaler (1995). "Anomalies: The flypaper effect." *Journal of Economic Perspectives* 9.4, pp. 217–226.

Honig, Dan (2018). *Navigation by judgment: Why and when top-down management of foreign aid doesn't work*. Oxford University Press.

Hood, Ronald, David Husband, and Fei Yu (2002). *Recurrent expenditure requirements of capital projects estimation for budget purposes*. Vol. 2938. World Bank Publications.

Human Rights Watch (2010). *Development without freedom: How aid underwrites repression in Ethiopia*. https://bit.ly/4bbbDik.

Humphreys, Macartan and Jeremy M. Weinstein (2012). "Policing politicians: Citizen empowerment and political accountability in Uganda." Mimeo. https://bit.ly/4aBQD47.

Hyde, Susan D and Nikolay Marinov (2012). "Which elections can be lost?" *Political Analysis* 20.2, pp. 191–210.

Ijaz, Syeda (2025). "Voter preferences and foreign aid: Experimental evidence from Pakistan." Working Paper.

International Monetary Fund (2018). "Malawi: Technical assistance report-public investment management assessment (PIMA)." *IMF Staff Country Reports* 259. https://doi.org/10.5089/9781484373750.002.

(2020). "Sierra leone public investment management assessment (PIMA)." *IMF Staff Country Reports*. https://bit.ly/4r2LSWn.

Isaksson, Ann-Sofie and Andreas Kotsadam (2018). "Chinese aid and local corruption." *Journal of Public Economics* 159, pp. 146–159.

Izzo, Federica, Torun Dewan, and Stephane Wolton (2018). "Cumulative knowledge in the social sciences: The case of improving voters' information." Available at SSRN 3239047.

Jablonski, Ryan and Brigitte Seim (2018). "How transparency affects distributional politics: A field experiment among elected incumbents in Malawi." AidData Working Paper. https://bit.ly/4cM2Nc2.

(2023). "What politicians don't know can hurt you: The effects of information on politicians' spending decisions." *American Political Science Review* pp. 1–21. https://doi.org/10.1017/S0003055423001132.

Jablonski, Ryan, Brigitte Seim, and Johan Ahlback (2025). "Foreign aid is neither a curse nor a blessing: Explaining the effects of foreign aid on voting behavior and accountability." Working Paper.

Jablonski, Ryan S (2013). "The effect of electoral politics on foreign aid spending." PhD thesis. University of California, San Diego.

(2014). "How aid targets votes: The impact of electoral incentives on foreign aid distribution." *World Politics* 66.2, pp. 293–330.

Jablonski, Ryan S et al. (2022). "Individualized text messages about public services fail to sway voters: Evidence from a field experiment on Ugandan elections." *Journal of Experimental Political Science* 9.3, pp. 346–358.

Jöst, Prisca and Ellen Lust (2022). "Receiving more, expecting less? Social ties, clientelism and the poor's expectations of future service provision." *World Development* 158, p. 106008.

Kagotho, Njeri, Alicia Bunger, and Kristen Wagner (2016). " 'They make money off of us': A phenomenological analysis of consumer perceptions of corruption in Kenya's HIV response system." *BMC Health Services Research* 16.1, pp. 1–11.

Keefer, Philip and Stuti Khemani (2005). "Democracy, public expenditures, and the poor: Understanding political incentives for providing public services." *The World Bank Research Observer* 20.1, pp. 1–27. http://jstor.org/stable/41261407.

(2009). "When do legislators pass on pork? The role of political parties in determining legislator effort." *The American Political Science Review* 103.1, pp. 99–112.

Keefer, Philip and Razvan Vlaicu (2008). "Democracy, credibility, and clientelism." *The Journal of Law, Economics, and Organization* 24.2, pp. 371–406.

Khamula, Owen (2015). "MPs accuse government of 'marginalising' North Malawi." *Nyasa Times* November 11, 2015. https://nyasatimes.com/mps-accusegovt-of-marginalising-north-malawi/.

(2016). "Malawi: Mutharika trashes ultimatums, donor pressure on information bill – spells out inconsistencies." *Nyasa Times* December 15, 2015. https://allafrica.com/stories/201512150799.html.

Kita, Stern Mwakalimi (2017). "'Government doesn't have the muscle': State, NGOs, local politics, and disaster risk governance in Malawi." *Risk, Hazards & Crisis in Public Policy* 8.3, pp. 244–267.

Knack, Stephen and Aminur Rahman (2007). "Donor fragmentation and bureaucratic quality in aid recipients." *Journal of Development Economics* 83.1, pp. 176–197.

Knutsen, Tora and Andreas Kotsadam (2020). "The political economy of aid allocation: Aid and incumbency at the local level in Sub Saharan Africa." *World Development* 127, p. 104729.

Koch, Susanne and Peter Weingart (2016). *The delusion of knowledge transfer: The impact of foreign aid experts on policy-making in South Africa and Tanzania.* African minds.

Kollman, Ken, Allen Hicken, Daniele Caramani, David Backer, and David Lublin. (2020). *Constituency-Level Elections Archive.* Accessed June 2023. http://electiondataarchive.org.

Kramon, Eric and Daniel N. Posner (2013). "Who benefits from distributive politics? How the outcome one studies affects the answer one gets." *Perspectives on Politics* 11.2, pp. 461–474.

Leeroy, Kabs-Kanu (2017). "Bankasoka, Makali and Charlotte dams are over 80% funded by the Chinese and not by UNIDO." *Cocorioko* November 18, 2017. https://cocorioko.net/bankasoka-makali-and-charlotte-dams-are-over-80-funded-bythe-chinese-and-not-by-unido/.

Lewis, David (2004). "On the difficulty of studying 'civil society': Reflections on NGOs, state and democracy in Bangladesh." *Contributions to Indian Sociology* 38.3, pp. 299–322.

Lewis, David and Shirin Madon (2004). "Information systems and nongovernmental development organizations: Advocacy, organizational learning, and accountability." *The Information Society* 20.2, pp. 117–126.

Liaqat, Asad (2020). "No representation without information: Politician responsiveness to citizen preferences." Working Paper. https://scholar.harvard.edu/files/asadliaqat/files/jmp.pdf.

Licht, Amanda A (2010). "Coming into money: The impact of foreign aid on leader survival." *Journal of Conflict Resolution* 54.1, pp. 58–87.

Lindberg, Staffan I (2010). "What accountability pressures do MPs in Africa face and how do they respond? Evidence from Ghana." *The Journal of Modern African Studies* 48.1, pp. 117–142.

Lio Rosvold, Elisabeth (2020). "Disaggregated determinants of aid: Development aid projects in the Philippines." *Development Policy Review* 38.6, pp. 783–803.

Malawi Ministry of Finance (2024). *Citizens budget: Investing in the future.* Accessed July 2024. https://finance.gov.mw/index.php/our-documents/budgetstatements.

Marć, Łukasz (2017). "The impact of aid on total government expenditures: New evidence on fungibility." *Review of Development Economics* 21.3, pp. 627–663.

Martin, Lucy and Pia J Raffler (2021). "Fault lines: The effects of bureaucratic power on electoral accountability." *American Journal of Political Science* 65.1, pp. 210–224.

Martin, Lucy ES (2023). *Strategic taxation: Fiscal capacity and accountability in African states*. Oxford University Press.

Masaki, Takaaki (2018). "The political economy of aid allocation in Africa: Evidence from Zambia." *African Studies Review* 61.1, pp. 55–82.

Mattes, Robert and Shaheen Mozaffar (2016). "Legislatures and democratic development in Africa." *African Studies Review* 59.3, pp. 201–215.

McFadden, Daniel (1973). "Conditional logit analysis of qualitative choice behavior." *Frontiers in Econometrics*. Academic Press.

McGillivray, Mark and Oliver Morrissey (2000). "Aid fungibility in assessing aid: Red herring or true concern?" *Journal of International Development* 12.3, pp. 413–428.

McGreal, Chris (June 4, 2008). "Mugabe accused of using food as a political weapon in Zimbabwe." *The Guardian*. http://theguardian.com/world/2008/jun/04/unitednations.zimbabwe (visited on 10/03/2018).

Mercer, Claire (2003). "Performing partnership: Civil society and the illusions of good governance in Tanzania." *Political Geography* 22.7, pp. 741–763.

Mesquita, Bruce Bueno de and Alastair Smith (2009). "A political economy of aid." *International Organization* 63.2, pp. 309–340.

Miguna, Miguna (2012). *Peeling Back the Mask: A quest for justice in Kenya*. Gilgamesh Africa.

Min, Brian et al. (2023). "Local partisan biases in allocations of foreign aid: A study of agricultural assistance in India." *World Politics* 75.1, pp. 43–98.

Mkandawire, Thandika (1999). "Crisis management and the making of 'choiceless democracies'." *State, Conflict and Democracy in Africa* pp. 119–136.

(2010). "Aid, accountability, and democracy in Africa." *Social Research: An International Quarterly* 77.4, pp. 1149–1182.

Mlusu, Felix (2021). "The 2020/21 budget statement delivered in the national assembly of the republic of Malawi." https://finance.gov.mw/index.php/our-documents/budget-statements (Accessed January 2024).

Mogha-Mana, Solister (2019). "Blantyre MPs 'fight' over secondary schools funded by the US." *Nyasa Times* October 1, 2019. https://nyasatimes.com/blantyremps-fight-over-secondary-schools-funded-by-us/.

Morrison, Kevin M (2007). "Natural resources, aid, and democratization: A best-case scenario." *Public Choice* 131.3–4, pp. 365–386.

(2014). *Nontaxation and representation*. Cambridge University Press.

Morrissey, Oliver (2015). "Aid and government fiscal behavior: Assessing recent evidence." *World Development* 69, pp. 98–105.

Moss, Todd J, Gunilla Pettersson Gelander, and Nicolas Van de Walle (2006). "An aid-institutions paradox? A review essay on aid dependency and state building in sub-Saharan Africa." *Center for Global Development Working Paper*, 74, pp. 11–05.

Moyo, Dambisa (2009). *Dead aid: Why aid is not working and how there is a better way for Africa*. Macmillan.

NGORA Malawi (2022). "2020 NGO sector report." *Non-Governmental Organizations Regulatory Authority (NGORA)*, https://ngora.mw/reports/.

(2024). “2024 NGO sector report.” *Non-Governmental Organizations Regulatory Authority (NGORA)*, https://ngora.mw/reports/.

Nichter, Simeon (2008). “Vote buying or turnout buying? Machine politics and the secret ballot.” *American Political Science Review* 102.1, pp. 19–31.

North, Douglass C and Barry R Weingast (1989). “Constitutions and commitment: The evolution of institutions governing public choice in seventeenth-century England.” *The Journal of Economic History* 49.4, pp. 803–832.

Nunnenkamp, Peter, Hannes Öhler, and Maximiliano Sosa Andrés (2017). “Need, merit and politics in multilateral aid allocation: A district-level analysis of World Bank projects in India.” *Review of Development Economics* 21.1, pp. 126–156.

Nyasa Times Reporter (2019). “M’mbelwa V accuses government of abandoning development projects in North Malawi.” *Nyasa Times* October 15, 2019. https://bit.ly/4qQBFvT.

OECD (2005). *Paris declaration on aid effectiveness: Ownership, harmonisation, alignment, results and mutual accountability*. Accessed June 2021. https://oecd.org/dac/effectiveness/34428351.pdf.

(2020). *Query wizard for international development statistics*. https://stats.oecd.org/qwids/.

(2024). *OECD credit reporting system*. https://stats.oecd.org/?lang=en. Accessed: 2024-23-01.

Ofosu, George Kwaku (2019). “Do fairer elections increase the responsiveness of politicians?” *American Political Science Review* 113.4, pp. 963–979.

(2024). “What do voters want from their legislators? Evidence from ghana.” *African Affairs* 123.491, pp. 165–192.

O’Brien-Udry, Cleo (2021). “Aid, blame, and backlash: The political economy of unpopular aid.” Working Paper. ...

Pack, Howard and Janet Rothenberg Pack (1990). “Is foreign aid fungible? The case of Indonesia.” *The Economic Journal* 100.399, pp. 188–194.

Paler, Laura (2013). “Keeping the public purse: An experiment in windfalls, taxes, and the incentives to restrain government.” *American Political Science Review* 107.4, pp. 706–725.

Paler, Laura et al. (2023). “Oil discoveries and political windfalls: Evidence on presidential support in Uganda.” *Political Science Research and Methods* 11.4, pp. 903–912.

Peratsakis, Christian et al. (2012). *Geocoded activity-level data from the government of Malawi’s Aid Management Platform*. Accessed June 2023. https://aiddata.org/data/malawirelease-17-april-2012.

Pereira, Miguel (2020). “Understanding and reducing biases in elite beliefs about the electorate.” *American Political Science Review* 115.4, pp. 1308–1324.

Persson, Torsten and Guido Tabellini (2002). *Political economics: Explaining economic policy*. Massachusetts: MIT press.

Prichard, Wilson (2016). “Reassessing tax and development research: A new dataset, new findings, and lessons for research.” *World Development* 80, pp. 48–60.

Przeworski, Adam, Susan C Stokes, and Bernard Manin (1999). *Democracy, accountability, and representation*. Vol. 2. Cambridge University Press.

Qian, Nancy (2015). "Making progress on foreign aid." *Annual Review of Economics* 7.1, pp. 277–308.

Rashid, Ahmed (Sept. 6, 2010). "Pakistani flood relief must start with fighting corruption." *Washington Post.* http://washingtonpost.com/wp-dyn/content/article/2010/09/05/AR2010090502816.html (visited on 10/03/2018).

Reinikka, Ritva and Jakob Svensson (2005). "Fighting corruption to improve schooling: Evidence from a newspaper campaign in Uganda." *Journal of the European Economic Association* 3.2–3, pp. 259–267.

Remmer, Karen L (2004). "Does foreign aid promote the expansion of government?" *American Journal of Political Science* 48.1, pp. 77–92.

Reno, William (1995). *Corruption and state politics in Sierra Leone.* Cambridge University Press.

Resnick, Danielle and Nicolas Van de Walle (2013). *Democratic trajectories in Africa: Unravelling the impact of foreign aid.* Oxford: Oxford University Press.

Rice, Xan (2007). "The Looting of Kenya." *The Guardian.* Accessed June 2025. https://theguardian.com/world/2007/aug/31/kenya.topstories3.

Robinson, James (2008). "Governance and political economy constraints to World Bank CAS priorities in Sierra Leone." Unpublished manuscript, Washington DC, World Bank. https://scholar.harvard.edu/files/jrobinson/files/jr_wb_sierraleone.pdf.

Rogger, Daniel and Ravi Somani (2023). "Hierarchy and information." *Journal of Public Economics* 219, p. 104823.

Ross, Michael (2012). *The oil curse: How petroleum wealth shapes the development of nations.* New Jersey: Princeton University Press.

Sacks, Audrey (2012). "Can donors and non-state actors undermine citizens' legitimating beliefs?" World Bank Policy Research Working Paper.

Seim, Brigitte (2015). "Voter response to scandal: Cashgate and the Malawian election. In democracy maturing?" *The 2014 Malawi Tripartite Elections.* Ed. by Nandini Patel and Michael Wahman. Lilongwe: National Initiative for Civic Education.

Seim, Brigitte, Ryan Jablonski, and Johan Ahlbäck (2020). "How information about foreign aid affects public spending decisions: Evidence from a field experiment in Malawi." *Journal of Development Economics* 146.

Sexton, Renard and Christoph Zürcher (2023). "Aid, attitudes, and insurgency: Evidence from development projects in Northern Afghanistan." *American Journal of Political Science* 68.3, pp. 1168–1182.

Sijpe, Nicolas Van de (2013). "Is foreign aid fungible? Evidence from the education and health sectors." *The World Bank Economic Review* 27.2, pp. 320–356. (Visited on 09/06/2024).

Simson, Rebecca and Elliott Green (2020). "Ethnic favouritism in Kenyan education reconsidered: When a picture is worth more than a thousand regressions." *The Journal of Modern African Studies* 58.3, pp. 425–460.

Slough, Tara (2024). "Bureaucratic quality and electoral accountability." *American Political Science Review* 118.4, pp. 1931–1950.

Springman, Jeremy (2023). "The political economy of NGO service provision: Evidence from an ancillary field experiment in Uganda." *World Politics* 1, pp. 523–563.

Steeves, Jeffrey (2006). "Presidential succession in Kenya: The transition from Moi to Kibaki." *Commonwealth & Comparative Politics* 44.2, pp. 211–233.

Stokes, Susan C. et al. (2013). *Brokers, voters, clientelism: The puzzle of distributive politics.* Cambridge University Press.

Svensson, Jakob (2000). "Foreign aid and rent-seeking." *Journal of International Economics* 51.2, pp. 437–461.

Swedlund, Haley J (2017a). "Can foreign aid donors credibly threaten to suspend aid? Evidence from a cross-national survey of donor officials." *Review of International Political Economy* 24.3, pp. 454–496.

(2017b). *The development dance: How donors and recipients negotiate the delivery of foreign aid.* Cornell University Press.

Swedlund, Haley J and Malte Lierl (2020). "The rise and fall of budget support: Ownership, bargaining and donor commitment problems in foreign aid." *Development Policy Review* 38, pp. O50–O69.

Tangri, Roger and Andrew M Mwenda (2006). "Politics, donors and the ineffectiveness of anti-corruption institutions in Uganda." *The Journal of Modern African Studies* 44.1, pp. 101–124.

Thornton, John (2014). "Does foreign aid reduce tax revenue? Further evidence." *Applied Economics* 46.4, pp. 359–373.

Throup, David and Charles Hornsby (1998). *Multi-party politics in Kenya: The Kenyatta & Moi States & the triumph of the system in the 1992 election.* (J. Currey).

Tierney, Michael J et al. (2011). "More dollars than sense: Refining our knowledge of development finance using AidData." *World Development* 39.11, pp. 1891–1906.

Tripp, Aili Mari (2012). *Donor assistance and political reform in Tanzania.* 2012/37. WIDER Working Paper.

Tweedie, Neil. (Mar. 26, 2005). "A hungry future for poor voters who oppose Mugabe." *Daily Telegraph.* http://theguardian.com/world/2008/jun/04/unitednations.zimbabwe (visited on 10/03/2018).

UNDP (Jan 2016). *Human Development Report.* Technical Report. Accessed June 2017. United Nations Development Programme (UNDP). http://hdr.undp.org/en/2016-report (Accessed June 2017).

UNICEF (2023). "National budget brief 2023/24." https://bit.ly/40zXrt2. (Accessed January 2024).

Van de Walle, Nicolas (2001). *African economies and the politics of permanent crisis, 1979–1999.* Cambridge University Press.

Wagstaff, Adam (2011). "Fungibility and the impact of development assistance: Evidence from Vietnam's health sector." *Journal of Development Economics* 94.1, pp. 62–73.

Walle, Dominique van de and Ren Mu (2007). "Fungibility and the flypaper effect of project aid: Micro-evidence for Vietnam." *Journal of Development Economics* 2.84, pp. 667–685.

Weigel, Jonathan L (2020). "The participation dividend of taxation: How citizens in Congo engage more with the state when it tries to tax them." *The Quarterly Journal of Economics* 135.4, pp. 1849–1903.

Weitz-Shapiro, Rebecca (2014). *Curbing clientelism in Argentina: Politics, poverty, and social policy.* Cambridge University Press.

Werker, Eric, Faisal Z Ahmed, and Charles Cohen (2009). "How is foreign aid spent? Evidence from a natural experiment." *American Economic Journal: Macroeconomics* 1.2, pp. 225–44.

Winters, Matthew S. (2014). "Targeting, accountability and capture in development projects." *International Studies Quarterly* 58.2, pp. 393–404.

World Bank (n.d.). *HIV/AIDS Disaster Response Project.* Accessed, August 2021. https://projects.worldbank.org/en/projects-operations/project-detail/P070920.

(1998). "Assessing aid: what works, what doesn't, and why." https://documents1.worldbank.org/curated/en/612481468764422935/pdf/Assessing-aidwhat-works-what-doesnt-and-why.pdf.

(2010a). *Financial management in action.* https://bit.ly/4s4MvPY.

(2010b). "The education system in Malawi." World Bank Working Paper No. 182.

(2012). *IBRD Articles of Agreement: Article IV.* Accessed June 2023. https://bit.ly/47oc6kZ.

(2017). *World development indicators.* Accessed June 2024. http://data.worldbank.org/data-catalog/world-development-indicators).

(2019a). *Kenya agricultural productivity program performance assessment report.* Accessed June 2021. https://bit.ly/4qWc9FG.

(2019b). *World development indicators.* Data retrieved from World Development Indicators, http://data.worldbank.org.

(2021). *Sierra leone public expenditure review: primary and secondary education.* World Bank Group. http://info.worldbank.org/governance/wgi/.

(2024). *World development indicators.* Accessed June 2024. http://data.worldbank.org/data-catalog/world-development-indicators.

Wright, Joseph and Matthew Winters (2010). "The politics of effective foreign aid." *Annual Review of Political Science* 13, pp. 61–80.

Yuichi Kono, Daniel and Gabriella R Montinola (2009). "Does foreign aid support autocrats, democrats, or both?" *The Journal of Politics* 71.2, pp. 704–718.

# Index


Accountability, 46, 67, 97, 163, 174
  and democratization, 55, 67
  and foreign aid, 10–12, 18–19, 46, 49, 52, 74, 93–95, 97, 120, 125, 155, 157–158, 162
  and taxation, 48, 120
  theories of, 11, 21, 53, 94, 95, 121, 156
African Development Bank, 76, 81, 175
Afrobarometer, 25, 160
Ahlbäck, Johan, 24, 96, 122
Aid curse, 18, 46–47, 56, 67, 127
  and democracy, 48, 67, 95
  criticisms of theory, 18, 47, 98
  and taxation, 18
  theory, 46, 98, 120
Aid delivery. *See* Foreign aid
Aid dependency, 15, 16, 20, 30. *See also* aid-dependent democracies
  changes over time, 28
  defined, 79–80, 88
Aid effectiveness. *See* Foreign aid
Aid officials. *See* Donors
AidData, 15, 76, 81–83, 96, 166, 176
Aid organizations. *See* Donors
Aid-dependent democracies, 2, 4, 6, 49, 50, 123, 152, 155–158
  characteristics, 1–2, 15, 23, 57, 77, 102
  compared, 14–17, 27–28, 158–160
  defined, 11, 23
  governance in, 2–6, 156
Attribution, 55, 162
  of credit, 8–9, 19, 31, 50, 78, 97, 99, 100, 110, 114–116, 118, 121
  misattribution, 31, 50, 54, 96, 98, 114–115. *See also* uncertainty effect
  voter beliefs about, 31, 50, 52, 77, 95. *See also* Uncertainty effect, beliefs
Authoritarian governments, 17, 46, 48, 87, 88, 98

Baldwin, Kate, 3, 18, 30, 51, 57, 64, 99
Banda, Hastings, 15, 87, 123
Banda, Joyce, 124
Banerjee, Abhijit, 25
Bangladesh, 128
  aid dependency, 3
  NGOs in, 3
Bargaining, 24, 47, 53, 156
  between donors and politicians, 2–6, 24, 47, 74, 80, 87, 100, 155, 157, 158
  game theory models, 53
  multilateral, 5, 24, 35–39
  over aid allocation, 6, 35–39, 58
  power, 63, 158
Beliefs. *See also* biases; knowledge
  about foreign aid, 31–32, 49–50, 55, 78
  about government spending, 31, 47, 77, 78, 97, 181
  biases in, 9, 55, 64, 67, 78, 98, 113
  effects on policymaking, 78
  effects on voting, 18, 50, 53, 57, 62, 66, 77, 97, 100, 102, 115, 119
  of politicians, 50, 78, 110
  of voters, 8–9, 12, 19, 21, 31–32, 54, 66, 77, 78, 95, 99, 100, 103, 116, 118, 119, 121, 125, 156–159

Bermeo, Sarah, 17, 47, 52, 74, 95, 98, 132, 163
Biases
in aid spending, 39, 64, 73–76, 78–81, 85, 86, 88, 90, 92, 93
in politician knowledge, 20, 31, 130, 139
in voter beliefs, 9, 31–32, 55, 64, 75, 98, 100, 101, 113, 157
Blessing
of foreign aid. *See* foreign aid
Brass, Jennifer, 3, 5, 13, 18, 39, 73
Bräutigam, Deborah, 3, 18, 48, 49, 52, 95
Briggs, Ryan, 3, 18, 34, 39, 52, 73, 79, 88, 89, 98
Budget support, 29, 47, 52, 82, 123, 124, 155, 159, 162, 163
decline in, 5, 29, 47, 82, 88
defined, 29
in Malawi, 17, 29, 89, 112
and politician influence, 58, 74, 82
Budgeting
constraints, 2–4, 10, 16, 25–28, 52, 89, 157, 158
and donor influence, 4, 6, 35, 157
government budgets, 26, 102
process of, 5, 26
Bueno de Mesquita, Bruce, 17, 18, 20, 51, 95, 98, 127
Bureaucrats, 3, 157, 173
and aid delivery, 5, 34, 37, 65, 75, 80, 89
interviews with. *See* interviews
knowledge of donor activities. *See* knowledge
Bypass aid, 32–35, 67, 68, 159
defined, 5, 32, 87
effects on accountability, 29, 68, 93
trends in, 17, 29

Choiceless democracy, 18, 155. *See also* democracy
Constituency Development Funds (CDF). *See* Malawi
Corruption, 46, 125, 126, 132, 148
and accountability, 10, 32, 49, 89
and aid, 18, 32, 46, 74, 82, 89, 161
donor concerns, 17, 32, 68, 82, 89, 158
Credit claiming, 7, 9, 19, 24, 30–32, 55, 56, 64, 66, 95, 129, 156–158, 162. *See also* Attribution
experimental evidence, 78, 103, 110, 121
and information, 21, 64, 78, 101
and voting behavior, 18, 65, 78, 93, 98, 117
Cruz, Cesi, 7, 10, 18, 19, 31, 51, 52, 64, 98, 159

Democracy, 46–48
in aid-dependent countries, 2, 6, 46, 77, 155–158
effects of foreign aid on, 10–11, 17–19, 21, 30–32, 47, 55, 93, 127, 129–130, 150, 155, 156, 163
legitimacy of, 30, 52
versus autocracy, 47, 98
Democratic Republic of the Congo (DRC), 16
Democratization, 18, 48, 56, 123
Department for International Development (DFID), 12, 162, 187
Deutche Gesellschaft fur Internationale Zusammenarbeit (GIZ), 187
Dietrich, Simone, 5, 29, 51, 159, 162
Dionne, Kim, 90
Discretionary spending, 52
limited in aid-dependent countries, 16
versus recurrent spending, 2, 28, 52
Distributive politics, 69, 130, 145
electoral motivations, 21, 38, 64, 69, 99
and foreign aid, 38, 64, 69, 73–78, 92
District Commissioners (DCs). *See* Malawi
Donor coordination. *See* donors
Donor fragmentation. *See* donors
Donor interviews with. *See* interviews
Donors, 2, 23, 47, 52, 122, 169, 173, 174, 187. *See also* foreign aid
bargaining with politicians. *See* bargaining
bilateral, 12, 35, 36, 57, 74, 76, 93, 166
branding, 102
budget support. *See* budget support
coordination with, 8, 20, 33, 93, 129, 152, 162
defined, 11
delegation, 13, 36–39, 63, 75
dependence on. *See* aid dependency
effect on democracy. *See* democracy
fragmentation, 20, 33, 68
incentives of, 32, 161–162
influence on policy, 2–4, 36, 73, 78, 87, 159

interactions with politicians, 1–2, 32–36, 39–44, 56, 73, 80, 156, 165, 166
multilateral, 5, 12, 35, 36, 57, 76, 86, 87, 93, 166
oversight, 7, 16, 67, 74, 75, 82, 88, 99, 122–125, 132, 150–153, 155, 159, 173, 183, 188
preferences, 6, 32, 47, 65, 66, 75, 88, 89, 93, 130
relationships with politicians, 23–44
Dreher, Axel, 39, 73, 74, 78
Dunning, Thad, 19, 26, 98

Easterly, William, 127, 129, 162
Elections, 6, 7, 9, 14, 38, 46–69, 73, 76, 83, 177–179. *See also* accountability, Voters
and foreign aid, 4–6, 9, 17, 43, 46–67, 69, 73–93, 95–120, 156, 158, 163, 165, 176
in Kenya, 76, 83–84, 87, 90
in Malawi, 83–84
in Sierra Leone, 83–84
theory of, 43, 98–100, 156
Electoral politics. *See* elections
Elite capture. *See* corruption
Ethiopia
aid dependency, 16, 28, 39
aid misuse, 39
European Union (EU) aid, 73, 124, 187
Experiments, 14, 133–134
field experiments, 13, 53, 99, 122
information experiments, 9, 49, 101, 142–143
with politicians, 8, 20, 22, 50, 76, 165, 166, 183
SMS experiment, 14, 97, 104, 108, 116, 121, 180–181
with voters, 9, 95–98

Findley, Michael G., 29, 50, 74, 128, 175
Fiscal policy
constraints, 2, 3, 23, 25–28, 52, 79
dilemmas of, 1, 25–28, 158
Focus groups. *See also* interviews
details, 14, 32, 173
findings, 7, 32, 80
Food aid. *See* Foreign aid
Foreign aid, 2–5, 14, 35, 46–69, 168
allocation, 21, 27, 54, 73, 76, 85, 96, 103–105, 155, 174
blessing, 19, 52, 56, 67, 157
budget support. *See* budget support
bypass aid. *See* Bypass aid
channels of delivery, 5, 37, 58, 67, 93, 99, 158, 162–163
composition, 27
criticisms of, 18–19, 33–34, 46–49, 51–53, 67–68, 93
curse. *See* aid curse
data, 75, 79, 81–83, 175–177, 187–188
defined, 27
displacement of, 125–126, 131, 147
distribution of, 3, 38, 64, 73–93, 101, 120, 175
effect on democracy. *See* democracy
effectiveness, 20, 32–34, 129, 130
effects of foreign aid on, 155
and elections. *See* Elections
flypaper effects, 126, 131, 134
food aid, 39
fragmentation, 158
government ownership of, 20, 38, 158–159, 161–162
humanitarian aid, 39
information, 122
modalities, 63, 159
and politician behavior, 100, 122, 158
programmatic aid, 58
statistics, 16, 81–83
transparency. *See* transparency
and voter behavior, 62–66, 95–120, 156, 157, 165, 180
Fungibility, 17, 68, 125–126, 132, 153. *See also* aid curse
of foreign aid, 68, 98

Game theory, 18, 57–62, 90, 130
German Development Cooperation (KFW), 187
Ghana, 28

Human Rights Watch, 39

International development. *See* foreign aid
Interviews, 13, 170. *See also* focus groups
with aid officials, 170
with bureaucrats, 14, 25, 38, 170, 173
with donors, 14, 24, 74, 151, 170
with politicians, 1, 6, 7, 14, 24, 30, 80, 124, 126, 129, 149, 170, 173

Japan International Cooperation Agency (JICA), 3, 30, 99, 187

Kenya, 3, 13, 39, 46, 69, 128, 160, 175
 2002 election, 21, 76, 87–92
 Agriculture Productivity Project (KAPP), 35
 aid dependency, 28, 79–80, 88
 aid distribution, 76, 79
 Constituency AIDS Control Committees (CACCs), 89
 Daniel arap Moi. *See* Moi, Daniel arap
 electoral politics, 21, 79, 85–87, 177–178
 HIV/AIDS Disaster Response Project, 89
 Kenya African National Union (KANU), 21, 35, 87, 90–92, 177
 Kibaki, Mwai. *See* Kibaki, Mwai
 National AIDS Control Council (NACC), 89
 National Rainbow Coalition (NARC), 21, 88, 91, 177
 NGOs, 3
 Odinga, Raila. *See* Raila Odinga
 voting data, 177
 World Bank and, 76, 81, 89
Kibaki, Mwai, 21, 87, 89, 177
Knack, Stephen, 20, 95
Knowledge, 50, 63–65. *See also* beliefs, biases
 about foreign aid, 31, 50, 57, 67, 96, 112
 about government spending, 31, 50, 94
 of bureaucrats, 34
 effects on policymaking, 8, 42, 65
 effects on voting, 63, 97, 104, 108, 116, 117
 of politicians, 8, 12, 14, 20, 22, 31, 75, 77, 122–123, 127–128, 132, 136–139, 152, 162, 166, 188
 of voters, 12, 21, 31–32, 53, 54, 57, 94, 96, 101, 112–115, 119, 155–159, 162

Learning. *See* Beliefs; Knowledge
Legislatures. *See* Parliaments
Levi, Margaret, 48
Lobbying, 8, 53, 156
 effects on elections, 30, 58, 73, 97, 101
 formal model, 21, 57–66, 68
 by politicians for aid, 3, 12, 30, 53, 62, 64, 73, 77, 78, 80, 84, 97, 99, 100, 117, 147

Malawi, 1–11, 13, 49, 51, 69, 122–124, 126, 128, 136, 152, 155–156, 158–160, 173, 175, 187
 aid dependency, 2, 15, 16, 28, 79–80, 102
 aid distribution, 73, 76, 79, 82, 86
 Aid Management Platform, 76, 82, 128, 175
 Area Development Committees (ADCs), 4, 5, 37, 38, 128, 136, 173
 budget constraints, 26
 budgeting, 15, 16, 26
 case study, 14–17, 102–103
 Cashgate, 17, 124
 compared to other countries, 14–17, 158–160
 Constituency Development Funds (CDF), 1, 136, 161
 Democratic Progressive Party (DPP), 43, 80, 167, 178
 District Commissioners (DCs), 34, 38, 80, 128, 129, 173
 donor spending, 15, 28, 74
 electoral politics, 14, 21, 79, 80, 103, 178
 government spending, 4, 15, 16, 28, 87
 Local Councillors (LCs), 1, 25, 39–44, 136, 165, 166, 183
 Local Councilors (LCs), 96, 103, 112, 122, 133, 135
 Local Development Fund (LDF), 4, 37, 112
 Members of Parliament (MPs), 3, 25, 39–44, 122, 126, 133, 135, 136, 166, 183
 NGO Regulatory Authority (NGORA), 15, 54
 NGOs, 3, 38, 54, 87, 128, 129
 poverty, 15, 16, 87, 104
 surveys in, 95, 103, 158, 165–167
 Village Development Committees, 37
 voting data, 178
Mali, 3, 16, 160
Marcos, Ferdinand, 46
Miguna, Miguna, 80
Mkandawire, Thandika, 18, 52, 125, 155
Moi, Daniel arap, 46, 177

and foreign aid, 82, 86, 88, 90, 92, 93
Kenya under, 21, 87
Morrison, Kevin M., 17, 18, 48, 95, 98, 127, 163
Moyo, Dambisa, 48, 52, 127
Mozambique, 16, 160
Mutharika, Bingu wa, 178
Mutharika, Peter, 124

Negotiations. *See* Bargaining
Non-Governmental Organizations (NGOs), 1, 5, 54, 124–127, 157, 173, 174, 176
and accountability, 4, 24, 65, 155
complexity, 127
defined in study context, 12
geographic presence, 3, 66
in Malawi, 15, 87, 103, 128
politician interactions, 1–2, 13, 37, 56, 74, 156, 158
and politicians, 152
role in aid delivery, 2, 4, 24, 54, 75, 96, 158, 159
versus government control, 162
North, Douglas, 48

Odinga, Raila, 80, 178
Official Development Assistance (ODA). *See* Foreign aid
Oxfam, 187

Pakistan, 31, 39, 46
Paler, Laura, 20, 49
Paris Declaration, 34
Parliaments, 2–4, 6, 18, 42, 155, 157, 163
in aid-dependent countries, 83, 89
legislating, 3, 6, 12, 42, 156
Philippines, The, 31, 39, 46, 98
Policymaking, 4, 20, 35, 69, 152, 156. *See also* public spending
donor influence, 123–124
effects of aid on, 6–8, 12, 22, 35–39, 93, 162
Politician interviews. *See* interviews
Politicians, 1, 47, 68, 122, 166, 168, 169, 173, 174
and aid delivery, 157–159, 162
and donors, 124
bargaining with donors. *See* Bargaining
behavior of, 1–6, 35, 53–54, 68, 74, 97, 99, 156
campaigning, 7, 31, 77, 110, 116
and elections, 73, 75, 76, 89
fiscal dilemmas of. *See* Fiscal policy
and foreign aid, 79, 81, 85, 89, 92, 93
incentives of, 51, 64
influence on aid allocation, 73, 75, 90
interactions with donors, 2–3, 12, 23, 30–44, 68, 74, 75, 80, 86, 94, 96, 103, 117, 152, 155, 156, 165, 166, 173
interviews of. *See* interviews
knowledge of. *See* knowledge
knowledge of constituents, 77
legislating. *See* parliaments
lobbying donors. *See* lobbying
Local Councillors (LCs), 1, 39–44
Members of Parliament (MPs), 3, 39–44, 50, 73, 89
prioritization of effort, 3, 6, 12, 19, 31, 39–44, 56, 75, 77, 156, 157
relationships with donors, 23–35, 42–44, 173
spending decisions, 7–8, 12, 14, 22, 32, 50, 74, 76–78, 80, 85, 87–89, 123, 126, 140–142, 156, 162, 165
surveys of. *See* surveys
Programmatic aid. *See* foreign aid
Public policy. *See* policymaking
Public spending, 1, 6, 7, 12, 46. *See also* policymaking
composition, 5, 25–28, 51, 98
coordination, 129, 152
donor influence, 2–4, 56, 153
duplication of, 129, 153
education spending, 4, 26, 47, 96, 102, 114
health spending, 2, 15, 26, 47, 89
social services, 2, 3, 15, 23, 25–28, 52
voter knowledge, 56, 96, 112

Recurrent spending, 2, 26–28, 157
in government budgets, 16
versus discretionary spending, 2, 28
versus donor spending, 26
Reinikka, Ritva, 49
Research methods, 13–100
experiments, 76, 84–85, 90, 103–110
Resource curse, 49. *See also* aid curse
comparison to aid curse, 20
Retrospective voting, 6, 47, 53–56, 95, 120, 156. *See also* elections
defined, 19, 47

Retrospective voting (cont.)
and foreign aid, 8–9, 31, 97, 157
models, 53, 81, 117, 118
theory, 18, 21, 77, 100–101
Ross, Michael, 20, 48, 49
Rwanda, 16, 46

Sampling. *See* surveys
Schneider, Christina, 7, 10, 18, 19, 31, 51, 64, 98
Seim, Brigitte, 3, 24, 52, 73, 75, 77–79, 96, 122, 165, 168
Sese Seko, Mobuto, 46
Sierra Leone, 28, 69, 95, 175
aid dependency, 3, 27, 79–80
aid distribution, 27, 76, 79, 80
All People's Congress (APC), 178
Development Assistance Database, 76, 82, 175
electoral politics, 178–179
Sierra Leone People's Party (SLPP), 178
voting data, 21, 178
Smith, Alastair, 17, 18, 20, 51, 95, 98, 127
State legitimacy, 18. *See also* democracy
Surveys, 1, 13, 155, 159–160
attrition, 166, 183
of citizens and voters, 14, 21, 25, 95–98, 103, 107, 112, 121, 167–169
details, 106–107
of politicians, 3, 6, 14, 20, 24, 39, 76, 122, 165–166
sampling, 168
of teachers, 14, 15, 96, 102, 103, 107, 112, 128, 144, 169
Svensson, Jakob, 49, 51
Swedlund, Haley, 33, 159

Tanzania, 28, 46
Taxation, 48–50, 158
and accountability, 18, 48–50, 53, 120
in aid-dependent countries, 16, 79
versus foreign aid, 16, 48. *See also* aid curse
Teachers, 96, 102, 106, 112, 144, 167, 169
surveys of. *See* surveys
Tearfund (NGO), 103, 133
Theory, 2, 14, 46–69, 158–159
of aid and elections, 17, 18, 46–69, 76–78, 81, 85, 100–101, 157
of aid and policymaking, 130–132
of aid and taxation, 48
of elite capture, 51
formal models, 21, 46, 57–66
game theory, 57–62
of policymaking, 77
of retrospective voting. *See* retrospective voting
of state legitimacy, 52
of voting, 66, 77, 81
Transparency, 20, 47, 67, 128, 155, 163, 183
in aid spending, 8, 10, 32, 47, 55, 74, 82, 102, 108, 115, 117, 156–157
unintended consequences, 68

Uganda, 3, 30, 31, 46, 49, 99
Uncertainty effect, 10, 19, 21, 55–56, 67, 97, 101–102, 112, 157, 158
United Nations Children's Fund (UNICEF), 37, 73, 126, 127, 187
United Nations Development Programme (UNDP), 187
United Nations Population Fund (UNFPA), 187
USAID, 73, 96, 103, 162, 166, 187

van de Walle, Nicolas, 5, 18
Visibility effect, 10, 19, 56, 67, 97, 157–158
Voter knowledge. *See* knowledge
Voters, 2, 6, 31, 66, 129, 167, 168
behavior of, 2, 4, 8, 9, 21, 31, 48, 57, 66, 73, 75–78, 81, 84, 95–120, 156–157
beliefs of. *See* beliefs
demands of, 1, 7, 25–26, 49, 77, 78, 80, 81, 88, 94, 103
intentions of, 21, 31, 52, 76, 97, 101, 103, 110, 115, 118, 120, 121, 181
knowledge of. *See* knowledge
pivotal, 73, 84, 92
surveys of. *See* surveys
theories of voting, 50, 57, 62–66
Voting. *See* Elections; Voters

Winters, Matthew, 3, 18, 20, 30, 51, 64, 99, 162
World Bank, 12, 31, 35, 76, 79, 81, 89, 98, 163, 175, 187. *See also* donors
World Food Programme (WFP), 187
World Vision, 73, 187
Wright, Joseph, 125

Zambia, 159, 160
Zimbabwe, 39

Printed in the United Kingdom by TJ Clays Ltd.

# ADVANCE PRAISE

*Making Sense of the University* is a daring and indispensable adventure in critical thought and historical inquiry. With enormous theoretical power and acute historical analysis, Debaditya Bhattacharya guides us through the history of contradictions that define the university and holds public universities in India accountable for decisive failures of justice and vision. With remarkable acuity, Bhattacharya gives us a way to think about institutional histories and radical democratic theory. This book compels us to understand the university as the institutional support for the desire for what has been unknown, insisting on an affirmative vision that calls for an end to repression and incursion. This book is unprecedented, brilliant and indispensable.

**Judith Butler,** author of *Gender Trouble: Feminism and the Subversion of Identity*

The university is commonly thought of as the place where 'sense' – that is, things like knowledge and understanding – is produced. This provocative and intensely argued book invites us, instead, to 'make sense of the university' itself at a time when universities are under attack in much of the world. Structured as an interrogation of the idea of the public university and its relationships with community, secularity, solidarity and freedom, this book will not only intrigue and challenge but also inform and inspire anyone who has thought seriously about higher education and its institutional frames.

**Satish Deshpande**, author of *Contemporary India: A Sociological View*

Why are universities being destroyed everywhere? This relentlessly thoughtful and innovative volume offers answers. Political and historical analyses are artfully combined to identify ways in which the university (and the idea of public good on which it depends) can be revalued, defended and salvaged. The argument exemplifies a strategic view of knowledge and knowing to which it points. This is a major intervention that deserves to be influential.

**Paul Gilroy,** author of *The Black Atlantic: Modernity and Double Consciousness*

This brilliant critique of the Indian university is informed by an alternative vision of what higher education might be. It is indeed 'a manifesto for our times' that is a vital read for anyone, anywhere concerned about the future of the university.

**Joan W. Scott**, author of *Knowledge, Power, and Academic Freedom*

# MAKING SENSE OF THE UNIVERSITY

Why are public universities across the world being decried and attacked as a waste of public money? How, in the history of the university, has 'publicness' come to be treated with such distrust and disdain? Importantly, what accounts for the 'publicness' of the public university? This book digs into four different concepts of 'publicness', and the university's relationship with each of them. These four concepts are: community, secularity, solidarity and freedom. Does looking at the university's historical negotiations with each of these concepts give us a possible way of realizing its 'will to publicness'?

The Indian case, and its contemporary university sector, ground this 'manifesto' for a 'public' university. But the case only serves as a demonstrative example for how the very 'idea' of the university is under attack across different continents and historical contexts. The manifesto is therefore – as the title says – for our *times* of democratic authoritarianism.

**Debaditya Bhattacharya** is an assistant professor in the Department of English at Jamia Millia Islamia University, New Delhi. He has worked on a historical sociology of Indian universities, and the place of 'critical humanities' in building alliances between institutions and their outsides. He is the author of *The Indian University: A Critical History* (2025). Two of his edited anthologies on critical university studies include *The Idea of the University: Histories and Contexts* (2019) and *The University Unthought: Notes for a Future* (2019). He is also co-editor of the anthology of essays *Sentiment, Politics, Censorship: The State of Hurt* (2016).

## SOUTH ASIA IN THE SOCIAL SCIENCES

South Asia has become a laboratory for devising new institutions and practices of modern social life. Forms of capitalist enterprise, providing welfare and social services, the public role of religion, the management of ethnic conflict, popular culture and mass democracy in the countries of the region have shown a marked divergence from known patterns in other parts of the world. South Asia is now being studied for its relevance to the general theoretical understanding of modernity itself.

*South Asia in the Social Sciences* features books that offer innovative research on contemporary South Asia. It focuses on the place of the region in the various global disciplines of the social sciences and highlights research that uses unconventional sources of information and novel research methods. While recognising that most current research is focused on the larger countries, the series attempts to showcase research on the smaller countries of the region.



Books in the series:
*Becoming Allies: Civil Liberties Activism in India*
Ankita Pandey

*Counting Caste: Census Politics, Bureaucratic Deflection, and Brahmanical Power in India*
Trina Vithayathil

*A Woman's Job: Making Middle Lives in New India*
Asiya Islam

*After the Exodus: Gender and Belonging in Bangladesh's Rohingya Refugee Camps*
Farhana Afrin Rahman

*The Backstage of Democracy: India's Election Campaigns and the People Who Manage Them*
Amogh Dhar Sharma

*Questioning Migrants: Ethnic Nationalism at the Limits of Universality in Pakistan*
Tahir H. Naqvi

*Syndicates and Societies: Criminal Politics in Dhaka*
David Jackman

*Performing Sovereign Aspirations: Tamil Insurgency and Postwar Transition in Sri Lanka*
Bart Klem

*Legalizing the Revolution: India and the Constitution of the Postcolony*
Sandipto Dasgupta

*Sovereign Atonement: Citizenship, Territory, and the State at the Bangladesh–India Border*
Md Azmeary Ferdoush

*Memories in the Service of the Hindu Nation: The Afterlife of the Partition of India*
Pranav Kohli

*Freedom in Captivity: Negotiations of Belonging along Kashmir's Frontier*
Radhika Gupta

*Founding Mothers of the Indian Republic: Gender Politics of the Framing of the Constitution*
Achyut Chetan

*An Uneasy Hegemony: Politics of State-building and Struggles for Justice in Sri Lanka*
Shyamika Jayasundara-Smits

*The Odds Revisited: Political Economy of the Development of Bangladesh*
K. A. S. Murshid

*Bureaucratic Archaeology: State, Science, and Past in Postcolonial India*
Ashish Avikunthak

*In Search of Home: Citizenship, Law and the Politics of the Poor*
Kaveri Haritas

*When Ideas Matter: Democracy and Corruption in India*
Bilal A. Baloch

*Colossus: The Anatomy of Delhi*
Sanjoy Chakravorty and Neelanjan Sircar (eds.)

*Deceptive Majority: Dalits, Hinduism, and Underground Religion*
Joel Lee

*Simultaneous Identities: Language, Education and the Nepali Nation*
Uma Pradhan

*Dynamics of Caste and Law: Dalits, Oppression and Constitutional Democracy in India*
Dag-Erik Berg

*Crafty Oligarchs, Savvy Voters: Democracy under Inequality in Rural Pakistan*
Shandana Khan Mohmand

*New Perspectives on Pakistan's Political Economy: State, Class and Social Change*
Matthew McCartney and S. Akbar Zaidi (eds.)

*Maoist People's War and the Revolution of Everyday Life in Nepal*
Ina Zharkevich

*Adivasis and the State: Subalternity and Citizenship in India's Bhil Heartland*
Alf Gunvald Nilsen

*South Asian Governmentalities: Michel Foucault and the Question of Postcolonial Orderings*
Stephen Legg and Deana Heath (eds.)

*Nationalism, Development and Ethnic Conflict in Sri Lanka*
Rajesh Venugopal

*Politics of the Poor: Negotiating Democracy in Contemporary India*
Indrajit Roy

*Development after Statism: Industrial Firms and the Political Economy of South Asia*
Adnan Naseemullah

*Courting the People: Public Interest Litigation in Post-Emergency India*
Anuj Bhuwania

*Government as Practice: Democratic Left in a Transforming India*
Dwaipayan Bhattacharyya

# MAKING SENSE OF THE UNIVERSITY

## *A Manifesto for Our Times*

DEBADITYA BHATTACHARYA

Shaftesbury Road, Cambridge CB2 8EA, United Kingdom
One Liberty Plaza, 20th Floor, New York, NY 10006, USA
477 Williamstown Road, Port Melbourne, VIC 3207, Australia
314–321, 3rd Floor, Plot 3, Splendor Forum, Jasola District Centre, New Delhi – 110025, India

Cambridge University Press is part of Cambridge University Press & Assessment, a department of the University of Cambridge.

We share the University's mission to contribute to society through the pursuit of education, learning and research at the highest international levels of excellence.

www.cambridge.org
Information on this title: www.cambridge.org/9781009722315



First published 2026

Cover image: Lisa Schaetzle/Getty Images

*A catalogue record for this publication is available from the British Library*

*A Cataloging-in-Publication data record for this book is available from the Library of Congress*

ISBN 978-1-009-72231-5 Hardback

ISBN 978-1-009-72232-2 Paperback